TEACHING AND LEARNING THROUGH INQUIRY

TEACHING AND LEARNING THROUGH INQUIRY

A Guidebook for Institutions and Instructors

Virginia S. Lee
Editor

Sty/us

STERLING, VIRGINIA

First published in 2004 by

Stylus Publishing, LLC
22883 Quicksilver Drive
Sterling, Virginia 20166

**Library of Congress
Cataloging-in-Publication Data**
Teaching and learning through inquiry:
a guidebook for institutions and instructors/
edited by Virginia S. Lee. — 1st ed.
  p. cm
Includes bibliographical references and index.
ISBN 1-57922-080-0 (hard cover : alk. paper)
—ISBN 1-57922-081-9 (pbk. : alk. paper
1. Questioning. 2. Active learning.
  3. Critical thinking. I. Lee, Virginia
Snowden.
LB1027.44.T43 2004
371.39—dc22   2004000348

First edition, 2004
ISBN: hardcover 1-57922-080-0
ISBN: paperback 1-57922-081-9

Printed in the United States of America

All first editions printed on acid-free paper.

The action of thought is excited by the irritation of doubt,
and ceases when belief is attained.
—*Charles Saunders Pierce,*
How to Make Our Ideas Clear (1878)

CONTENTS

"It all began with the van ride home from Charlotte," people like to say, refer-ring to the ride a dozen university faculty took home from a workshop 150 miles away led by Richard Paul, the critical-thinking guru, on a cold January weekend in 1996. Since then the Inquiry-guided Learning Initiative at North Carolina State University has grown considerably. Today it is a complex, mul-tipronged initiative that has engaged well over 6,000 students, more than 200 faculty and staff, and 60 academic and administrative units on our campus. The initiative comprises a growing First Year Inquiry Program, a First Year Seminar Program in the College of Humanities and Social Sciences, selected courses throughout the undergraduate program, both general education and the major, and nine lead departments in 7 of the university's 10 colleges that have transformed a sequence of courses in the major. And we are forging stronger connections with the University Honors Program and the new Office of Undergraduate Research.

This book both documents and explores the Inquiry-guided Learning Ini-tiative from a variety of perspectives: how we've arrived at our current under-standing of inquiry-guided learning; how we've interpreted inquiry-guided learning at various levels—the individual course, the major, the college, the uni-versity-wide program, and the undergraduate curriculum as a whole; how we've dovetailed the initiative with other complementary efforts and programs; and how we've tried to assess its impact on our campus. We hope the volume will highlight both the promise and challenges of managing an undergraduate reform effort in a complex, research university like ours. We further hope that the book will be of interest to instructors who want to use inquiry-guided learning in their classrooms; faculty developers who may support comparable efforts on their campuses; administrators who are interested in managing similar undergraduate reform efforts; and instructors of courses in the administration of higher educa-tion who are looking for relevant case studies of reform, particularly in the research university, to use in their classes.

We've organized the book into four parts. Part I provides a framework for the rest of the volume by articulating our current, mutual understanding of inquiry-guided learning and some of the tensions inherent in it and by briefly summarizing the history of the initiative. Part II, the largest section, describes how various instructors, departments, and colleges in a range of disciplines have interpreted inquiry-guided learning. It also describes indicators of the potential for even broader dissemination of inquiry-guided learning in the undergraduate curriculum as a whole. Part III describes two inquiry-guided learning programs for first-year students and the interesting ways in which our university-wide writing and speaking program and growing service-learning program support inquiry-guided learning. Part IV documents the various ways we've supported instructors (and they have supported themselves) as they grow into inquiry-guided learning as well as the methods we've used to try to assess the impact of inquiry-guided learning—on our students, faculty, and the institution as a whole.

In addition to the dedication and support of the contributors to this volume, the Inquiry-guided Learning Initiative has benefited greatly from the efforts of others. Not the least of these are the many faculty, staff, and students not represented in the volume who have contributed to the continued growth and development of inquiry-guided learning on our campus. We have also been fortunate to have strong support from North Carolina State University administration. While the initiative has been largely faculty driven, without the support of administration, we would have never achieved the degree of institutional penetration we enjoy today. Finally, we have benefited greatly from the support of the William and Flora Hewlett Foundation as well as the U.S. Department of Education's Fund for the Improvement of Postsecondary Education.

Virginia S. Lee
North Carolina State University

PART I

SETTING THE CONTEXT

Part I provides a framework for the rest of the volume. In Chapter 1 we articulate our current, mutual understanding of inquiry-guided learning and some
of the tensions still inherent in that understanding. In Chapter 2 we briefly
summarize the history of inquiry-guided learning on our campus and the various projects that have stimulated its growth.

I

WHAT IS INQUIRY-GUIDED LEARNING?

By Virginia S. Lee, David B. Greene, Janice Odom,
Ephraim Schechter, and Richard W. Slatta

In May 2003 five of us who have been involved collectively with inquiry-guided learning (IGL) on campus for a number of years in a variety of leadership capacities sat around to discuss, what is inquiry-guided learning? We represented a number of units on campus with quite different functions—First Year College, First Year Inquiry Program, Faculty Center for Teaching and Learning, First Year Seminar Program of the College of Humanities and Social Sciences, University Planning and Analysis—as well as our various academic homes. We also came to IGL at North Carolina State University through different avenues and at different times, which has in turn colored our experience and practice of inquiry-guided learning. While sharing certain common features, each IGL project at the university has had a slightly different character, depending on its focus, leadership, and participants. Nevertheless we are all sitting around a table to talk about it.

As our conversation began to unfold, certain questions emerged as parameters for framing our understanding of inquiry-guided learning.

1. Does inquiry-guided learning refer to a specific teaching strategy or is it an umbrella term that refers to an array of teaching strategies? Is inquiry-guided learning simply another term for active learning?

2. What do we mean by inquiry-*guided* learning, and who or what is doing the guiding? Is inquiry-*guided* learning the same as inquiry-*based* learning?

3. What is the relationship between inquiry and critical thinking? Have some projects emphasized one more than the other? What effect has this had on how inquiry-guided learning is practiced in the classroom?

4. To what extent is the disciplinary context important in our understanding and practice of inquiry-guided learning?

5. When we refer to inquiry-guided learning at NCSU, what do we really mean? Do we mean a clearly defined pedagogy through which we are intentionally reforming undergraduate education at the university or the entire living initiative—its history, conversations, community of faculty, staff, students, administrators—that unfolds in often unpredictable ways?

The questions themselves point to diversity in both the understanding and practice of inquiry-guided learning at our institution, probably a sign of a vibrant undergraduate education reform initiative in the process of unfolding. We felt that it was important to acknowledge these differences, tensions, and inconsistencies as essential aspects of our dynamic understanding of inquiry-guided learning on this campus. At the same time we felt that we wanted to stake out the territory and offer an extended definition developed by those of us who have thought deeply about the concept and are guiding its practice on the campus, whether as administrators, faculty developers, and/or advanced practitioners. In the following pages of this chapter, we explore these questions further and conclude by offering a description of inquiry-guided learning, bracketed by what has preceded it.

Specific Pedagogy or Umbrella Term?

The term *inquiry-guided learning* has been used widely, both on this campus and nationally, but its reference and meaning are unclear. Like problem-based learning or the case study method, does it refer to a particular teaching method or pedagogy? Or is it a broader term that refers to a constellation of strategies that promote student learning through the process of inquiry? As the five of us, all in various leadership capacities in the IGL initiative, talked about inquiry-guided learning, different understandings of the term emerged.

On this campus we have defined inquiry-guided learning as much by the student commitments (or outcomes) it brings about than the teaching methods used. Since 1998, critical thinking, independent inquiry, responsibility for one's own learning, and intellectual growth and development have been the mortar of our initiative, binding the diverse teaching and learning experiences of students, instructors, departments, and colleges engaged in inquiry-guided learning. As later chapters will show, having a common understanding of inquiry-guided learning in terms of the overarching student learning outcomes has been extraordinarily useful. It has allowed us to speak across disciplines, because each of these terms has meaning no matter what the discipline. And as departments have begun to articulate curricular-level outcomes as part of our undergraduate academic program review process (see Chapter 15), the extent of the four student commitments across the entire undergraduate curriculum has become increasingly apparent. While falling short of a *lingua franca*, the four commitments point to a common intention within an otherwise highly fragmented undergraduate curriculum.

Still what do we mean by inquiry-guided learning in terms of what actually happens in the classroom? For most of us it refers to a range of strategies used to promote learning through students' active, and increasingly independent, investigation of questions, problems and issues, often for which there is no single answer (see p. 9). A range of teaching strategies is consistent with inquiry-guided learning including interactive lecture, discussion, problem-based learning, case studies, simulations, and independent study. In fact, probably the only strategy that is not consistent with inquiry-guided learning is the exclusive use of traditional lecturing. It also connotes a developmental range, perhaps beginning with raw questioning and curiosity and continuing through successive refinements to the more sophisticated lines of inquiry characteristic of the disciplines.

Who (or What) Is Doing the Guiding?

We refer to inquiry-*guided* learning, but who or what is doing the guiding? For some of us, inquiry itself was driving the learning or, more particularly, a question or questioning was driving the process. In the context of this understanding, it is vital for the student to be an active questioner and do the majority of the questioning. What motivates learning is students really having a question to which they want an answer. The challenge then becomes taking undergraduate students, many of whom have become accustomed to the numbing passivity bred by years of traditional schooling, and trying to reignite in them a spirit of curiosity, will, and purpose that manifests itself in independent questioning and inquiry. As students progress through the undergraduate curriculum and their chosen major, we anticipate their ability to question and seek answers to those questions becomes increasingly refined in ways that are appropriate to their chosen discipline. But in the end (and the beginning) it is the raw and vibrant interest and curiosity that we see in very young children that drives learning.

Others of us focused more on the guidance provided by faculty in inquiry-guided learning. In this view, inquiry is a developmental process; there's some skepticism that first-year students, for example, will be able to ask good, robust questions that will yield productive inquiry. In the early stages, instructor guidance may be substantial, but over time guidance as a driver of learning decreases while inquiry as the primary driver of learning increases. This view is consistent with a view of inquiry-guided learning expressed by the inquiry continuum: In the early stages the instructor defines most stages of inquiry (e.g., question, methods), while in the later stages such as in undergraduate research the student defines most stages of inquiry with the instructor serving as a resource only if needed.

How we respond to this question may reflect differences in personality, our current understanding of teaching and learning, and in our implicit view of the purpose of undergraduate education. After all there are the free spirits and the control freaks among us. Some of us are naturally more comfortable going with the flow, buoyed on the tide of experience; others maintain a firm hold on the tiller, navigating against the tide in an attempt to direct it. Researchers (e.g., Kember, 1997; Pratt, 1998) have identified different conceptualizations of teaching that range from wholly teacher and content centered to increasingly student centered with a focus on student development. Finally, often our instructional practice reflects an implicit view of the purpose of undergraduate education including preparation for responsible citizenry or cultivation of disciplinary experts (Clewett, 1998). Depending on our particular profile, some of us may weigh the nurturing of student curiosity, will, and purpose more heavily. In turn others may stress instructor control and guidance.

Critical Thinking or Inquiry? Does Disciplinary Context Matter?

At NCSU we have defined inquiry-guided learning in terms of four student commitments—critical thinking, independent inquiry, responsibility for one's own learning, and intellectual growth and maturity. We continue to struggle with the relationships among them and what we must do in the classroom to bring them about. But one question that has been particularly salient is the relationship between critical thinking and inquiry and the relative weight of one or the other in our courses and curriculum. As you will see in the next chapter, the importance of critical thinking in the context of IGL at NCSU is in part historical. The conversation about IGL emerged from a recognition that we were not guiding students intentionally in critical thinking. Core members of the first initiative had attended an intensive critical-thinking workshop by Richard Paul that had a deep impact on them. Paul's view of critical thinking; its emphasis on the distinctions between fact, opinion, and judgment; and the importance of universal standards continued to influence the first initiative and the subsequent practice of those who had participated in it. In addition the focus of the first IGL initiative here was in general education. One of the most tangible and important outcomes that emerged from it was a pilot inquiry-guided learning seminar program for first-year students, which has grown to become the First Year Inquiry Program. In the context of the patchwork of disciplines that comprise general education, critical thinking may have been more important. Critical thinking represents an intellectual core and key qualities of mind, and the disciplines simply represent variations (or "flavors") of this core quality. The ability of faculty from a variety of different disciplines to learn from one another and profit from interdisciplinary discussions as they have throughout the IGL initiative reinforces this belief.

For a few reasons the dynamic of subsequent initiatives was different from the first. Successive initiatives moved increasingly into later courses in the undergraduate curriculum and the major. In addition, unlike the first initiative that was largely faculty-guided exploration, a faculty developer with a formal background in pedagogy and cognitive psychology led the effort and designed many of the workshops. She tended to interpret inquiry-guided learning more purely and focus on the student commitment of independent inquiry. As a result the student commitment of independent inquiry and what it means in the context of individual disciplines became more salient. Later initiatives were less influenced by Paul's work and more influenced by the importance of disciplinary context and standards. While critical thinking was important, we felt that it emerged in the context of disciplinary inquiry, the types of judgments made, evidence used to support those judgments, and the different forms of argumentation used (Walvoord & Anderson, 1998; Donald, 2002, 1995, 1983). We tended to use Bloom's taxonomy as our operational definition of critical thinking. Many instructors find the taxonomy helpful as a planning tool and easier to use with their students. Used together with one of several heuristics for inquiry or problem solving, the taxonomy serves as a reminder that processes of inquiry also reinforced critical-thinking skills. Later in this chapter when we lay out a more formal definition of inquiry-guided learning, we also show how critical thinking and inquiry are related in our minds.

In later initiatives we also explored the question of the relationship between general education and the major and the idea of transferability: for example, what aspects of students' general education experience transfer to their later work in the major? How do we cultivate the ability to transfer? What skills and competencies can we count on as students move into higher level courses in the major? Here also the question of the relationship of the disciplines has emerged. For example, what relationship do the problem-solving capabilities developed in a general education mathematics requirement have to later coursework in sociology? Or what is the relationship between an introductory music course and later work in a highly technical and applied field such as food or pulp and paper science? Is it useful to talk about critical thinking as a single competency that develops across the disciplines?

Clearly Defined Pedagogy or Living Initiative?

Like the ancient Indian tale of the blind men and the elephant, how we perceive the IGL initiative may depend on where we stand in relation to it. Consider, for example, the instructor using inquiry-guided learning for the first time in her classroom, the administrator negotiating with departments and soliciting and engaging faculty, the faculty developer designing and delivering workshops, the grant writer identifying a program need and articulating a vision, the project director implementing and guiding a program. IGL is at once each of these experiences, all of these experiences, and none of these experiences: IGL truly is a plural term.

In an email exchange between Virginia Lee and David Greene, Virginia titled the subject header "Making IGL Work," one of the early working titles for this volume. In his return message, David changed the subject header to "Letting IGL Happen." While playful, the original message and its retort reflect an implication of the clearly defined pedagogy versus living initiative dilemma. And like the meaning of *guided* in inquiry-guided learning, where we fall on the horns of the dilemma may reflect philosophical orientation and personality as well as our role in the initiative. As a faculty developer and project director, Virginia sometimes feels as if she is trying to make IGL work: finding ways to guide instructors in the practice of IGL in useful and compelling ways, planning programs, and guiding the efforts of project participants in the daily rough-and-tumble of the university. As the director of the First Year Inquiry Program, David can acquire and protect resources and solicit faculty, but beyond that, he can simply "let things happen," trusting that with certain conditions in place, interesting and productive things will happen in classrooms and when faculty meet. In fact, we are at once making and letting inquiry-guided learning happen.

Like a variation on Yeats's dancer and dance, inquiry-guided learning may be inseparable from the community that practices it. Below we do stake out the territory and define what we mean by inquiry-guided learning as a set of teaching and learning practices; but like dancing, inquiry-guided learning is a performance. And like other performances such as music or drama, the score and script are guides to performance but not the performance itself. This is particularly true of inquiry-guided learning, because of the dynamic nature of teaching and learning. Instructors come with a variety of assumptions about teaching and learning that affect how they interpret what they hear in a workshop or conversation among other instructors and how that translates into what they do in the classroom. Their own teaching preferences as students, the nature of their discipline and its teaching traditions, the amount of time they devote to teaching, and a host of other factors affect how they interpret inquiry-guided learning in their classrooms. And, of course, students who often behave in unpredictable ways are another key element in the process.

Further, the IGL initiative is more than what goes on between instructors and students in classrooms or other learning spaces. It also comprises the larger community of administrators and staff, academic support units and administrative units, departments and colleges that both directly and indirectly affect how the initiative has unfolded. While this book presents a coherent and organized view, the initiative itself has unfolded quite differently: in fits and starts, pockets of activity here and there, influenced by this personality and that personality as they come and go. And it is inseparable from its history, opportunities recognized and ignored, the series of grants that have supported it, and other initiatives that have both complemented and competed with it.

We acknowledge these points of tension in our collective understanding of IGL. At the same time, inquiry-guided learning has meaning on our campus as a shared set of outcomes and constellation of teaching and learning practices. In the chapters ahead written by instructors and staff from a range of disciplines who have participated in one or more of several IGL projects on the campus, certain common features emerge: a way of talking about teaching and a common vocabulary; students' active engagement; teaching critical thinking and the processes of inquiry explicitly and intentionally; an emphasis on induction or moving from the concrete to the abstract; encouragement of questioning; and teaching through engagement in the methods of the discipline rather than simply about the discipline. Like a coral reef capable of behaving as a single organism despite its vastness and extraordinary diversity, the IGL initiative has a common intention and loose coherence that the single performance of this or that instructor belies.

Claim Staking

Now is not the first time we've met to discuss inquiry-guided learning and what we think it is. Feeling that IGL was probably more than the four student commitments and a set of pedagogical tools and principles (e.g., Bloom's taxonomy, Paul's universal standards, Perry's stages of intellectual development), in the fall of 2000 the Hewlett Steering Committee, a loosely organized coordinating body for the various IGL programs on our campus, met and endorsed the following definition of inquiry-guided learning.

What Is Inquiry-Guided Learning?

Inquiry-guided learning (IGL) refers to an array of classroom practices that promote student learning through guided and, increasingly, independent investigation of complex questions and problems, often for which there is no single answer.

Rather than teaching the results of others' investigations, which students learn passively, instructors assist students in mastering and learning through the process of active investigation itself. This process involves the ability to formulate good questions, identify and collect appropriate evidence, present results systematically, analyze and interpret results, formulate conclusions, and evaluate the worth and importance of those conclusions. It may also involve the ability to identify problems, examine problems, generate possible solutions, and select the best solution with appropriate justification. This process will differ somewhat among different academic disciplines.

Learning in this way promotes other important outcomes as well. It nurtures curiosity, initiative, and risk taking. It promotes critical thinking. It develops students' responsibility for their own learning and habits of life-long learning. And it fosters intellectual development and maturity: the recognition that ambiguity and uncertainty are inevitable, and in response, we must learn to make reasoned judgments and act in ways consistent with these judgments.

A variety of teaching strategies, used singly or, more often, in combination with one another, are consistent with inquiry-guided learning: interactive lecture, discussion, group work, case studies, problem-based learning, service learning, simulations, fieldwork, and labs as well as many others. In fact the only method that is not consistent with IGL is the exclusive use of straight lecturing and the posing of questions for which there is only one correct answer.

In addition, because of the nature of the outcomes it promotes and the necessity for active engagement, inquiry-guided learning must also involve writing and speaking both in classroom instruction and in the methods used to evaluate students.

While inquiry-guided learning is appropriate in all classes, it is most effective in small classes (i.e., approximately 10 students). It is particularly appropriate for first year students who are forming habits of learning that they will exercise throughout their undergraduate years and beyond. Finally, the rest of the undergraduate curriculum should reinforce these early learning experiences.

Prepared by
Faculty Center for Teaching and Learning and Hewlett Steering Committee, NC State University, September 2000

However useful the statement has been, it falls short of a prescription for practice that many instructors want: "Okay, so how do I do inquiry-guided learning?" Like a recipe with all the ingredients but no instructions, all the elements of inquiry-guided learning are there—the key outcomes, teaching strategies, and a hint about appropriate assignments, but guidance on how to orchestrate them to achieve the desired end is missing. Providing useful and compelling guidance on how to implement inquiry-guided learning for a highly diverse group of instructors has been a constant challenge. Table 1.1 is our latest effort to provide this guidance. It is a heuristic for instruction—while it offers a prescription, it is not prescriptive. For example, it permits many points of entry into IGL for the novice instructor and guidance for growth. It also acknowledges many of the critical questions posed earlier, offering some flexibility in response.

The table draws on several sources: the work of Novak and Gowin (1996/1979) and Donald (2002, 1995, 1983) to describe the underlying structure and methods of inquiry of the disciplines, Bloom (1956) and Paul (1993) to define more specifically what we mean by critical thinking, Kolb (1983) to provide a mechanism for the dynamics of learning, Knefelkamp (1974) to describe a developmental approach to instruction derived from the work of Perry, and, fundamental instructional design principles. In addition, Svinicki and Dixon (1987) provided a useful mapping of Kolb's cycle as an instructional cycle with different teaching strategies associated with each stage. Together their work provides a theoretical and research grounding for describing what we mean by inquiry-guided learning.

As we review Table 1.1, let's return to the questions posed at the beginning of the chapter.

Specific Teaching Strategy or Umbrella Term?

Inquiry-guided learning encompasses a range of teaching strategies, but the teaching strategies alone do not constitute inquiry-guided learning. Rather instructors need to use selected teaching strategies intentionally to facilitate students' ability to engage in inquiry and think critically. Similarly, because inquiry and critical thinking are active processes, students must also engage actively as they acquire these new skills. But active learning and engagement alone do not constitute inquiry-guided learning.

Actively engaging students, perhaps in carefully controlled question and answer sessions or in small group discussions, may be the initial entry point into inquiry-guided learning for instructors who have used content-driven lectures as their primary teaching strategy. Or it could be an assignment that departs from the conventional multiple-choice or short answer exam. At the outset, the instructor may simply use the strategy, but with no particular outcome related to inquiry or critical thinking in mind. With careful reflection, peer observation, conversation with other faculty, and other assessment techniques, over time the instructor will learn to exploit a range of teaching strategies more intentionally and more flexibly given the perceived needs of the students.

Who (or What) Is Doing the Guiding?

Table 1.1 points to multiple sources of guidance that instructors may exploit to varying degrees according to their predilection, will, or desire. The stages of inquiry or problem solving themselves, presented to students as heuristics, are a source of guidance. Likewise, the design of learning experiences—the orchestration of outcomes, teaching strategies, and assignments—is a source of guidance. Instructors can offer high levels of support in the form of guiding questions, carefully chosen problems, modeling and the like or lower levels of support again depending on their judgment, philosophy, or personality. Then again, the process of inquiry and problem solving itself provides guidance as a question or problem posed, whether by instructors or students, naturally asks for resolution.

Critical Thinking or Inquiry?

In Table 1.1 we characterize inquiry (or problem solving) as a series of generic stages beginning with the development of a question (identification of a problem). Using Bloom's taxonomy, we suggest parallels between the processes of inquiry and critical thinking. According to this model, the entire process of inquiry or problem solving constitutes the making of a reasoned judgment based on appropriate evidence—the hallmark of critical thinking. In the actual making of the

Table 1.1 Current Understanding of Inquiry-guided Learning

Stages of inquiry	Critical thinking	Kolb's learning cycle	Teaching strategies	Continuum of support	Selected methods of assessment
Content	Knowledge Comprehension		Various (see below)	✓ Various (see below)	Quizzes, exams Outlines Concept maps Briefing (paper) (Mini-) Papers, reports Oral presentations (Annotated) Bibliography
Develop question Design/frame experiment/study Select raw data [Define/represent problem] →	Synthesis	Active Experimentation →	Laboratories Direct observation Primary text reading Simulations/games Field work Problems Case studies Service learning Problem-based learning Project (e.g., design) Performance Internships	✓ Question/problem provided ✓ Readings selected ✓ Parameters provided ✓ Site selected ✓ Guiding questions provided ✓ Prompts provided ✓ Heuristic provided ✓ Modeling ✓ Coaching	Research proposal Study design/plan Problem statement Develop question/hypothesis Chart, diagram, flowchart

				✓ Questions provided ✓ Worksheet provided ✓ Guidelines provided	Log Lab/field notes Observation lists Idea lists Tables, charts Alternative drafts/solutions
Observe Record [Explore, generate strategies] →		Concrete Experience →	See above [Role play]		
Organize Analyze [Analyze alternative strategies] →	Analysis	Reflective Observation →	Logs/journals Other writing assignments Discussion Brainstorming [Debate/panel]	✓ Questions provided ✓ Format provided ✓ Articulation	Charts, tables, diagrams, flowcharts (Mini-) Papers Memo Taxonomy/set of categories Journal
Interpret Evaluate [Select strategy] →	Synthesis Evaluation	Abstract Conceptualization →	Lecture Readings Films/videotapes Concept maps Demonstrations	✓ Outlines ✓ Note-taking guidelines ✓ Concept maps ✓ Guiding questions	Briefing paper Abstract (Mini-) Paper Statement of assumptions Performance (e.g., clinical, artistic) Reflective journal Case analysis Diagnosis Regulation, law, rule Plan (e.g., nursing, construction)

Developed by Virginia S. Lee, Ph.D., Faculty Center for Teaching & Learning, NC State University.

judgment, particular emphasis may fall on the final stage involving interpretation and evaluation of the worth of the knowledge claim or problem solution made. The criteria for making warranted claims or selecting appropriate strategies often represent the professional standards of the disciplines.

Some of us foreground critical thinking more prominently and have drawn on the work of Paul more heavily, particularly his emphasis on the distinction between fact, opinion, and judgment and the use of universal standards (e.g., breadth, depth, precision, accuracy). In the early stages we may encourage student questioning for its own sake, not worrying too much about the conventions of our discipline. However, in seeking answers to those questions, we encourage students to make responsible distinctions between fact, opinion, and judgment and the conditions under which each is warranted. Further we help students use the universal standards to evaluate their thinking and how they arrive at the conclusions they do. For those of us using this approach, perhaps in first-year seminars or general education courses, the disciplinary context may be less important than the development of generic critical-thinking skills.

Is Disciplinary Context Important?

Table 1.1 uses generic stages of inquiry and problem solving, but it also allows for disciplinary variations on them. The so-called content of each discipline comprises a distinct set of concepts and the nature of the relationships among them and perhaps principles and theories derived from them as well; and often inquiry proceeds from questions about these concepts, such as quark, power, meaning, and foraging. Of course, the nature of the concepts influences the nature of the research questions asked and the data or phenomena examined. In some fields of science, research questions may need to include independent and dependent variables and the suggested relationships among them. In contrast the types of questions asked by an anthropologist or a zoologist may be far more open ended. Likewise, different disciplines may interpret each stage of inquiry or problem solving differently or emphasize some stages more than others. For example, as a variation of problem solving, a musician encountering a new score may explore it by running straight through it or exploring first this passage and then that, trying out alternative fingerings in challenging passages, and experimenting with different dynamics and interpretations, before settling on the final performance strategy. In contrast, the clinician, whether doctor, veterinarian, or management consultant, may spend far longer defining and representing the problem before generating alternative strategies to resolve it. As we suggest above, disciplinary context may matter more in advanced courses in the major than in general education courses. Nonetheless the more instructors teach through rather than about their disciplines as they do in inquiry-guided learning, the more the teaching and learning process takes on the distinctive characteristics of the discipline, even in introductory courses.

Clearly Defined Pedagogy or Living Initiative?

Just like the relationship between a score and musical performance, the table alone is not what we mean by inquiry-guided learning at NCSU. As a guide to instructional practice, it grew out of our own reading and struggle to understand what the term *inquiry-guided learning* meant, refinements of presentations of inquiry-guided learning in workshop settings in response to participant reactions, conversations among faculty, and wider conversations at the university stimulated by assessment and technology, for example. Some instructors have come to inquiry-guided learning on their own, without the benefit of the formal IGL projects. And through the university's undergraduate program review process, many departments are defining curricular-level outcomes that require some form of inquiry-guided learning to adequately address them (see Chapter 15). Further, as we alluded to previously, most instructors grow into inquiry-guided learning rather than instantaneously transforming their teaching like a light switched on. How they grow into it depends on the individual personalities of the faculty members, their assumptions about the teaching and learning process, the amount of time they have to devote to teaching, their discipline, and a host of other factors. Some instructors may begin by articulating clear learning outcomes as a guide for instruction. Others may jump in, try out an interactive teaching strategy, like the way students respond, and then gradually refine it. Others may begin by assigning a project and then realize that they need to provide students more explicit instruction in how to do it. And so inquiry-guided learning proceeds by fits and starts.

References

Bloom, B. S. (Ed.). (1956). *Taxonomy of educational objectives: The classification of educational goals: Handbook I cognitive domain.* New York: Longman.

Clewett, R. M., Jr. (1998). A general education focus for the coming years. *The Journal of General Education, 47*(4), 265–281.

Donald, J. G. (1983). Knowledge structures: Methods for exploring course content. *Journal of Higher Education, 54*(1), 31–41.

Donald, J. G. (1995). Disciplines with an affinity for the improvement of undergraduate education. In N. Hativa & M. Marincovich (Eds.), *Disciplinary differences in teaching and learning: Implications for practice* (pp. 7–17). San Francisco: Jossey-Bass.

Donald, J. G. (2002). *Learning to think: Disciplinary perspectives.* San Francisco: Jossey-Bass.

Hewlett Steering Committee. (2000). *What is inquiry-guided learning?* Raleigh, NC: Faculty Center for Teaching & Learning, North Carolina State University.

Kember, D. (1997). A reconceptualization of the research into university academics' conceptions of teaching. *Learning and Instruction, 7*(1), 255–275.

Knefelkamp, L. (1974). *Developmental instruction: Fostering intellectual and personal growth of college students.* Unpublished doctoral dissertation. University of Minnesota.

Kolb, D. A. (1983). *Experiential learning: Experience as the source of learning and development.* Englewood Cliffs, NJ: Prentice Hall.

Novak, J. D., & Gowin, D. B. (1996/1979). *Learning how to learn.* New York: Cambridge University Press.

Paul, R. W. (1993). *Critical thinking: What every person needs to survive in a rapidly changing world.* Santa Rosa, CA: The Foundation for Critical Thinking.

Pratt, D. D. (1998). *Five perspectives on teaching in adult and higher education.* Malabar, FL: Krieger Publishing Co., Inc.

Svinicki, M., & Dixon, N. M. (1987). The Kolb model modified for classroom activities. *College Teaching, 35*(4), 141–146.

Walvoord, B. E., & Anderson, V. J. (1998). *Effective grading: A tool for learning and assessment.* San Francisco: Jossey-Bass.

2

INQUIRY-GUIDED LEARNING AT NORTH CAROLINA STATE UNIVERSITY

A BRIEF HISTORY

By David B. Greene,
Virginia S. Lee, and J. Douglas Wellman

Introduction

NCSU's Inquiry-guided Learning (IGL) Initiative began in 1995 and represents a bridge between the teaching and research missions of the university. It is a complex, multipronged initiative that has engaged well over 6,000 students, more than 200 faculty and staff, and 60 academic and administrative units on campus. The initiative comprises a growing First Year Inquiry Program, a First Year Seminar Program in the College of Humanities and Social Sciences, selected courses throughout the undergraduate program, both general education and the major, and nine lead departments in seven of the university's 10 colleges that have transformed a sequence of courses in the major. All facets of the initiative share a commitment to (1) four broad student learning outcomes: critical thinking, developing habits of independent inquiry, responsibility for one's own learning, and intellectual growth and development; and (2) promoting student learning through the active investigation of complex questions and problems. A shared commitment to these outcomes has furthered the integration of the IGL Initiative with four other key initiatives on campus—writing and speaking across the curriculum, undergraduate academic program review, various accreditation efforts, both disciplinary and university-wide, and assessment—in ways that leverage the impact of these separate initiatives. The IGL Initiative is also intertwined with broader, ongoing conversations concerning general education and the undergraduate curriculum. Although inquiry-guided learning is not pervasive in the curriculum, nevertheless there are now pockets of inquiry-guided learning practices at key points throughout the undergraduate curriculum in forms that are replicable in other courses, sequence of courses, and undergraduate programs. Figure 2.1 captures the extent of inquiry-guided learning practices in the undergraduate curriculum. The progressively darker graying within the 10 colleges represents students' developmental progression as they advance through the major.

Early Beginnings

It hasn't always been this way. Like all good stories, the story of the IGL effort at NCSU was well under way before anyone realized there was anything happening at all. And like all good stories, this one has invented a beginning for itself. "It all began with the van ride home from Charlotte," people like to say, referring to the ride a dozen university faculty took home from a workshop 150 miles away led by Richard Paul, the critical-thinking guru, on a cold January weekend in 1996. The excursion was organized by a graduate student

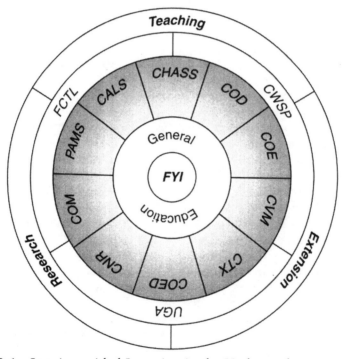

Figure 2.1 Inquiry-guided Learning in the Undergraduate Curriculum at NCSU.

who worked in the office of the dean of undergraduate affairs and served as support staff for the Council on Undergraduate Education (CUE or "the Council"), which is charged by the provost to tend to the general education of all the students in all curricula of the university. She was aware that the university required students to think critically and that most faculty modeled critical thinking. But she also felt that very few faculty provided students *explicit* guidance on how to think critically themselves. When she heard about the two-day workshop in Charlotte, she persuaded a dozen members of the Council and others to give up a weekend for the sake of critical thinking and the dean to fund the trip.

The workshop was stimulating and constructively irritating. The Charlotte Dozen found themselves talking about how they might change some of their assignments and classroom practices to help students learn how to monitor their thinking and think more critically. Over dinner at a Thai restaurant, they discovered that a small change in a math course could be adapted to become a big change in an arts course. Grateful for what they learned about critical thinking, they were energized by what they were learning from each other. During the van ride home they promised each other to keep meeting and exchanging ideas.

During the spring of 1996 CUE discussed the futility of general education requirements if students satisfied the requirements by taking unwanted courses and then forgot their content as quickly as possible. So long as students saw their education as the faculty's responsibility, the Council saw, education wasn't going to happen. The Council drew up and passed a position paper on students' responsibility for and commitment to their education (see Chapter 15, Appendix A), which charged faculty to help students take responsibility for their own education. The position paper also charged faculty to offer students "guided practice in critical thinking" in order that students would increasingly take charge of their own thinking. These two new emphases in defining the role of the faculty provided the groundwork on which specific classroom practices could be built.

In December 1996 the provost received an invitation from the William and Flora Hewlett Foundation to apply for a grant to "improve general education at a Research I University." This challenge was passed along to the Council's chair, who worked with a small committee and a grant writer on a proposal that put these two emphases together under the banner of "inquiry-guided instruction" (later changed to "inquiry-guided learning"). They made the case that with Hewlett funding these emphases could appear on a continuum of inquiry running from entering-level general education courses to individual or group research projects in the student's final semester.

The following sections describe the three major projects that have contributed to the growth of inquiry-guided learning on our campus, as summarized in Table 2.1.

Table 2.1 Inquiry-guided Learning at NCSU

Dates	Program title	Participating units	Focus	Program features
Before 1997	Independent Faculty Initiatives CUS Report CUE Position Statement Richard Paul Workshop	Individual Faculty Faculty Senate CUE Div. of Undergraduate Affairs	Early exploration	
1997–1999	**Hewlett I** ($150,000—funded by Hewlett Foundation)	Individual Faculty, Staff and Graduate Students (50) Div. of Undergraduate Affairs	Exploration of inquiry-guided learning with classroom experimentation in general education courses	Self-directed faculty groups Retreats/workshops with external facilitators Assessment study
1999–2002	**First Year Inquiry Courses** (2001/2002— $271,000 funded by Div. of Undergraduate Affairs)	Sections: 1999/2000— 10; 2000/2001— 28; 2001/2002—46 Div. of Undergraduate Affairs	Small seminars for first-year students taught with inquiry-guided learning	Small (i.e, 22 students) classes Faculty development Program assessment
2000–2001	**Hewlett Continuation** ($59,500—funded by NCSU Office of the Provost)	Individual Faculty, Staff and Graduate Students (40) Hewlett Steering Committee	Integration of inquiry-guided learning in individual courses	Outcomes-based course development process Common under-standing of inquiry-guided instruction

Table 2.1 (Continued)

Dates	Program title	Participating units	Focus	Program features
2000–2001 (*continued*)		Faculty Center for Teaching and Learning		Resource handbook Retreats/workshops with external/internal facilitators Small working groups Embedded classroom/program assessment Campus-wide dissemination
2000–2002	**Hewlett Campus Challenge** ($150,000—funded by Hewlett Foundation)	Departmental Teams (10) Faculty Center for Teaching and Learning Campus Writing and Speaking Program Div. of Undergraduate Affairs University Planning and Analysis	Institutionalization of inquiry-guided learning in the departmental major with multiunit collaboration	Outcomes-based curricular-level outcomes and course/curriculum planning Orchestration of campus initiatives Resource handbook Retreats/workshops with external/internal facilitators Embedded classroom/program assessment Departmental dissemination Campus-wide dissemination

(*Continued*)

Table 2.1 (Continued)

Dates	Program title	Participating units	Focus	Program features
2001–2002	**FIPSE Planning Grant** ($30,000)	Div. of Undergraduate Affairs College of Humanities and Social Sciences Faculty Center for Teaching and Learning	Assessment of impact of IGL initiatives on faculty and student perceptions of teaching and learning and effects on student learning	Construction of an assessment model
2002	**Teaching with IGL Seminar**	Faculty Center for Teaching and Learning	Integration of IGL into courses in department teams of two	See **Hewlett Continuation** above
	Other Reform Efforts	Office of the Provost Faculty Center for Teaching and Learning Campus Writing and Speaking Program		Service learning, curriculum diversity, writing/speaking across the curriculum

Hewlett I (1997–1999)—Exploring Inquiry-guided Learning and Early Experimentation with Inquiry-guided Learning in the Classroom

Hewlett funded the proposal and provided $150,000 over the two-year period (1997–1999) for an initial exploration of inquiry-guided learning. Sixty-two faculty and staff were identified as "Hewlett Fellows" and organized into working groups around issues of pedagogy, curriculum, and institutional impediments to successful learning experiences. A parallel group of 25 Hewlett Graduate Student Fellows worked independently for 18 months. In retrospect, we realized how beneficial it would have been to link the faculty/staff and graduate student working groups; at our capstone retreat when the two groups came together, the faculty were dazzled by the energy and insight of their graduate student colleagues. In addition to the bimonthly meetings of the working groups, we held an off-campus two-day workshop each year. The first, led by Peter Frederick of Wabash College, focused on ways of understanding the goals of education and how to shape the curriculum and the individual class meeting to accord with those goals. The second, led by Craig Nelson of Indiana University-Bloomington, focused on interventions faculty can use to rouse students out of dualistic thinking. In addition, the initiative benefited from campus visits by Richard Paul of Sonoma State and Robert Orrill of The College Board.

The Hewlett Initiative, as the program was called, produced several outcomes. Faculty from every college of the university pooled their wisdom and their frustration and worked together from their individual practices toward a common understanding of teaching as providing opportunities for inquiry-guided learning. The excitement and insight that emerged from this extended cross-disciplinary experience helped sustain participant motivation and allowed us to build a learning community. Substantively, participants identified three principles, called for a while the "Hewlett Principles," that characterized the outcomes of a course with opportunities for inquiry-guided learning: a sense of independent inquiry, the ability to think critically, and the capacity to take responsibility for one's own learning. Together these capacities encourage intellectual growth toward maturity, understood in the terms of the William Perry model of intellectual development from dualistic thinking to mature thinking in which there are no single correct answers, only better and less well reasoned judgments. Many of the participants discovered for the first time the usefulness of tools like Bloom's taxonomy for thinking about inquiry-guided learning.

Hewlett I created a critical mass of faculty versed in the concept, practice, objectives, and outcomes of IGL. In addition, through the leadership of a subgroup of Hewlett Fellows, the Hewlett Initiative spawned the First Year Inquiry Program, consisting of small (i.e., no more than 22 students) freshman seminars taught by faculty versed in IGL principles and practices. With strong administrative backing, the First Year Inquiry Program (combined with the parallel First Year Seminar Program offered by the College of Humanities and Social Sciences) has grown to over 70 courses each year serving approximately one-third of all new freshmen at NCSU (see Chapter 16).

Hewlett Continuation (2000–2001)—Transforming Individual Courses Through Inquiry-guided Learning

A new provost came on board in the fall of 1999. Impressed by the accomplishments of the first Hewlett project, he provided $59,500 to fund three semesters of programming for a second-generation project, ultimately called the Hewlett Continuation (HC) Project. Directed by the Faculty Center for Teaching and Learning, the HC Project was very different from Hewlett I, in part due to how much the Hewlett I had accomplished. Whereas the first initiative wandered around many topics, unsure of which ones to pursue, Hewlett Continuation had a definite focus: classroom practices that made IGL real in individual courses. Forty-five faculty, graduate students, and staff worked together on transforming their courses in ways consistent with the Hewlett principles.

Instead of bimonthly meetings with uncertain agendas, the HC project had a comprehensive program of retreats, seminars, workshops, outside speakers (i.e., Peter Frederick, Barbara Walvoord, Tim Riordan and Ann van Heerden from Alverno College, Sheila Tobias) and luncheons. It had an outcomes-based course development process and a resource handbook to facilitate a common understanding of IGL. The HC project was well documented and carefully assessed using techniques such as external assessment, instructor course-development reports, and peer review and observation. The project concluded with a series of luncheons in which selected participants made short presentations about their transformed courses and a final celebratory dinner. Perhaps most important was a campus-wide, daylong symposium, called Inquiry-guided Instruction at NC State, that took stock of the many ways in which inquiry-guided learning was taking place, including service learning and study abroad programs (see Chapter 19 for a fuller discussion). As never before, people were struck by the power of inquiry-guided learning to help students feel the power of their own questions and the importance of learning how to answer them.

As we moved into the HC Project, the steering committee that had been put together to oversee Hewlett I decided to continue to meet as a way of coordinating a number of initiatives occurring around the campus, all of which supported or touched on IGL in one way or another. Among others, the committee included the director and associate director of the newly formed Faculty Center for Teaching and Learning, the director of the Alcoa-funded project to build increased effective attention to curriculum diversity issues, the leader of the College of Humanities and Social Sciences' new First Year Seminar Program, the director of the new Honors Program (which emphasized first-year seminars and undergraduate research), the director of the Freshman

Writing Program, and the director of the Campus Writing and Speaking Program. The steering committee still continues as a coordinating body, now under the name "IGL Group" with a slightly different membership.

It was sometime in this period that people began to use the word *movement* to describe what IGL was coming to mean at NCSU. The term was earned, for more and more faculty were teaching general education courses using principles of IGL, more and more faculty were volunteering to teach First Year Inquiry and First Year Seminar courses, and participants in both Hewlett I and the Hewlett Continuation Project were now engaged in the numerous educational reforms on campus, including but not limited to the following:

- Faculty Center for Teaching and Learning that supports faculty instructional development through a wide variety of programs and services and seeks to nurture a positive campus culture for teaching and learning
- Campus Writing and Speaking Program that provides support for both faculty and students involved in "across-the-curriculum" courses intended to improve students' communication, thinking, and group-process skills
- DELTA (Distance Education and Learning Technology Applications), the Learning Technologies Service, and the Teaching and Learning with Technology Roundtable that support faculty development in teaching with technology and emphasize the importance of pedagogy driving technology
- Curriculum Diversity Initiative that recognizes that student-centered approaches to teaching and learning are essential to inclusive education and that diversity is essential to the development of higher order thinking
- Service Learning Program, in which students in service learning courses engage in meaningful community service and are guided through reflection on how what they learned in the course informs their service and vice versa
- Undergraduate Academic Program Review process that focuses attention on the assessment of student learning outcomes
- University Standing Committee on the Evaluation of Teaching that over the past three years has made great headway in pursuit of improvements in student course evaluation, peer review of teaching, and the scholarship of teaching and learning
- New teaching awards, including the Board of Governors Award, the Departmental Award for Teaching and Learning (provides $5,000 one-time and $15,000 ongoing additions to departmental operating budget), the Gertrude Cox Award for innovative excellence in technology-assisted teaching, and awards for outstanding service in support of teaching by both faculty and staff
- Faculty Senate Select Committee on Reappointment, Promotion, and Tenure that adapted the work of Ernest Boyer and colleagues for a major revision of the faculty reward system at NCSU intended to raise the status of teaching and outreach/extension

Hewlett Campus Challenge (2000–2002)—The Institutionalization of Inquiry-guided Learning in the Departmental Major

In Spring 2000 we applied for a second Hewlett grant—Hewlett Campus Challenge: General Education and the Major—to extend inquiry-guided learning into the departmental major. We believed that failing to move IGL into the majors would undercut the progress we had made in transforming teaching and learning in general education courses. Once again, Hewlett funded our proposal, providing another $150,000 over two years. Unlike the earlier two initiatives whose primary focus was general education and the individual course, the focus of the HCC Project was a sequence of courses in the departmental major. At the outset the project included 10 departmental teams each comprising three faculty members, a graduate student, and an undergraduate student. Each team identified a sequence of three or four courses in the major to transform through the introduction of IGL. In transforming these courses, the team had to consider how these courses were related developmentally to one another, for example, how a first semester junior's problem-solving ability is different from a first semester senior's ability and how instructors develop that ability intentionally through instruction. Toward the end of the project, teams were also asked to develop an internal dissemination model, a kind of faculty development plan for the rest of their department, in an effort to move the project beyond early adopters and on to the next tier of faculty engagement.

In addition, four units on campus, each with a common focus on student learning outcomes and outcomes-based assessment, collaborated on the project.

- The Campus Writing and Speaking Program began to assist individual departments in articulating curricular-level outcomes in response to changes in the general education requirements regarding writing and speaking. The outcomes described what a graduating senior in the major would know and be able to do. Many of these outcomes emphasized students' ability to utilize the modes of inquiry in the discipline that could be assessed using writing and speaking assignments. (Among the 10 departments participating in the Hewlett Campus Challenge, 5 departments had curricular-level writing and speaking outcomes in place at the outset of the project.)

- The Faculty Center for Teaching and Learning utilizes a student learning outcomes approach to course development. It had also coordinated the Hewlett Continuation Project that had stressed the outcomes of inquiry: the ability to formulate good questions, identify and collect appropriate evidence, present results systematically, analyze and interpret results, and the like. These outcomes represent in more general terms what it means to conduct inquiry in the disciplines.

- University Planning and Analysis supports outcomes-based planning and assessment and would coordinate the university's self-study as part of the institution's reaccreditation process. Outcomes-based planning and assessment will drive portions of the self-study.

- The Division of Undergraduate Affairs administers the departmental undergraduate academic program review process, portions of which are based on student learning outcomes. As part of that effort, departments develop curricular-level outcomes and determine how they will assess them using a combination of indirect and direct methods, derived from student performance on classroom assignments.

By coordinating the efforts of these four units, we hoped that departments would recognize these efforts as related and complementary. We wanted the work of the four units to support and reinforce one another in the interest of undergraduate education reform. This kind of coordination occurs all too rarely in higher education and particularly in large, decentralized research-extensive institutions.

To support the departmental teams, the project provided a program of retreats, seminars and workshops, outside speakers, luncheons, and the like. Other project elements include outcomes-based curricular-level outcomes and course/curriculum planning, orchestration of campus initiatives, a resource handbook, departmental and external dissemination, and assessment. Finally, each team received $9,000 over the project period to support travel and internal dissemination.

Over the past three and one-half years, after two extensions on the grant, departmental teams have made significant progress in moving toward the project goals. (Two departments—Microbiology and Paper Science and Engineering—describe their progress later in this volume.) We are also beginning to develop a model of transformation in the academic department based on their work.

Other Projects

In addition to these larger projects, there have been some other smaller but still important efforts, many of which are preparing us for a new and deeper level of inquiry-guided learning activity in the years ahead. In 2001, we received a small Fund for the Improvement of Postsecondary Education (FIPSE) planning grant that supported deeper assessment of ongoing projects as well as a one-day Inquiry-guided Learning Institute described in later chapters (see Chapters 19 and 20). We have also experimented with less resource-intensive faculty development projects including a seminar for five two-person departmental teams, an all-day workshop for newer faculty cofacilitated by faculty who are more experienced with IGL practices, and a four-session IGL workshop series. We are also in the process of developing a comprehensive inquiry-guided learning website for the university, which we hope will help disseminate IGL practices even more broadly, foster scholarship related to inquiry-guided learning, and encourage deeper reflection on how we practice inquiry-guided learning at various levels of the university.

At the moment we are at a crossroads with inquiry-guided learning. Over the past seven years we have developed successful programs like the First Year Inquiry Program that cut across departments. We have good models of IGL practices in individual courses from a variety of disciplines. We have examples of departments that have successfully transformed a sequence of key courses in their undergraduate major or an entire program using inquiry-guided learning. And we have good evidence, based on the curricular-level outcomes articulated by all undergraduate programs, that inquiry-guided learning should be pervasive throughout the undergraduate curriculum (see Chapter 15). The writing of this volume represents an opportunity to reflect on what we've accomplished to date and move to the next level of extending and institutionalizing inquiry-guided learning at NCSU.

PART II

INTERPRETING AND IMPLEMENTING INQUIRY-GUIDED LEARNING

Part II, the largest section of the volume, describes how various instructors, departments, and colleges in a range of disciplines have interpreted and implemented inquiry-guided learning. In Chapters 3 through 10, individual instructors share how they have implemented inquiry-guided learning in their courses in disciplines ranging from music to food science and for first-year through graduate students. Chapters 11 and 12 describe the efforts of the Department of Microbiology and the Paper Science and Engineering Program in the Department of Pulp and Paper Science to introduce inquiry-guided learning more broadly into the undergraduate major. In Chapters 13 and 14 two of our 10 colleges—Engineering and Design—consider college-wide mechanisms for disseminating inquiry-guided learning. In Chapter 15, we explore the potential for even broader dissemination of inquiry-guided learning in the undergraduate curriculum in part through our undergraduate academic program review process.

3

ALL IN THE BALANCE

PSYCHOLOGY 201 "CONTROVERSIAL ISSUES IN PSYCHOLOGY"

By Samuel B. Pond, III

A foolish consistency is the hobgoblin of
little minds . . .
          —*Ralph Waldo Emerson*

Like all introductory psychology courses, Psychology 201 "Controversial Issues in Psychology" (PSY 201) exposes students to fundamental concepts and applications of psychology, aiming to develop in students a richer understanding of themselves, of others, and the intricacies of human relationships. Unlike such courses, however, PSY 201 operates largely on the principles of inquiry-guided learning, offers specific instruction in critical thinking, and endeavors to develop students' abilities and inclinations to scrutinize various subjects in psychology and academia. Using an inductive form of pedagogy, I endeavor primarily to help students develop an appreciation of the field—its methods, its paradoxes, its past, present, and future—by exposing them to various controversies in psychology. I cover selected content areas in psychology in the process of addressing the types of problems with which psychologists struggle and their methods of exploring and resolving these problems.

Some controversial topics addressed in the course include the effects of genetics testing, the appropriateness of using nonhumans in psychological research, the value of intelligence testing, the effectiveness of spanking children, the veracity of long-term memories of abuse, the diagnosis of mental disorders, the efficacy of psychotherapy, and the role of religion in mental health. To help ensure a reasonably comprehensive survey of the field, I tap controversies in such diverse areas of psychology as research methodology, biological psychology, human development, cognitive processes, mental health, and social psychology. By tackling controversial issues such as these, students develop, employ, refine, and practice systematic searching skills that apply to other subjects in psychology and even other disciplines. If students seriously probe the depths of challenging controversial topics, they come to realize that there can be no wholly satisfying answers without significant investigative effort (Slife & Yanchar, 2000).

As I expose students to controversies in psychology, I encourage them to actively explore the positions held by their classmates, knowing that in so doing, their own positions may be challenged. This is often an uncomfortable time, but when conducted candidly, these discussion sessions can eventually increase a student's tolerance for uncertainty and ambiguity, at least temporarily, in the interest of learning. Through such healthy explorations, a student's position may become more firmly solidified or it may be drastically revised. A main objective of the course, therefore, is to refine the way students think about and use controversy and uncertainty in the learning process (Lee, 1998).

A Learning Model

The model of learning I use in the course is chiefly based on a fundamental aspect of human nature: people tend to avoid incongruity, dissonance, and imbalance (Brown, 1962). Classic work in psychology has shown that human nature seems to abhor imbalance and inconsistency as nature abhors a vacuum (Zajonc, 1960). That said, however, human nature is perhaps a bit more fickle about it. While we generally avoid inconsistency and find it uncomfortable, we sometimes find it intriguing or entertaining and something desirable. Like teasing the cat, tempting fate, or taking a risk to try something new, there are occasions when we enter a state of imbalance for amusement or the opportunity to feel efficacious. Researchers have drawn upon this phenomenon to explain attitude formation and change, reactions to conflict, and perceptual bias. Langer (2001) and Hansen (1998) have also shown its relevance to how people resist or actively engage themselves in the learning process.

The model presented in Figure 3.1 illustrates the role that balance plays when we ask students to learn about both sides of a controversial issue and to come to a defensible position. From the perspective of the students, a currently held position is comfortable mainly because it is balanced and consistent with other things they know. On the other hand, the work required to appreciate the counter position is often cognitively uncomfortable because the students perceive it to be inconsistent and dissonant with their position. In other words, the model assumes that the students are reluctant to explore the counter position because their present cursory understanding of it actually hinders further serious consideration.

The bottom arrow pointing to the left side of the figure signifies a cognitive gradient of sorts and portrays students' natural inclination to defend their current position. The task of instruction is to get students to move into the "learn-

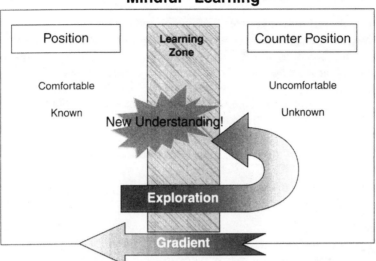

Figure 3.1   A Model of "Mindful" Learning.

ing zone." Because this is a location of incongruity, dissonance, and imbalance, I exhort students against inclinations to stay comfortable. I think that the degree of discomfort students experience is probably proportional to the extent to which they are fixed in their original position. In the model, the sweeping curved arrow indicates an act of exploration encouraged and shaped by the learning activities and structure of the course. The guidance offered students through instruction in guided inquiry, critical thinking, and various methods of persuasion mitigates the discomfort produced by wandering into the unknown.

The final result of working within the learning zone is always some degree of new understanding of the controversy based upon new information the student obtains through connecting in a deeper way with the topic at hand. Students move to a new position, actually a temporary resting spot. Sometimes students subscribe to the counter position. More often than not, though, I find that students' work produces a more refined and internalized understanding of an issue that is closer to the position held originally, although tempered by the counter position.

Although this model begins to capture the type of cognitive commotion I believe students probably experience when they seriously address positions counter to their own, I have not assessed this systematically. For now, I rely on conversations I have had with students and on the work in psychology and education that seems to bear upon it. (Argyris, 1969, 1976; Crossan, 2003; Hansen, 1998; Irving & Williams, 1995; Lee, 1998) And although the model portrays the dynamics of the learning process, it does not directly address the pedagogy relevant to shepherding students through it.

Layout of the Course

The first one-fifth of the course introduces aspects of learning and psychology that stimulate students' awareness of the linkages among inquiry-guided learning, academic freedom, and critical thinking, as summarized in Figure 3.2.

This "front-loading" is designed to prepare students for the remainder of the course in which they address controversial issues in psychology and put learning into practice. Interspersed throughout this second part of the course are brief training sessions on skills that are needed to implement and integrate inquiry-guided learning and critical thinking (e.g., how to work in groups, how to listen and communicate, and how to recognize propaganda).

Part One: Front-loading for Controversy

I have tried to organize the course so that it is consistent with the tenets of inquiry-guided learning, which assume that knowledge is a constructed entity based on students' active exploration of topics together rather than the passive reception of information primarily through lectures. By structuring the course so that one component builds upon another and stressing to students that they should find points of connection across all new material, I acknowledge and reinforce the idea that prior learning plays a direct role in future learning. During this segment of the course, all class activities and homework assignments focus on the following topics: the psychology of balance and consistency, mindful learning, academic freedom, critical thinking, and philosophical assumptions in psychology. At the end of this period, students discuss how all of these topics are interrelated.

Front-loading for Controversy	*Practicing on Controversial Issues*
Desire for balance and consistency	Four-step cycle for covering controversial issues
"Mindful" learning	"Process review" days and skills trainings
Academic freedom	
Critical thinking	
Philosophical assumptions in psychology	

Figure 3.2   The Structure of PSY 201 "Controversial Issues in Psychology."

Desire for Balance and Consistency. A foundation of my learning model is that we are motivated to explain and deal with events that create imbalance and that we often work hard to find meaning, connectedness, and closure in a series of events. Rather than directly announcing these psychological phenomena, I use in-class demonstrations to illustrate them and elicit student comment and to get students working together in groups.

For example, I divide the class into four teams and ask one player from each team to play a game of Twister, a party game where players are directed to position their hands and feet on different colored dots on a 5' × 4' sheet of white plastic. With four or five players, this becomes a challenging game of balance and interpersonal entanglement. I alter the playing conditions, even having teams blindfold a representative player, so that some psychological points about social space, balance, personal control, and dissonance are discovered and discussed by the students. After the game the players describe how they felt while playing.

Using another demonstration involving auditory stimulation, I ask students to listen for a message contained in a recording of a phrase of a song played backwards. Unless they have heard the demonstration before, none of the students is usually able to hear the message. After being told what they should be hearing, however, most students hear the message in a subsequent playback. Subsequent discussion most frequently addresses how we usually dislike confusion and try to make sense of all incoming information, how we can be lazy and immediately lock on to what others suggest, and similarly, how we often resist alternative suggestions inconsistent with what we are expecting. I deliberately create discussion groups consisting of four to five members and try to make the membership of these groups as diverse as possible with regard to ethnic background, gender, and knowledge of psychology to increase the likelihood that multiple positions will be considered and discussed within each group throughout the semester.

Mindful Learning. Overall, these demonstrations and the discussions they engender provide a good lead into Langer's (2001) work on "mindful learning." Students are prepared experientially to reflect on how mindsets might limit the way they learn and on how many of their beliefs about learning itself are, perhaps, based on blindly accepted mindsets. By considering what it means to be more fully mindful of the world around them, students begin to acquire a better understanding of both the effort inquiry-guided learning sometimes takes and of the way learning occurs in a university environment.

Academic Freedom. Because students take the course in their first year, the course enjoys the power of the first impression of university life, particularly its foundation of academic freedom. Designed to put academic freedom into operation in the classroom, the course encourages students to learn how to learn together and teach each other. It demonstrates how the university community is active, thriving on complexity and differing opinions. I urge students to take an informed position on any issue, actively exchange ideas, expect to be challenged, and be prepared to develop measured and respectful responses.

To help them extend the ideas developed within the academic community beyond its walls, I ask students to reflect upon Cronon's (1998) article, "Only Connect . . .", and to consider the many types of "connecting" they will undertake. Around this time I present specific information about inquiry-guided learning, critical thinking, and the learning model previously described.

Instruction in Critical Thinking.   Students receive formal instruction in critical thinking because they need a common framework and terminology to which they can hold one another accountable. Richard Paul's (Paul & Elder, 2001) approach to critical thinking has been most helpful in this endeavor: I allocate class time to review the elements and standards of critical thinking and the intellectual traits of critical thinkers. At the end of the first one-fifth of the course, I formally assess students' knowledge of the terminology and structure of critical thinking and their ability to integrate what they have learned about psychology, critical thinking, and academic freedom.

Philosophical Assumptions.   Just prior to tackling controversial issues in psychology and initiating the second part of the course, we discuss some basic philosophical assumptions that often drive controversy in the field of psychology. With minimal prompting, students readily identify the following: free will and determinism, nature and nurture, mind and body (albeit not necessarily using these words). As a homework assignment, each student explores the assumptions further while reviewing the controversial issues we will address during the semester. Students note in their journals their current position on each of the issues and how stances endorsed in each of the philosophical sets might support their position. This exercise gives students a quick glance at the complexity of upcoming controversial issues and opens the possibility that equally viable and conflicting positions on controversies can exist.

Part Two: Practicing on Controversial Issues

I introduce the second part of PSY 201 by reviewing a four-day, four-step approach to exploring and discussing controversial issues in psychology. Because it contains a valuable compilation of point–counterpoint articles on controversial issues addressed in the course, I use Slife's (2000) *Taking Sides: Clashing Views on Controversial Psychological Issues* as a textbook. For each controversy, the author briefly highlights the main points of contention and presents two articles with opposing viewpoints.

For each controversy, I include on my required reading list articles from academic journals, scholarly magazines, and the popular press to provide students additional background information. For example, *Current Directions in Psychological Science* contains succinct, readable examinations of issues across all areas of psychology. *American Psychologist* often contains articles addressing the application of psychology and associated social and ethical issues. We also consult other interdisciplinary journals including *Journal of Social Issues* and *American Scientist*. Popular magazines such as *Time* and *Newsweek* serve as good "connecting points" for deeper investigation, because they often contain articles that are timely and relevant to issues being studied.

In addition to these required readings, I have linked websites containing multiple online supporting resources to the PSY 201 online syllabus. These include the American Psychological Association, the American Psychological Society, CNN, FOX, the Public Broadcasting Service, online supporting resources provided by Dushkin, the publisher of *Taking Sides,* and some materials (e.g., guidelines, outlines, diagrams) that I have gathered, made, or adapted specifically for the course. These resources provide the initial scaffolding for the topics of study, but I also remind the students to use the university library page and the various databases and resources offered there (e.g., PsychInfo, Eric, Library Catalog, dictionaries, and encyclopedias).

Covering the Issues.   We explore five to seven controversies over the course of a semester, each in a four-step cycle.

1. Review background information on the issue (e.g., a videotape, assigned readings, a mini-lecture) to stimulate interest and to help students select an appropriate initial line of inquiry into the controversy. Students jot down their immediate reactions and questions to pursue with others on their teams in subsequent brainstorming sessions.

2. Assemble in groups to share and analyze additional information students have gathered relevant to the controversy and their interest in it. Guided by the elements and standards of critical thinking, each group determines how to further refine and extend the research on the topic.

3. Exchange information they have found with other groups. After taking stock of what they have learned about the topic, the group focuses more specifically on the controversy and tries to establish a clear understanding of the controversy as presented in the *Taking Sides* readings.

4. State and explain their group's positions and share them with the class. Sometimes we debate in an online forum. In this final step, I always give a six- to eight-item multiple-choice quiz to assess how well students are reading and understanding the main points of opposing arguments.

Process Review Days.   Occasionally we need "process days" when we remind ourselves of the overall objectives of the course. Sometimes I provide special training on topics such as groupthink, effective listening skills, and teamwork.

Once students learn techniques for monitoring critical thinking and stimulating appropriate group discussion, group investigation often becomes easier and more productive. Students engage in higher quality debate and acquire a good exposure to the field of psychology to boot. In a week they do not all learn the same "facts," but what they learn is relevant to the topic at hand and arguably well integrated with their personal experiences and interests and with those of their workgroup.

I want to try out some new approaches to process training. For example, I would like to develop some brief, online "just-in-time" training modules pertaining to areas such as interpersonal communication, group dynamics, critical reading, and critical thinking to support class activities. With these modules in place, students could spend time "inquiring" into the course process as well as its content.

Challenges in Implementing Inquiry-guided Learning

When I first taught PSY 201 to stimulate inquiry-guided learning, I optimistically thought that all I needed to do was provide a fascinating introduction to a controversial topic. Students would become immediately and deeply engaged and excited about the opportunity to explore it on their own terms. Alas, with most new freshmen, I discovered it just doesn't happen that way. Many of these students need significant preliminary instruction pertaining to both the "how" and "why" of inquiry-guided learning—at least initially. The library skills of most freshmen are rudimentary at best. Reflecting together on introductory material, talking about the parts that really draw interest, and thinking together about ways to further explore unique perspectives on a subject rarely occur naturally in a neophyte discussion group. To some students, being allowed the freedom to explore in this way is threatening and frustrating, especially since they have to coordinate their investigations with other students. Since insecurities do arise, I've found students need guidelines that support them while we move into the "learning zone." Discovering such strategies has been the focus of course refinement over the past three years I have taught PSY 201.

As indicated by the literature on inquiry-guided learning, another challenge arises, because a number of assumptions about motivation and learning style must hold for students to gain from the method. For example, students must want to be autonomous learners in an environment that demands curiosity and initiative. Unfortunately, many students who have not had educational experiences that reinforce these qualities of mind resist inquiry-guided learning because of their habitual passivity (Hansen, 1998; Langer, 2001). For some, however, resistance is rooted in a lack of maturity and readiness for the approach (Perry, 1970).

Resistance reveals itself in various ways, but most often it comes in the form of work avoidance. Some students think inquiry-guided learning requires an inordinate amount of ill-defined homework compared to high school (Hansen, 1998). An unfortunate result is their deciding they do not care enough about an issue to fully invest themselves in it. Another avoidance strategy involves "rushing to an answer." Here students do what they think is expected of them: hastily solving a problem so that they can move on to the next.

In keeping with the learning model, however, I maintain that the purpose of the course is to get students to linger longer in the learning zone, the place of tension between having a final answer and not having one. The process itself requires time, scaffolding, practice, patience, and affirmation that students are doing the right thing by not coming to immediate conclusions. But it is gratifying when students reach the end of the course and acknowledge every so often that the process of discovery is at least as important as the discovery itself. Because the course has drawn out some of the best as well as some of the worst student attitudes, the teaching experience has been both extremely enjoyable but also demanding and, at times, even unpleasant.

As one of a growing number of inquiry-guided learning courses developed for and integrated into the curriculum at NCSU, PSY 201 "Controversial Issues in Psychology" serves a special purpose of introducing first-year students not only to the field of psychology but also to another entirely new arena of learning, the university.

References

Argyris, C. (1969). The incompleteness of social-psychological theory: Examples from small group, cognitive consistency, and attribution research. *American Psychologist, 24*(10), 893–908.

Argyris, C. (1976). Theories of action that inhibit individual learning. *American Psychologist, 31*(9), 638–654.

Brown, R. (1962). Models of attitude change. In T. M. Newcomb (Ed.), *New directions in psychology* (Vol. 1, pp. 1–85). New York: Holt, Rinehart & Winston.

Cronon, W. (1998). Only connect . . . *American Scholar, 67,* 73–80.

Crossan, M. (2003). Altering theories of learning and action: An interview with Chris Argyris. *Academy of Management Executive, 17*(2), 40–46.

Emerson, R. W. (1950). Self-reliance. In B. Atkinson (Ed.), *The Complete Essays and Other Writings of Ralph Waldo Emerson* (pp. 145–169). New York: Random House.

Hansen, E. J. (1998). Creating teachable moments . . . and making them last. *Innovative Higher Education, 23*(1) 7–26.

Irving, J. A., & Williams, D. I. (1995). Critical thinking and reflective practice in counseling. *British Journal of Guidance and Counseling, 23*(1), 107–114.

Langer, E. J. (2001). Mindful learning. *Current Directions in Psychological Science, 9,* 220–223.

Lee, V. S. (1998). The uses of uncertainty in the college classroom. Essays on *Teaching Excellence, 10*(1). Fort Collins, CO: The POD Network.

Paul, R., & Elder, L. (2001). *Critical thinking: Tools for taking charge of your learning and your life.* Upper Saddle River, NJ: Prentice Hall.

Perry, W. (1970). *Forms of intellectual and ethical development in the college years.* New York: Holt, Rinehart & Winston.

Slife, B. (Ed.) (2000). *Taking sides: Clashing views on controversial psychological issues.* (11th ed). Guilford, CT: Dushkin.

Slife, B., & Yanchar, S. C. (2000). Introduction: Unresolved issues in psychology. In B. Slife (Ed.), *Taking sides: Clashing views on controversial psychological issues* (11th ed.). Guilford, CT: Dushkin.

Zajonc, R. B. (1960). Balance, congruity, and dissonance. *Public Opinion Quarterly, 24,* 280–296.

4

MUSIC 200
"UNDERSTANDING MUSIC"
AN INQUIRY-GUIDED APPROACH
TO MUSIC APPRECIATION

By Jonathan Kramer and Alison Arnold

Introduction

Music 200 is an introductory level music appreciation course for undergraduate students at NCSU. Since 2000, the Department of Music has offered the course both as a general class open to all undergraduate students (Music 200) and as a First Year Inquiry (FYI) (see Chapter 16) class for freshmen only (Music 200Q). The class size differs between the two, with an average of 35 students in Music 200 and a restricted 20-student enrollment in Music 200Q. Both courses fulfill the visual and performing arts requirement for the university's undergraduate general education program.

The common goals of both classes are to acquaint students with the elements of music (melody, rhythm, harmony, etc.), musical styles, instruments, and so forth, and with the contexts and purposes of music-making in contemporary life and in the past; and to broaden students' understanding of music in social and cultural life. The geographical coverage of musical traditions varies according to the interests and expertise of the instructor. Because various Music Department faculty members teach the class, the focus ranges from European and American music to a more global perspective including Asian, African, and other music of the world. The class format similarly differs among faculty, ranging from a primarily lecture-based structure with quiz and exam evaluation to a more interactive lecture format with class and group discussion and assessment through essays and other written and oral assignments. A further common goal for "Understanding Music" is to encourage students to listen to and to think critically about a wide variety of musics.

When the Music Department decided to offer Music 200 as an inquiry-guided learning course in 2000, we had to rethink the existing syllabus and course goals in light of the objectives of the First Year Inquiry Program. Up to that time, the music appreciation class had primarily emphasized the learning of facts and recognition of specific musical styles through the study of "masterworks" and formal elements in order to provide students with knowledge of the history of Western music. The FYI Program presented a new approach: Its primary aims were to promote student learning through active investigation rather than passive instruction, to help students take responsibility for their own learning, and to foster intellectual development and growth.[1] FYI instruction sought to provide guided practice in asking good questions, collecting evidence, analyzing results, and formulating and evaluating conclusions. The task was then to create an inquiry-guided learning course that no longer fed students information and required its periodic regurgitation, but challenged students to discover ways of studying and inquiring into the phenomenon of music in our world, ways that lead to an understanding of the place and role of music in human experience. This essay is the story of that journey, beginning with Jonathan's introduction of an inquiry-based approach and continuing with Alison's involvement in the FYI class. We describe the current structure of Music 200Q (so designated in 2002), present some of our assignments and activities, and identify how they promote the FYI goals of critical thinking, independent inquiry, intellectual growth, and taking responsibility for one's own learning.

JK: Establishing an Inquiry-guided Approach to Music Appreciation

What does it mean to "understand" music? Or to understand anything for that matter? How do I know whether students have successfully *understood* music by the end of a semester, thus fulfilling the premise of the course title? What constitutes understanding, and how do I measure and grade the extent to which understanding has occurred? Do I myself understand music?

At NCSU, Music Appreciation—a catch-all term for the study of music by nonmajors with no prior necessary background that is universally included in undergraduate curricula—has been labeled "Understanding Music" since before I arrived in the mid-1980s. I taught the course for years, using the standard college textbooks[2] and presenting the usual historical survey of Western

---

[1] See www.ncsu.edu/firstyearinquiry/faculty_info/faculty_info.htm# Objectives_of_FYI_Courses

[2] Popular texts include Joseph Kerman, *Listen;* Joseph Machlis, *The Enjoyment of Music;* and Roger Kamien, *Music: An Appreciation.*

art music with a token of jazz, pop, and ethnic music thrown in at the end of the semester as a nod to "diversity," but not with a clear conscience. The notated art music of the West, from Bach to Stravinsky in my syllabus, constitutes a miniscule portion of all the world's music. This repertoire, which I had been taught to value as akin to Scripture, was far from the musical experience of most of my students, and was in its forms and contexts quite atypical of most of the music that most people made and listened to. For a number of years, I assuaged my conscience by offering parallel courses in World Music, thereby providing students with more choices in how they would fulfill the distribution requirement that brought them into the classroom in the first place. Still, it was the course title "Understanding Music" that finally inspired me to rethink the whole approach. I needed, and my students needed, to understand *understanding!* Then and only then could I begin to develop a syllabus, a methodology, a theory, a canon, a course that lived up to the name.

In the first place, it seemed that if the "appreciation" of music were the desired outcome (I had been told at faculty meetings that we were "educating the audience members of tomorrow") then the substance of the course I was teaching—stylistic periods, composer biographies, technical terms and concepts like *fugue* and *sonata form*—was perhaps beside the point. Freud had questioned the relationship between knowledge and appreciation in his famous essay on daVinci: "It is not true that human beings delay loving or hating until they have studied and become familiar with the nature of the object to which these affects apply. On the contrary, they love impulsively, from emotional motives that have nothing to do with knowledge and whose operations [may be] weakened by reflection and consideration" (Freud, 1964, p. 25). I wondered if the methods I was using to teach music were in fact counterproductive. When I learned to love Beethoven, I knew nothing about modulations and keys and sonata form. I certainly was never tested and graded on how well I could identify a flute; and if I had been, that would have killed at the outset what became a life-long passion for me. If the goal of the course was appreciation, why not simply turn off the lights and spin the discs? Take the students to concerts? Sing with them? But (and here was the rub in that strategy) on what basis do I grade them? How do I evaluate appreciation?

Then it hit me . . . the goal was not appreciation but understanding. I had arrived at the questions posed at the beginning of this essay. I recalled Tennyson's (1869) poem "Flower in the Crannied Wall":

> Flower in the crannied wall,
> I pluck you out of the crannies,
> I hold you here, root and all, in my hand,
> Little flower—but if I could understand
> What you are, root and all, and all in all,
> I should know what God and man is.

I began my first inquiry-guided version of "Understanding Music" with this poem on day one. Tennyson's reverie is not about appreciating the flower, but understanding, which does not derive "from emotional motives that have nothing to do with knowledge and whose operations [may be] weakened by reflection and consideration." Understanding has *everything* to do with knowledge, and its operations may lead to appreciation or not; but appreciation seemed a happy epiphenomenon of the learning process. After all, biology professors didn't seem to worry much whether students developed a love of nematodes because of their pedagogical efforts.

I asked the students, "Is this true, what Tennyson claims? Can you really know what 'God and man is' by understanding the flower?" The question seemed to me to be not rhetorical in the least, but testable. "Where would you begin?" I asked. "What is the flower made of?" a student suggested, and we began. I gave the students the resources of the university. We first imagined a visit to the Botany Department and categorized the flower according to its taxonomy; then to Histology, Genetics, Molecular Biology, Organic Chemistry, Particle Physics as our inquiry led us deeper and deeper into the stuff of the flower, now crushed, pulverized, atomized. When we had exhausted that line of questioning (not having arrived at God and man yet) we took a different tack: "What was it doing there in the wall?" In trying to understand walls and other products and functions of living processes, we went to the History Department, Sociology, Anthropology, Meteorology, Soil Science, and Agricultural Economics as students suggested further lines of inquiry. Questions of purpose, meaning, and value—such as "What is the flower for?"—took us into areas more and more abstract, interpretive, qualitative. Understanding, we discovered, is an ongoing, open-ended, perhaps infinite process of *inquiry*.

We then tried the "Flower in the Crannied Wall" experiment on a song: Antonio Carlos (Tom) Jobim's "The Girl from Ipenema." We divided our inquiry into four types of questions, as shown in Table 4.1.

We began with "What is it made of?" and identified the sounds themselves: the voice, the guitar, the saxophone, melody, chord progression, rhythm. We surrounded the sounds with imagined social contexts and socially constructed meanings. We began a long archeology of music codes that connected the sounds with Afro-Brazilian samba, with roots in African religious practices, with Portuguese fado, and the "cool" jazz of Miles Davis and Frank Sinatra that made its way into the soundworld of Brazil via broadcast radio. Our interrogation situated the song at the confluence of slave trade routes, colonial powers, industrial and commercial processes of production, distribution and consumption. We followed the song from its creation by the team of Antonio Carlos Jobim and Vinicius de Moraes on its journey from the lounges of the Copa Cabana to the top-40 hit lists of North America and the nightclubs of Paris. This investigation established a pattern for musical inquiry—beginning with the sounds themselves and working outward through a process of interrogation to ever wider circles of context, meaning, and value.

Table 4.1   Perspectives for Understanding Music*

Analytical. What are you hearing? What is making the sounds? How are they organized in terms of music's elements: timbre, melody, harmony, rhythm, texture, form, etc.?

Contextual. What circumstances give rise to the music? Who makes it, who listens to it, who pays for it, how/why is it (re)produced, taught, remembered, learned, preserved, marketed, etc.? What are people doing *in order* to make this music; what are they doing *as* they make this music? When, where, and how did the song and song-type emerge/evolve?

Semiotic. What does it mean to those who make it and respond to it? What occasions does it mark, what messages does it convey? How does it function as (part of) a communicative code? How does it transform consciousness? What does/can it mean to *you*?

Performative. How is it created in real time? What learning/rehearsing/ organizing preceded it? (How) Is it preserved for future performances? How does it change in the processing/preserving/recording/engineering/marketing/ sampling phases? Is it good music? By what criteria is it evaluated by those who make and listen to it? What constitutes a good rendition? What is the relationship of performance or recording to text/template/ideal?

*Based on a class handout developed by Jonathan Kramer for Music 200.

AA: Variation on a Theme of Understanding

In the summer 2000, I received an invitation from Jonathan Kramer and the NCSU Department of Music to teach one class section of Music 200 "Understanding Music." While the course title was intriguing, I found Jonathan's syllabus inspiring. Having taught undergraduate World Music classes at other universities, I was familiar with many of his topics and resources. Yet his course structure was neither the standard Western music history sequence of so many music appreciation classes nor the country-by-country musical tour typical of introductions to world music. It focused on themes common to human cultural and social experience—music and identity, music and religion, music and narrative—through which one could explore and compare the rich diversity of music in our world.[3] I accepted the offer and began musing on its exciting possibilities and challenges.

---

[3] This approach to teaching music has since appeared in published form in Kay Kaufman Shelemay's (2001) textbook, *Soundscapes: Exploring Music in a Changing World,* New York: Norton.

Jonathan's exploration of the meaning of *understanding* on the first day of class seemed so natural and so important to this course, if not to education in general, that the search for a musical topic comparable to Tennyson's poem was compelling. I sought a musical example or even a musical puzzle that similarly challenged the students to consider the nature of *understanding* through a process of inquiry. I wished to embrace inquiry-guided learning even though my class at this time was not a designated FYI class. After some thought, I found the solution in my own home. The students would simulate an inquiry to identify and evaluate an unknown musical instrument (selected from my own instrument collection from India, Iran, and Egypt) that they had been given as a gift. Their task was to discover whether its destiny was Carnegie Hall or the trash bin and also, through exploring its purpose and its value, to determine what connection or relevance this instrument might have to their own lives and musical experience. Like Jonathan's "Flower in the Crannied Wall" exercise, the students would use this inquiry to probe the nature of understanding.

On the first day of class, I showed my 30 Music 200 students a musical instrument that none of them recognized and asked them questions to stimulate their inquiry. Did they recognize anything? Did it remind them of anything? What knowledge could they gain simply by observing? The students then considered where they might go to find answers to their own questions: What was the instrument made of? How old was it? Where had it come from? How did people value it in its homeland? What kind of music was played on it? Was it connected structurally, historically, symbolically with other instruments or other cultures? Role-playing the various sources of information, I offered leads that sent them in new directions: As a violin maker, I suggested a local Turkish musician who played a similar stringed instrument; as an anthropology professor, I owned a CD with music played on this instrument. The students discovered, described, defined, distinguished, analyzed, assessed, and evaluated; they considered contradictory explanations from varied sources; they recognized biases. They used the tools of critical thinking without receiving any theoretical introduction to them. Solving the mystery of the instrument opened up new worlds of *understanding* and of musical inquiry, worlds we would explore in detail in the coming semester.

JK: The Four Units of the Course

Throughout the semester, inquiry into music's procedures, contexts, and materials is informed by O'Brien's challenge to the College Music Society (1992): "We must state boldly that the aim of our studies is the revelation of world visions, not proficiency in the statistics, jargon, footnoting, and other double-stoppings and roulades of the academic trade. If we are courageous enough to say straight off that the reason we pursue these studies is to create a dialogue of world visions, that we are engaged in a wayward search for wisdom, our students will leave us not only scientific and professional but perhaps, well, if not wholly wise—at least filled with that awe and wonder which lead to wisdom" (p. 11).

I devised the syllabus for "Understanding Music" based on the premise that music is a global phenomenon and a commonality of human social experience. In the first part of the semester, the students are occupied with fundamental questions about the nature of music: What is music? How is it made? What is it made of? What is it for? When and how did it originate? Their attempts to answer these open-ended questions lead to the development of a working vocabulary and conceptual base: Terms such as *melody, harmony, rhythm, affect, art form, aesthetics, culture* become familiar and useable. Through many and varied examples, we learn that while the sounds humans use to project musical meaning are as diverse as human languages, worldviews, and diets, the contexts and functions of human music-making suggest broad areas of similarity and convergence. For the remainder of the semester I chose three of these areas to explore, around which I organized the course reading and listening materials: music's expressive power in the exposition of *narrative and drama;* its roles in the formation, expression, and contestation of *social identity;* and its complex relationships with *religious belief, observation, and experience.* We examined specific case studies in each category based upon general concepts derived from scholarly readings. In our unit on Music and Religion, for example, we read in Ellingson's (1987) article, "Music and Religion," that ". . . music is widely used as a demarcator of ritual time and space" (p. 169). We explore the applicability of this principle among Sinhalese drummers, in ancestral rites of the Shona of Zimbabwe, in the Islamic call to prayer, and in the ringing of church bells down the street. Thus, the study of music for us becomes, indeed, a "dialogue of world visions" as we examine, through videos, readings, and performances (both recorded and live) from diverse world regions, the occasions and purposes of music-making and listening. At the same time we attempted to account for the ways in which tradition and change, identity and hegemony, belief systems and patterns of social change are encoded and made manifest in musical practices.

AA: Engaging Students

In the fall of 2000, my Music 200 class meetings consisted primarily of lectures followed by discussions related to required reading and listening assignments. I enhanced lectures with video and audio recordings ranging from clips of Tibetan Buddhist monks chanting scriptures to excerpts of Beethoven's Fifth Symphony. I believed that this approach together with my own effervescent enthusiasm for the subject would sufficiently engage and motivate students in their college-level introductory music class. Beyond the classroom, I required the students to attend three music concerts during the semester and write reports on their experiences, and to attend a worship event of their choice for a written paper on music and religion. This combination of in-class and out-of-class learning experiences suited the class size of 30 students, encouraged breadth and variety in the students' musical experiences, and enabled some independent research. But in the fall of 2002 when I was approached to teach Music 200Q, the First Year Inquiry class taught solely by Jonathan Kramer, I wondered whether my approach would sufficiently address the needs of 20 freshmen registered for an inquiry-guided learning class, seeking to experience active learning and to develop critical reading, writing, and discussion skills. The required concert attendance and classroom discussions already promoted inquiry-guided learning, but what new "engaging" strategies could I employ?

My first strategy was to organize class field trips, an activity now possible with the smaller class size. I arranged two: a class visit to a black Baptist church worship service in downtown Raleigh in place of the individual assignment to attend a religious event, and a beginner workshop on playing the Javanese gamelan housed at the University of North Carolina, Chapel Hill. The general goal and purpose of the first trip was to experience black gospel music in the context of a worship service with several specific outcomes, such as the consideration of how music functions in the service and how it relates to the service's structure. The second trip served to introduce students to a musical culture far removed from their own through the direct hands-on experience of playing musical instruments. The benefits gained by the students were certainly worth the time and effort arranging the trips. One especially valuable outcome was community building, the opportunity for the students to get to know one another and to share in a real-life experience that could then be discussed, analyzed, and explored in the classroom. Other outcomes closely matched the IGL goals for Music 200Q: The trips provided practice for the students in asking questions, and in speaking and writing about their understanding of a musical experience; they also fostered a sense of inquiry into the meaning of music in social and cultural life.

A second strategy was to create a mini-field research project feasible for non music majors that would introduce the students to research methods used in ethno-musicological inquiry. I was fully aware of the importance of field research in my scholarly discipline but now considered its benefits for undergraduate inquiry-guided learning. Field research projects embrace active involvement in the learning process; they encourage students' responsibility in planning and implementing their own research; they provide practice in critical-thinking skills; and, from my own teaching experience, they introduce a greater level of excitement and enthusiasm in the class by allowing students to explore topics of personal interest to themselves. The project I designed, linked to the students' final paper on music and identity, required students in groups of two to collect their own data by interviewing musicians and to draw their own conclusions on what kinds of identity the musicians were expressing through their music. For some students, the project was their first experience in planning and carrying out an interview and in considering ethical questions about documenting people's private lives. Others were challenged and/or stimulated by formulating and asking questions about what people express in their music. The field research strategy clearly offered enormous potential for inquiry-guided learning, from project preparation and implementation, to data analysis, synthesis, and evaluation.

A third means of engaging students arose when I invited a group of visiting musicians in the area to present a lecture-demonstration to the class. With the world music perspective of Music 200Q it was not difficult to link the presentation to the course themes, in this case to music and identity. A group of North Indian musicians introduced the Hindustani classical tradition; they talked, played, demonstrated, and answered questions about their music, their instruments, their training, and their lives as artists and performers. The event turned out to be a highlight of the semester. It not only offered my students the privilege of learning about another distant musical tradition directly from some of its most renowned artists and practitioners, but also enabled and encouraged them to ask questions, to form opinions, to compare Indian music with their own musical culture, and to think critically about this area of Asian music. Furthermore, it brought my students face-to-face with the realities of musical performance and the global music marketplace in the 21st century: the necessities of travel, of technology, and of translation for new audiences. The lecture-demonstration requires perhaps more advance planning (e.g., time scheduling, invitations, room reservations) and resources (e.g., sound equipment, honoraria) than other strategies for engaging students, but the educational rewards for both students and faculty are invaluable.

Conclusion

Our joint experience teaching Music 200Q has confirmed our beliefs that the exploration of music lends itself well to inquiry-guided learning. Investigations into the scientific aspects of music, such as the properties of sound, acoustics, the mechanism of hearing, and recording technology, allow the students to discover, to test, to experiment, while inquiry into artistic areas—musical expression, interpretation, meaning, value—invite opinions and judgments. Questions relating to the latter often open up students to viewpoints and worldviews different from their own, and allow them to experience uncertainty where there may be no right or wrong answers. Such questions necessitate critical thinking (i.e., analysis, synthesis, evaluation) and offer opportunities for our students to discuss, debate, and make reasoned judgments about music-related issues both individually and with their peers.

References

Ellingson, T. (1987). Music and religion. In Mircea Eliade (Ed.), *Encyclopedia of religion* (p. 169). New York: Macmillan.

Freud, S. (1964). *Leonardo da Vinci and a memory of his childhood.* Translated by Alan Tyson. New York: W. W. Norton and Company, p. 25.

O'Brien, D. (1992). In *College Music Society Annual Report 7,* 11.

Tennyson, A. L. (1869/1958). Flower in the crannied wall. In J. H. Buckley (Ed.), *Poems of Tennyson.* Boston: Houghton Mifflin.

5

SCALE-UP

BRINGING INQUIRY-GUIDED LEARNING TO LARGE ENROLLMENT COURSES

*By Maria Oliver-Hoyo
and Robert Beichner*

Developed in our Department of Physics, the Student-Centered Activities for Large Enrollment University Programs (or "SCALE-UP") provides an alternative to traditional large lecture, introductory chemistry, and physics classes[1] and opens the door to implement inquiry-guided learning practices more extensively in classes of up to 99 students. It promotes an active learning environment through special classroom management techniques, a unique

---

[1] At NCSU, we offer the following courses in both traditional and SCALE-UP formats:
- CH 101, required for all science students, is a conceptually driven course that lays the foundation of basic concepts including the principles of atomic structure, bonding, reactivity, energetics, intermolecular forces, and types of reactions as well as introductions to organic and inorganic chemistry.
- CH 201, takes a second look at the concepts studied in CH 101 and applies quantitative aspects of problem solving to the areas of stoichiometry, thermodynamics, kinetics, equilibrium, electrochemistry, and nuclear chemistry.
- A two-semester required sequence for engineering students: PY 205 covers mechanics, including the description of motion and its causes, gravitation, oscillation, sound, and waves; and PY 208 deals with electricity and magnetism, including current at the microscopic level, fields, some of the basic laws of electricity and magnetism, circuits and components, along with geometric and physical optics.

classroom design, collaborative work, and the extensive use of technology. Contemporary research supports the instructional practices used in SCALE-UP, now replicated at many other colleges and universities in this country and abroad.

Moving from traditional to IGL practices over time, we've made fundamental changes in the way we think about the learning process, which has in turn influenced what we do in the classroom.

1. *We select materials, activities, and technology consciously to meet learning outcomes.* We choose to define technology as "a carefully considered approach to solving a problem." The problem is how to improve learning for large numbers of students. There have been many research and development efforts that have produced wonderful curricular materials. The task of the SCALE-UP project has been to make a conscientious effort to find ways to use those proven techniques in large enrollment courses. Working on this project has forced us to think hard about each topical area, what we want students to learn, where they have difficulties, and how to craft an instructional event to address those issues.

2. *We shift the meaning of and responsibility for the learning process.* Earlier in our careers we believed that if we didn't "cover" material, then we hadn't really taught it. But in SCALE-UP, students read assigned material and take quizzes on it *before* class starts. As a result we can use class time to move topics forward and challenge students with more advanced problems and applications. Only then can we challenge students' cognitive skills beyond basic knowledge and comprehension. Students hear over and over again that the learning process is a partnership; the teacher does his or her share and the students do theirs.

3. *We've also come to believe that "[g]enuine uncertainty and doubt are the natural provocations for real learning"* (Lee, 1998, p. 1). Students demand right answers from us as the instructors initially, with very little interest in finding the right approach themselves. But in the science-oriented IGL classroom, nature must replace the teacher as the ultimate authority. We constantly encourage students to think about and explicitly ask, "Why are we doing this? What are we supposed to get out of this?" We also focus on providing different views of the same problem, often using published articles in referred journals, or we present topics with the whole spectrum of possible answers. This is a difficult transition, since the majority of students have learned to passively accept whatever the teacher presents. The social nature of the SCALE-UP classroom supports students through this transition.

The SCALE-UP Learning Environment

The most distinguishing features of the SCALE-UP integrated format are as follows:

1. Full integration of key concepts and applications into a seamless session blending lecture and lab components
2. Shift from a teacher-centered classroom to a student-centered environment (Through carefully designed activities, students discover or investigate concepts while the instructor facilitates this process.)
3. Minimized lecture with a focus on hands-on activities as the driving force of the class time (In a typical two-hour session, we may interject one or two short lectures of 15 to 20 minutes between activities.)
4. Promotion of collaborative work through classroom design and management techniques
5. Incorporation of technological advancements that promote collaborative work and communication between groups of students
6. Resources (e.g., teaching assistants, funds) comparable to and, at times, less than traditional settings

Through this rich environment, SCALE-UP promotes the following learning objectives.

- To improve student understanding of basic chemical/physical phenomena
- To improve higher order cognitive skills of students through "real world" problems and applications
- To increase the interest and/or decrease the apprehensions of students toward chemistry and physics
- To improve graphical skills including representation and interpretation of graphs
- To develop teamwork and communication skills
- To decrease the attrition rate in chemistry and physics courses

Classroom Design and Management Techniques

At NCSU a special room houses SCALE-UP courses. The room holds up to 99 students seated at 11 round tables and then further divided in teams of three, each with a laptop and Internet access. We chose round tables to promote collaboration among team members as well as among the group of three teams. Teams can readily access mounted white boards around the entire room. We also use computer technology and multimedia projectors with screens at both ends of the room to ensure visibility for all students. Figure 5.1 shows our current room design; Figure 5.2 offers a side-by-side picture of a smaller renovated classroom.

Figure 5.1   The SCALE-UP Room.

We have incorporated specific classroom management techniques that are crucial to effectively manage an active class of up to 99 students. First, all students have name cards placed in front of them to help us establish a sense of community and facilitate communication. Tables are numbered to facilitate collection and distribution of papers. Electronic homework is due every class period, but we can collect other group or individual assignments by the roll of a special, 12-sided die. As a result, every student is responsible for doing assignments, but grading is reduced to a fraction of the student population. Because of the interactive nature of the classroom, we can assess team comprehension quickly by scanning answers that team members write on the white boards. Each of these techniques encourages individual accountability, positive interdependence, development of interpersonal skills, and communication as well as the effective use of time to make an active class this size manageable.

Classroom Dynamics

An important goal for us in SCALE-UP classes is to establish a highly collaborative environment. Various researchers have reported the necessity and success of cooperative grouping in the classroom (Cohen, 1994; Johnson et al., 1991; Qin et al., 1995) and specifically in the chemistry classroom (Bowen, 2000). We closely monitor group arrangements and have found over the years that placing students in teams of three with three teams per table is the optimal seating

Figure 5.2   Traditional Classroom (55 desks) Converted to SCALE-UP Classroom (54 desks).

arrangement (Beichner et al., 2000a; Cox & Berger, 1985). Team effectiveness is assessed using peer evaluations and test grades. And in order to enhance collaboration, teams earn bonus points on their exam scores when they average above a specified minimum. This practice seems to encourage better students to help group members that may be struggling with the material, while slower students tend to show a deeper sense of responsibility (Beichner et al., 2000b). In grouping students we try to maximize heterogeneity with respect to ability, gender, race, and ethnicity (Beichner et al., 2000b; Felder & Brent, 1994).

Curriculum Development

We present content materials through hands-on activities that allow students to reason through data and observations (see Appendix 5.A). In chemistry courses, we consider several factors in the development of these activities including chemical handling, implementation of microscale techniques, and incorporation of technology. To guide instructors in their facilitation of class work, we developed the specific format shown in Figure 5.3.

Incorporation of Technology

Technology plays a critical role in the SCALE-UP classroom in five major areas: class management, electronic homework, data collection, graphical analysis, and simulations/animations. Every laptop has Internet access; basic software such as Microsoft Excel, Word, and PowerPoint; and special discipline-related programs such as WebLab Viewer Lite.[2] An instructor station equipped with a camera projector displays material onto two screens located at both ends of the room. We can also project student work on the white boards to the entire class.

The learning management system WebCT[3] allows us to organize, manage, and distribute class materials and notes, and WebAssign[4] to assign daily electronic homework. In chemistry courses, we collect data with computers coupled with chemical probes and then analyze these data including graphical form. The Internet provides access to many simulations and animations that involve re-creating historical experiments or offer tools for students to study chemical behavior. These simulations use student-controlled parameters that allow students to perform experiments on the computer.

Assessment

NCSU's Physics Education Research & Development group looked at a variety of outcomes to ascertain whether the SCALE-UP approach was successful. Students performing well on traditional problems posed on common exams was still a primary concern. To determine this, we randomly selected questions from exams given to students in traditional mechanics and electricity/magnetism courses and gave them to the SCALE-UP students. Percentages correct for the two-item sets were 73 versus 62 and 80 versus 75, both in favor of the SCALE-UP students. The results were strong enough that further comparisons were not made since the traditional tests, in their multiple-choice format, did not sufficiently challenge the SCALE-UP students.

---

[2] See www.accelrys.com/viewer/index.html
[3] See www.webct.com
[4] See www.webassign.com

TITLE

Time: *time suggested for completing activity*

Topic: *topics covered by activity*

Type: *probe or investigation*

Level: *introductory, intermediate, or advanced*

Overview: *statement outlining the activity*

Materials and Equipment: *items needed to complete the activity*

Objective(s): *statements identifying the intended learning outcomes*

Misconceptions: *common misunderstandings that conflict with scientific theory*

Other Student Difficulties: *areas that should be given special attention*

Prerequisites: *concepts or material needed to complete the activity*

Activity Table: *outlines every step of the activity for instructors*

Task	Reason	Notes
Action to be taken by students or instructors	Why the action is important	Helpful information for instructors

Related Activities: *activities that incorporate related concepts*

References: *the resources used in developing the activity*

Supplementary Material: *discussion of concepts, explanation of demos and procedures*

Figure 5.3 Activity Form.

We also assessed students' conceptual learning of physics with a nationally normed test, The Force Concept Inventory, and compared the results to a national sample of more than 6,000 students. The results are shown in Table 5.1. (We have similar results from other institutions that have adopted the SCALE-UP approach.)

In addition to improved student attitudes and depth of questioning, the attrition rates of different student groups served as a coarse measure of success. The ratio of percentage failing a traditional section versus a SCALE-UP section was 2.8. African Americans are 3.5 times as likely to fail in a traditional section, while women fail 4.7 times as often. (See http://scaleup.ncsu.edu for more details.)

In addition to the studies conducted by the Physics Education R&D group, rigorous studies were conducted in chemistry classrooms using quantitative and qualitative chemical education methods (Oliver-Hoyo et al., in

Table 5.1   Comparison of Students' Conceptual Understanding of Physics in Traditional Lecture versus SCALE-UP Courses*

Semester	Traditional lecture	Interactive
National Sample**	0.22	0.48
Spring 1997		0.55
Fall 1997	0.206	
Fall 1998		0.41
Spring 1999		0.52
Fall 1999		0.35
Fall 2000		0.36
Spring 2001		0.41
Spring 2002		0.34
Fall 2002	0.23	

*From Beichner, R., Saul, J., Abbott, D., Morse, J., Deardorff, D., Allain, R., Bonham, S., Dancy, M., & Risley, J. (nearing completion). *The Student-Centered Activities for Large Enrollment Undergraduate Programs (SCALE-UP) project. Part II: Objectives, outcomes, and learning what works.*

**Hake, R. (1998). Interactive-engagement vs. traditional methods: A six-thousand-student survey of mechanics test data for introductory physics courses. *American Journal of Physics,* 66(1), 64.

press; Oliver-Hoyo et al., in review). These studies evaluated the effects of the SCALE-UP environment on student understanding of basic chemical concepts, the development of higher order cognitive skills, problem solving and graphical abilities, as well as on attitudes and anxiety levels toward chemistry.

The results of a quantitative study show significant statistical differences between traditional and SCALE-UP sections of CH 101. Students in SCALE-UP outperformed students in the traditional lecture on higher order cognitive skills as questions carefully chosen to address these skills were compared in the study. Figure 5.4 shows the comparison between both sections where the results for the first and third exam questions were not statistically different but results on the second and fourth exams were.

These results strongly suggest to us that SCALE-UP students' understanding of basic chemical concepts and the development of higher order cognitive skills were superior to students in the traditional lecture.

We also monitored attitudes and anxiety levels in three areas: chemical handling, chemistry evaluation, and learning chemistry. To monitor attitudinal changes we compared pre- and post-attitudinal survey scores for both the traditional class (control group) and the SCALE-UP class (experimental group). To do this, we first plotted pre- and post-survey scores for the traditional class and conducted a regression analysis (see Figure 5.5). The resulting line equation was used to monitor changes in the SCALE-UP class. Using the pre-scores for the

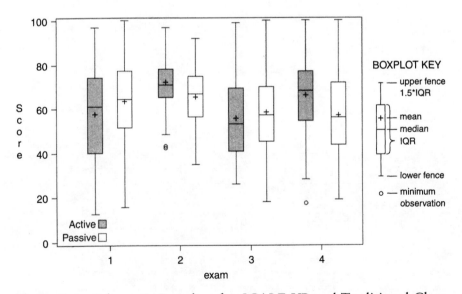

Figure 5.4 Schematic Boxplots for SCALE-UP and Traditional Class Formats Exam Data.

SCALE-UP class (*x* values), we obtained *predicted* post scores (*y* values) for the experimental class. When predicted post-scores were compared to actual post-scores from the SCALE-UP class, the difference gives a residualized gain (see Figure 5.5). Positive gains mean more positive attitudes relative to the control group. Seventy-seven percent of the SCALE-UP section yielded positive gains, demonstrating that SCALE-UP students achieved greater attitudinal change than the corresponding lecture section.

Qualitative data collected from 54 student interviews, 280 reflective journal entries, 514 copies of student work, and 116 survey responses provide overwhelming evidence that students favor the SCALE-UP approach. The most meaningful findings are as follows:

1. Students responded positively to working in groups and, in some cases, changed their attitudes toward group work. Students who once considered groups an obstacle to learning viewed them as a necessary and important part of their SCALE-UP experience.

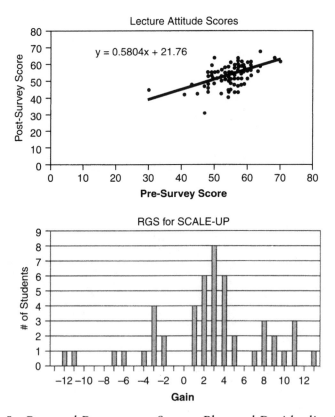

Figure 5.5   Pre- and Post-survey Scatter Plot and Residualized Gains.

2. Approximately half of the students agreed that the course had increased their interest in science, chemistry, and pursuing a science-related field. A third of the students agreed that the course had increased their interest in taking more chemistry and pursuing a chemistry-related major.

3. The majority of students (63%) indicated positive attitudes toward the class and its structure (i.e., responded either "strongly agree" or "agree"), while only 9% reported negative attitudes.

Conclusion

The features responsible for SCALE-UP's success include an emphasis on cooperative learning techniques, a focus on carefully constructed hands-on activities, and the effective use of technology. We believe these features work together to make the classroom a community of students seeking answers to provoking questions in an intellectually challenging environment that explores content knowledge and exposes students to necessary scientific skills. The studies we have conducted show that students exposed to the SCALE-UP format did better than students in traditional science lecture formats as measured by standardized tests, higher order cognitive skills testing, and graphical and problem-solving performance. We were also able to monitor changes in attitudes toward the sciences using qualitative research methods that show SCALE-UP having positive effects on students' attitudes and course attrition rates.

References

Beichner, R. J., Saul, J. M., Allain, R. J., Deardorff, D., & Abbott, D. S. (2000a). Introduction to SCALE-UP: Student-centered activities for large enrollment courses. *Proceedings of the 2000 Annual Meeting of the American Society for Engineering Education.*

Beichner, R. J., Saul, J. M., Allain, R. J., Deardorff, D., & Abbott, D. S. (2000b). Promoting collaborative groups in large enrollment courses. *Proceedings of the 2000 Annual Meeting of the American Society for Engineering Education.*

Bowen, C. W. (2000). A quantitative literature review of cooperative learning effects on high school and college chemistry achievement. *Journal of Chemical Education, 77,* 116–119.

Cohen, E. G. (1994). Restructuring the classroom: Conditions for productive small groups. *Review of Educational Research, 64,* 1–35.

Cox, D., & Berger, C. (1985). The importance of group size in the use of problem-solving skills on a microcomputer. *Journal of Educational Computing Research, 1*(4), 459–468.

Felder, R. M., & Brent, R. (1994). *Cooperative learning in technical courses: Procedures, pitfalls, and payoffs.* ERIC Document Reproduction Service, ED 377038.

Johnson, D. W., Johnson, R. T., & Smith, K. (1991). *Active learning: Cooperation in the college classroom.* Edina, MN: Interaction Book Company.

Lee, V. S. (1998). The uses of uncertainty in the college classroom. *Essays on Teaching Excellence, 10*(1). Fort Collins, CO: The POD Network.

Oliver-Hoyo, M. T., Allen, D., Hunt, W. F., Hutson, J., & Pitts, A. (in press). Effects of an active learning environment: Teaching innovations at a research I institution. *Journal of Chemical Education.*

Oliver-Hoyo, M. T., & Allen, D. (in review). Attitudinal effects of a student-centered active learning environment. *Journal of Chemical Education.*

Qin, Z., Johnson, D. W., & Johnson, R. T. (1995). Cooperative versus competitive efforts and problem solving. *Review of Educational Research, 65,* 129–143.

APPENDIX 5.A

SAMPLE SCALE-UP
ACTIVITY FROM PHYSICS

Bouncing Ball   plan for 30 minutes

Students have a great deal of difficulty making the connection between motion events and the graphs representing that motion. The purpose of this exercise is to help students make that connection and see an example of the strengths and shortcomings of Interactive Physics simulation software.

Objectives

After completing this exercise, students should be able to sketch graphs of position, velocity, and acceleration versus time when they are presented with a simple motion event. They will recognize the relationships between these graphs and be able to produce either of the other two graphs when given one of them. They will also be able to create simple simulations using Interactive Physics.

Misconceptions

Students have a great deal of difficulty interpreting kinematics graphs. They can often construct graphs from data points, but don't really know what those graphs represent. The most common mistake is called the "graph as picture" error. They expect graphs to be similar to a photographic representation of the motion event. Basically they believe all kinematics graphs will look like a graph of y vs. x. Making the transition from an abscissa of x to one of t is a very subtle point that we often skip over.

Task	Reason	Notes
1. **Drop a racquetball** from rest, let it bounce three times, and catch it. Have each individual write down as thorough a description of the motion as they can, using words.	Eventually we want them to see how compact, yet complete graphs can be. They allow trends to be seen without obscuring the details.	Warn students that "gravity" and "force" are not allowed words since they haven't been covered yet.
2. Have a few **people read** what they wrote. Discuss the motion as a large group.	We want them to thoroughly examine the motion situation.	Make sure everyone hears what is said. You will probably have to repeat it.
3. Have students follow along while you (and they) **create a ball** with IP and run the simulation. Ask where is it going slowly, where is it going fastest, does it rebound to the same height each time, etc.	See if they recognize that it is accelerating.	Stress the similarity to a graphics package. Show them what is different by having them run the simulation and watching the ball fall.

4. Ask how one would simulate the bouncing ball. Someone will probably suggest that you draw a floor somehow. Have them use the rectangle tool to do just that. Ask the students to predict what will happen when they run the simulation this time. They'll quickly see the need for the anchor tool, so show it to them. Now they will have a good **simulation** of the bouncing racquetball.	If you like, you can discuss the equal accelerations of the ball and the rectangle before it is anchored.	Note: watch out for students going off and trying all kinds of strange things. In fact, if you suspect that this will be a problem, specifically assign two minutes to drawing whatever they want, just to get it out of their systems. Tell them to stay away from the menus for the time being.
5. After telling them to just watch, create a graph of vertical position vs. time, but don't run the simulation. Ask student groups to sketch their predictions of the graph shape. Circulate and when you see that a group has made a reasonable guess, have them draw it on the board. Then give that group permission to have IP **create the graph.** Continue until all groups are done.	Building their interest.	Don't take too much time or the faster groups will get bored or be distracted.

65

(Continued)

Task	Reason	Notes
6. Resize your IP graph so that the vertical axis directly corresponds with the vertical motion of the ball. This will help them make the connection between the motion and the graph. **Compare** to the graphs on the board.	Talk about differences between the graphs in terms of the motion they describe. Ask them what a graph of y vs. x would look like. (Just a vertical line.)	Just about everyone will have noted that the ball does not go as high after each bounce. You will probably see some with cusps representing the times when the ball hits the floor, others will look like sine waves.
7. Ask about whether the bounces happen at **uniform intervals.** Listen for a student suggesting that as you let it bounce many times, the ball is in the air for shorter and shorter intervals. Actually let the ball bounce and have students listen for the sound of the bounces. Tell the students to carefully sketch the correct graph onto their paper, taking special care to account for the details you have discussed.	They are learning to be careful observers.	Be sure to look at their work. Many will be sloppy and not attend to the important little differences that are so important.

8. Now ask them to **predict** what a graph of vertical **velocity** versus time would look like. This will be much more difficult for them than the first graph. Have the four groups at each table compare their work. If you can, bring the entire class to consensus about the shape of the graph.	We are trying to get them away from thinking of the graph as a photograph.	There will often be at least one student who is close in each supergroup of 12. A very common mistake is to think that the graph will look like a series of "V" shapes. Lead them through a discussion of the meaning of that type of graph. You may need to "manufacture" some numbers for the vertical axis to make it more real.
9. Have everyone **create** the IP graph and compare it to their prediction.	Make the connection between the two kinematics graphs.	Step through the simulation and discuss the bouncing points and the maximum height points. Ask what the slope of the position graph represents, if they haven't used this fact to determine the velocity graph. Show how the varying slope of the position graph shows up as varying velocities on that graph.
10. Ask what the **slope** of the **velocity** graph should be. Most will now see that it is the acceleration due to gravity.	Start connecting to the acceleration graph.	This seems to be fairly straightforward for them.

(Continued)

11. Ask them to **predict** the **acceleration** graph. Have them create it and compare it to their expectations.	To understand the acceleration graph, to build confidence in their abilities, and to recognize limitations of the simulation engine.	They will be quite confident at this point and will very surprised when the simulation does not match what they expect. Because the collision between the ball and the floor takes so little time, the simulation engine does not model it very well. Even though it is clear that there should be a large positive acceleration when the ball hits the floor (how else could the velocity go from large negative to large positive values?), and this can be seen as a slope on the velocity graph, the large spikes do not appear on the acceleration graph.

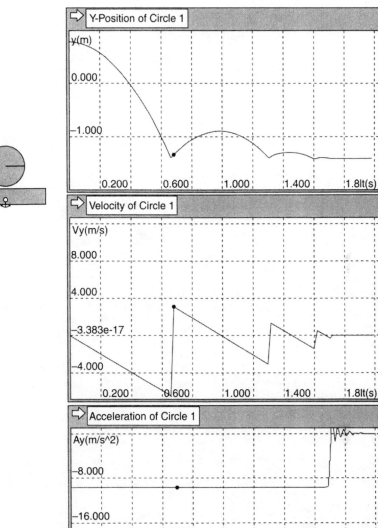

6

INQUIRY-GUIDED LEARNING AND THE FOREIGN LANGUAGE CLASSROOM

*By Ana Kennedy
and Susan Navey-Davis*

The central tenets of inquiry-guided learning are not new to effective language teachers, although they may not be aware of them as such. Language instruction that does not rely upon rote memory, mechanical application of lifeless rules, and memorization of obscure and virtually useless vocabulary has long applied the principles of inquiry-guided learning to make language instruction vibrant and exciting.

Consciousness of inquiry-guided learning, however, allows the instructor to sharpen and refine the focus on critical thinking, independent inquiry, responsibility for one's own learning, and intellectual growth and maturity. Recognizing the centrality of these learning outcomes to what instructors do can help them to rethink their strategies and energize their classrooms.

What ignites the classroom is the students' excitement about what they are studying. Inquiry-guided learning provides the tools to create that excitement. Students learn best when they are actively engaged in using their critical faculties to take ownership of their intellectual journeys and in seeing the practical benefits of their endeavors. The most sophisticated of students may even recognize that the IGL skills are powerful thinking tools that extend to other disciplines and beyond the classroom. Inquiry-guided learning can confer, then, not simply a dynamic way to acquire and harness knowledge, but habits of intellectual discipline that transform the individual from pupil to a life-long independent thinker and learner.

What we have just described is the ideal, the theory. It is up to the instructor to translate theory into practice, and to the language instructor to apply IGL principles to language acquisition. What follows is the description of experimental approaches to language learning, which simultaneously aim to achieve and incorporate the principles and outcomes of IGL.

Inquiry-guided Learning in a Traditional Foreign Language Classroom

The National Standards for Foreign Language Learning emphasize several key components of IGL. The goal areas of the standards, which are communication, cultures, connections to other disciplines, language and cultural comparisons, and participation in communities, indicate that students are expected to be active participants in the learning process and that they must employ higher order thinking skills. I (i.e., Ana Kennedy) use active learning strategies in all classes I teach, but I was charged with formalizing this approach in two intermediate-level Spanish classes. The classes were open only to freshmen, and enrollment was capped at 20 students.

I added a new component to these classes, an inquiry notebook. Each student had to prepare this four-section notebook and contribute to it regularly throughout the semester. The sections were *My Dictionary, Encounters, Investigations,* and *Reflections.* Students submitted the notebook to me a minimum of three times during the semester, and response to the comments I offered at each submission was an important part of the assessment of the notebook.

My goal was to have the students use the notebook to become more actively involved in their own learning and to have them address issues that are not part of the prescribed curriculum for intermediate foreign language students. I designed the notebook so that they would need to use higher order thinking skills and would become more independent learners by making decisions about their learning.

In the first section, students recorded words, phrases, and other language items that they wanted to learn or believed they needed to know. Intermediate-level students have a vocabulary of some 1,500 to 2,000 words, but they have learned almost all of these, because they were presented in a textbook or by an instructor. Intermediate students need to develop a personal vocabulary so they can talk and write about topics that interest them. This section of the notebook encouraged students to make decisions about content they wished to learn. Some students just recorded new words and phrases in the notebook, some commented on their entries, others included grammar points that they wished to review. Many students chose to learn vocabulary associated with their fields of study, and many recorded words that they encountered when completing other sections of the notebook, particularly *Encounters* and *Investigations.*

During the semester I asked students to seek out encounters with Spanish language and Hispanic culture and to pay careful attention to chance encounters that were almost certain to occur. In the second section of the notebook they recorded information about these encounters and often included related artifacts such as advertisements, brochures, and correspondence. A significant number of students commented that they had trouble finding entries for this section during the early part of the semester, but as the semester progressed they were having encounters on a regular basis. They reported that their awareness of the Spanish language and Hispanic culture increased dramatically and that they began noticing references to the language and culture in other classes as well as in everyday activities such as shopping, listening to music, and watching television.

In the third section of the notebook students had to choose topics to research, select sources to use, and evaluate their sources. They often did additional investigation of topics that were treated in class, but many also chose new topics. Students were required to use at least two sources for each investigation, and they were limited to one Internet source. Each entry had to include an evaluation of all sources used. My feedback on the evaluation of sources proved to be very important, and I was pleased that many students demonstrated great progress in the ability to offer a critical evaluation based on evidence as the semester progressed.

Students reflected upon their learning in the final section of the notebook. They were expected to use higher order thinking skills such as analysis, synthesis, and evaluation. They often reflected on their own learning process, but they also explored linguistic and cultural phenomena in this section and in several cases examined stereotypes about the language and culture they were studying. I offered the most extensive feedback in this section of the notebook and through that established a conversation with students about their reactions to what they were learning and about what they learned about themselves as students of foreign language and culture.

Numerous times during the semester students used information from their notebooks during class time. Students were required to do class presentations and most chose topics that they had investigated for notebook entries. The evaluation of sources proved to be an interesting and important part of many presentations. In class, students often worked in pairs or small groups to improve their conversational skills and it was common for notebook entries to play a part in these discussions. On several occasions I had students present a question or provocative statement from a notebook entry so that their classmates could offer responses. These interactions often led to additional notebook entries. I believe the notebooks were effective in tying the mandatory content of an intermediate-level foreign language class to the interests and experiences of the students in the class.

I also devised a rubric for grading the notebook:

The notebook meets 100% or nearly 100% of the requirements. There may be more than the required number of entries and/or the entries may include notable detail and/or depth. Originality is demonstrated in the choice and/or the treatment of topics. There is evidence of probing, that is to say searching for information, finding it, evaluating it and using it. The notebook is well organized and entries are easy to read and understand. The notebook is turned in on time and includes the proper number and type of entries each time it is submitted. The student has included response to instructor feedback on entries when appropriate.

Students reacted quite positively to the notebooks:

"If I learn something or hear something in class that interests me, I learn more about it on my own. My *Investigations* helped me learn to do this. I learned more about things I was interested in."

"I definitely ask my own questions more now because the . . . journal forces you to do that in your *Encounters* and *Reflections* sections. You can't simply write down just what you take in because you have to process it."

"I think this class [by requiring the notebook entries] has inspired me to actually go out and explore the Spanish language more. Rather than taking notes and studying, I feel like learning."

"This course has allowed me to become more aware of things I might not have ever investigated. Using the notebooks as an example, I was able to look up things and was more prone to try and hear or be in situations involving Spanish language."

And perhaps my favorite comment, written after the last notebook submission:

"I am definitely noticing encounters much more than in January— now, when an *encuentro* occurs, I am almost disappointed that I don't have to write it down. The . . . notebook became a challenge, a sort of hobby, and a resource for the future."

These comments lead me to believe that many students achieved the goals I had established for the notebook assignment. They became actively involved in their learning, they chose topics that interested them and sought information about the topics on their own, and they tried to process the information in a critical way. Many students indicated that they were excited about learning a foreign language and about the cultures that the language represents, and many sought opportunities to use the language and to be exposed to the culture outside of class. I believe that some students will continue to seek opportunities to speak Spanish and participate in Hispanic culture, fulfilling an important area of the National Standards: participation in communities beyond the classroom. I hope that students will take with them to other classes the inquiry-guided model of learning that I believe they employed successfully in these intermediate Spanish classes.

Inquiry-guided Learning, Laptops, and Spanish for Engineers

When faced with the challenge of teaching Spanish to engineers in an honors course which required the use of wireless laptop computers, I was determined to follow the tenets of inquiry-guided learning: How could we harness the computer to enhance learning in a foreign language with IGL outcomes in mind? Does a computer help a student to become a more active learner or will the opposite occur—passivity behind the computer screen? It turned out that the most important use of the laptop was the linking of foreign language acquisition and global culture and technology to the students' interest in computers and engineering. Engineering students arrive on campus predisposed to this learning tool, and we made the most of it in their research, daily class work, and group work.

Our learning goals were ambitious in encompassing not only foreign language literacy but also cultural literacy.

- To master grammatical structures required in an intermediate Spanish class
- To communicate with newly learned structures in written and oral form
- To learn vocabulary commonly used in engineering and technology contexts
- To develop the ability to comprehend and use Spanish in settings inevitably encountered in our technological society
- To demonstrate an awareness and appreciation of target culture and understand the cultural and historic importance of artifacts in the Hispanic world such as Roman aqueducts, cathedrals, castles, and paintings
- To interact in a more formal setting such as the presentation of an engineering project
- To demonstrate historical and aesthetic knowledge of certain historical/ art sites

The essential features of objects such as aqueducts, castles, cathedrals, weapons, and clothing are independent of the forces of culture. That is, in order to perform the function for which they are designed, they must have certain characteristics whether they were built by Slavs, Morrocans, Japanese, or western Europeans. A sword, for example, must have a handle and must be sharp, whoever makes it. But the blade can be decorated, shaped, or engraved. These features are irrelevant to the function of the sword, but they may be distinctive expressions of the culture that produced the sword. Culture, then, in the sense in which we use it in this course, is a manifestation in an object of the individuality of a people, a country, a time.

Spain, because of its unique historical mixing of diverse cultures, is an ideal focus for students who are considering questions of the relationship between technology and culture. Modern Spanish culture is a fascinating product of the admixture of Romano-Hispanic, Moorish, and Sephardic Jewish traditions. In short, in addition to the intermediate language curriculum, the students learn to appreciate cultural awareness as a practical tool in their professional careers as engineers. The great mosque in Cordoba, the Mesquita, would be a dramatic example for the students of the way culture shapes technology. After the Moors were expelled from Cordoba, Charles V built a Catholic church in the center of the mosque. Its elaborate appearance presents a stark and riveting contrast to the elegant simplicity of the mosque. Both buildings serve the same function as a place of worship, but they could hardly be more different. The student who passes from one to the other cannot help but ponder the way in which culture informs the appreciation of technology.

Much of the students' daily work was computer centered. Wireless technology was integrated into research projects, daily class activities, and outside work. My goal was to use this technology to make them independent learners. The course, for example, featured an interactive website. Students submitted projects and work to the website and important class information was available there. This worked well for the more mature students who kept up with assignments without reminders; but the freshmen commented that it was too much responsibility: We think it was good training.

Texts from the website of *How Stuff Works* (www.howstuffworks.com) were provided via the class website; permission was kindly granted from the *How Stuff Works* team. The video for the text was available on the web as were the lab book and workbook. Did this enhance learning? Did it lead to more engagement in the material and consequently in class? Students overwhelmingly stated that they preferred this to the traditional language lab tapes.

Students created their own website. Included in the website was a portfolio of the student's work. We were able to share and comment on portfolios in an easy and quick way. Student correction of errors of written work was required before it was put on the web; the goal was student learning from mistakes and responsibility for correction.

All in all, it was a remarkable experience and the coordination of the use of laptop, language acquisition, and inquiry-guided learning was a positive one. Students learned more Spanish, culture, and technology simply because they enjoyed working with the laptop. We were able to cover more text material, more culture modules, and the added engineering/technology themes to the curriculum. One student expressed it this way: "Technology is so much more interesting when tied to culture." It was a felicitous partnership.

Inquiry-guided Learning and Spanish for Design Students

The critical evaluation of evidence is an important component of inquiry-guided learning. Academics in foreign languages use written evidence in their work as they make judgments about the merits of literature and criticism. We help our students learn how to make similar judgments about written texts in our literature classes. But how do we assess evidence that is not written? Even more fundamentally, what counts as evidence? This was the challenge I faced when I prepared to teach a class in Spanish language and culture for a group of students in our College of Design. Design students are consistently visual learners who look to the visual for their evidence. The making of pictures, reproductions, and diagrams is the basis for their active evaluation, comparison, and appreciation of the cultural artifacts. Asked how a Hispanic artifact reflects the culture, design students immediately sit down to draw the artifact or to find materials to reproduce it. Their peers in turn judge their work on the quality of its workmanship and its truth in reproduction.

In designing a major project for the course, I tried to imitate the culture of the design school. Evidence would be presented in a "crit" session in the design school gallery with design faculty and peers in attendance who would evaluate the evidence. The project simply called for research of an artifact from a Hispanic country. What is it? What societal needs or functions guided its creation? Who uses it? How was it built? What does it reveal about the time and place and people?

Students worked all semester on evaluating evidence in art. They were required to bring in a reproduction or an interpretation of the artifact and to evaluate the artifact in the context of culture. For their individual presentation I asked them to create a notebook. (Design students carry drawing notebooks as a matter of course to draw or diagram what they see—their visual evidence.) They described in the notebook the weekly progress of their project from their research to their visual evidence. I checked their notebooks periodically. I used rough guidelines for completion of the parts of the project. Design students do not think in a linear fashion, and they tend to go back and forth in written research and design of artifact. The oral presentation was scheduled for the end of the semester, and students were charged with presenting a board, a poster, and/or a replica to use as the visual evidence.

The students rose to the challenge, producing creative responses to the project assignment. One student studied the designs on the tiles of the Alhambra for color and the composition and placement of each individual tile. Using her art history research and visual evidence, she described how the use of tiles and the designs reflected the Moorish culture. She then did a silkscreen scarf, which replicated a favorite design of the tile. Her research became a thing of beauty for her to wear. Another student researched the history of the Spanish Civil War. He then studied Picasso's *Guernica* for the themes, composition, and color. He used this evidence to paint his own work inspired by the themes and colors of *Guernica*. The artifact and history were a springboard to his own creation. Another student in landscape architecture worked on the pilgrimage route to Santiago. He studied the history, artistic value of the churches along the route, and the landscape of the route itself. His artifact was a poster he designed featuring the walk as a crusade with medieval images of man and Saint James. In short, these design students used both written and visual evidence to prepare a project on the cultural underpinnings of important artifacts in Hispanic culture.

Study Abroad: Inquiry-guided Learning in Segovia, Spain, for (Mostly) Engineering Students

Inquiry-guided learning is driven and vitalized by active investigation. Formulating questions, coming to conclusions, analyzing results, and evaluating one's own learning—these are the goals of the program. This particular experience took place in Europe in both a classroom and a city. Twenty-eight students traveled to Segovia where they took two classes: a culture and technology language class and a Spanish history and culture class. The program was sponsored by the College of Humanities and Social Sciences and the College of Engineering.

Segovia, a small city 55 miles northwest of Madrid, is an ideal locus for students considering questions of the relationship between technology and culture in our society: Among other features, it boasts a Roman aqueduct, a Gothic cathedral, and a castle. It provided a perfect introduction to the richness of Spanish artifacts and processes as well as to the lifestyle of the Spanish people.

The city itself became our learning lab. The students' charge was to learn as much culture and language as they could and to learn about their own personal learning styles. To that end we assigned a project that tied in technology with culture. The goal was simple: to study and understand in depth how artifacts or processes reflect the culture. Different students approached this question differently, but the common thread was their excitement about their project and the high quality of the work they produced.

One of our mechanical engineers, Erica, brought an interest in blacksmithing to Spain. With the help of a grant from our Park Scholarship Foundation, she apprenticed with Monica Ferrer, a master blacksmith who restores ironwork for the 17th century La Granja Palace nearby. Erica worked at her forge four hours a week and learned the history and vocabulary of blacksmithing in Spain. The life and times of Baroque Spain, the process used by these craftsmen, the life of a woman in 21st century Spain working to restore precious artifacts—all this was part of our student's research. She made a study plan, arranged times with Monica, managed to travel by local bus, solved the problems attendant with creating locks typical of Renaissance Spain, and wrote a report which covered a remarkable list of blacksmithing terms in Spanish and the process of making the artifact.

Another student, a chemical engineer, studied the distillery process in making DYC whisky, a popular Spanish product. With the project manager, Amanda made a project plan and learned how the distillery works. She worked with the project manager to understand the process and learned enough to take us on a tour of the whisky plant. Her report included important vocabulary used in this industry and a discussion of the process of making whisky supplemented with diagrams.

A social work major with a special interest in children interviewed numerous social workers in Segovia on how children are protected in Spain. Caroline formulated questions that helped her understand the child welfare system, arranged and interviewed three social workers, and visited a social work office and a food kitchen. I was present at one interview where I saw Caroline grow from a concrete thinker in Spanish to an abstract thinker as she discussed social issues in the foreign language. Her report was a cogent commentary on social issues in Spain, a comparative study of families at home and abroad, and a synthesis of Spanish protective laws for children.

As a final example, two students studied the 11th-century aqueduct in Segovia. They researched the technology, did some onsite study, talked with experts in the city about this most important artifact, and finally brought the class to the aqueduct to view it from a variety of different perspectives that highlighted its structural features. Again the students planned the project, posed important questions, did visual and written research, and shared their findings with the class, with the aqueduct as a background.

All students kept a daily journal of their impressions of Spain and a more academic journal about their progress on their projects and what they discovered about their independent research. Anecdotes from the students tell us that this independent research in a foreign country has made them more confident of their ability to seek answers and evaluate information. They honed their skills in critical thinking and accepting responsibility for their learning. They all became more engaged in the class learning because of their projects. The personal part of the journal showed students becoming more committed to learning and inquiry.

The dread of foreign language courses among high school and college students may not be universal, but it is certainly widespread. And while the causes of this phenomenon are complex, at least some of the blame is due to outmoded, stultifying methods of language instruction. Frequently, foreign language teachers find that they have much to overcome before class begins. Here is where IGL can literally come to the rescue. It certainly won't energize and excite all students about language study; some will find it impenetrable and unrewarding whatever the approach. But foreign language instructors who use inquiry-guided learning will certainly find themselves in classrooms that are more lively and vital. At the end of the term they will also undoubtedly find that many of their students have learned more, enjoyed the process more, and kindled in themselves a hunger for more inquiry, more investigation, and more excitement for learning.

7

INCORPORATING ACTIVE LEARNING, CRITICAL THINKING, AND PROBLEM-BASED LEARNING IN AN ADVANCED FRENCH CULTURE AND CIVILIZATION COURSE

By Arlene Malinowski

> We teach to change the world. The hope
> that undergirds our efforts to help students
> learn is that doing this will help them act
> towards each other, and to their environ-
> ment, with compassion, understanding,
> and fairness.
> —*Stephen Brookfield, Becoming*
> *a Critically Reflective Teacher (1995, p. 1)*

For the past several years, I have been working to transform my upper-level French course on culture and civilization following the guidelines of inquiry-guided learning. This course, FLF 315 "French Culture and Civilization," is a required course at the third year, advanced level for all French majors in the Department of Foreign Languages and Literatures. FLF 315 is offered every spring semester and is a rather popular course in our department, averaging approximately 25 students each semester that it is taught. The course generally follows a traditional format in that is it taught on campus, three days a week, in a regular university classroom.

In 1999, I first taught this course in a traditional way by selecting a textbook, dividing up how much material I would need to cover each week, determining how many exams I would administer, and then settling upon an appropriate number of written assignments. I didn't pay much attention to student learning outcomes other than my concern that the students learn the course material. Although I very much enjoyed teaching this course and I felt that students were benefiting from the instruction, I felt that it could be organized in a better way. I was worried that students were merely memorizing facts and not probing deeply enough in order to gain a significant appreciation of cultural issues. I was unaware of a number of alternatives that were available to me for modifying the course to enable students to do so. When I began to learn about the rationale and the many facets of inquiry-guided learning, I was intrigued by the possibilities to apply some of these to my course. I also discovered the work of Claire Kramsch and was delighted to find that my new ideas for this course fit nicely within her pivotal discussion of the need for depth and complexity in cross-cultural competence and cultural perceptions (Kramsch, 1993, pp. 205–232).[1] By defining specific goals and objectives for my students and by integrating a number of active learning strategies in the course, including critical-thinking questions and problem-based learning, I was able to transform the course. I also offered students a more coherent approach to the course material whereby students became actively involved in developing a critical understanding of the culture and civilization of France.

My starting point was to address three major questions for the restructuring of my course: (1) What is the big or overarching question for the course?[2] (this involves the establishment of goals and objectives); (2) What kinds of course activities will lead students to inquire and to think critically? (this requires devising and planning for active learning strategies to achieve these goals); and (3) How do I know if the students have achieved the intended outcomes? (this necessitates the development of assessment measures that assist in determining if the goals have been met). I will treat each of these broad categories in turn and elaborate on the contents and approach of each one as I have developed them within the context of this course.

---

[1] In addition to the work of Claire Kramsch, I have also found the following texts to be helpful in providing insights and perspectives on the complexity of cultural diversity and cultural understanding: Ferraro, G. P. (2002). *The cultural dimensions of international business* (4th ed.). Upper Saddle River, NJ: Prentice Hall; Hall, E. T., & Hall, M. R. (1990). *Understanding cultural differences*. Yarmouth, ME: Intercultural Press.

[2] I was first introduced to this concept of the "Big Question" for a course by Kenneth R. Bain of Northwestern University in a workshop entitled, "What Do the Best Teachers Do?" at NCSU on October 12, 1999.

The Big Question

In arriving at the overriding question for my course, I settled upon the following: How can the study of French history and civilization help us to understand the complexity of contemporary life and thought in France? Articulating the question at the outset of the course more or less turns topsy-turvy the orientation that I had taken in the past and provides a coherency that I perceived as lacking before. Instead of focusing on starting at the beginning and continuing until the end, I chose to focus on where I wanted the students to end up at the end of the course, which helped me to know exactly where I wanted to be headed every step along the way. This goal was accomplished through reading, writing, and discussion in French of topics pertaining to the social, cultural, economic, and political structures of France, including its geography, history, music, art, and national consciousness. The material in the course is thus designed to support student learning and to lead students to an understanding of the forces and events that have shaped modern France and the French people. Basing the specific intended student outcomes on Bloom's taxonomy included in Appendix 7.A, I was able to shift the focus of the course to inquiry-guided learning, in which students are asked to analyze and evaluate relevant cultural topics and questions. Students are presented with perplexing or puzzling cultural dilemmas or situations, which I ask them to analyze and interpret based on the facts and knowledge that they have learned in the course. Basically, critical thinking and inquiry-guided learning, as I have defined it for this course, is the ability to analyze and interpret French historical and contemporary facts and cultural information (somewhat as social scientists, especially anthropologists, do) and to acquire the knowledge and resources needed to produce a well-organized, carefully articulated, important and meaningful research question and written and oral presentation at the end of the term. These goals and objectives are graphically illustrated in Table 7.1.

Course Activities and Assignments

Using the intended student outcomes and the "big question" for my course as a guide, I then addressed the second major question indicated which refers to the kinds of activities and assignments used to promote inquiry-guided learning and critical thinking. In that regard, I have developed over the last couple of years a number of active learning techniques involving critical-thinking questions and problem-based learning scenarios in the French culture and civilization course. To support these activities with resources for students (e.g., lists of reference texts and articles, online links to the French press, lists of possible research topics, steps involved in a process approach to writing term papers), I find it helpful to maintain an active website containing this information. One example of an activity during the course of the semester is a student assignment

Table 7.1 FLF 315 Student Learning Outcomes for an IGL Classroom

Know *basic facts and ideas*	*Analyze* *cultural issues and questions*	*Synthesize* *research findings*
Historical dates and events	Critical analysis of French news articles	Formulating research questions
Important people	Comparison and contrast of cross-cultural dilemmas and situations	Brainstorming, peer review using rubric
Artistic endeavors		Written and oral reports
Inventions		
Political developments		
Bloom's Taxonomy		
Knowledge	Application	Synthesis
Comprehension	Analysis	Evaluation

for an oral report in class based on a current French newspaper article. The purpose of this assignment is to enable students to begin to "close the loop" between the historical background of France and the present-day ramifications of past developments, thereby leading students to address the "big question" for the course. Specific guidelines are given to the students for this activity (see Appendix 7.B).

Another assignment that I have developed for my students is a series of study questions to promote critical thinking and inquiry. These questions are specially designed to address problematic issues and events in French history and culture, for which no *one* answer is available and which will require students to think, research, and discuss with others possible responses or solutions. These critical-thinking questions serve to synthesize the course material in a meaningful way for students by illustrating to them how knowledge from the course work can assist them in addressing difficult issues and problems in French society. These questions are used during the course of the semester for homework and class discussion. I also include one or two of them on the final exam and even ask students to develop one of their own critical-thinking questions as part of the final assessment at the end of the semester. An example of these IGL questions are listed in Appendix 7.C.

An additional course assignment and instructional strategy that I have used for promoting IGL in this course is the use of problem-based learning scenarios. By presenting students with a cultural dilemma or problem to solve, I find that I can more easily integrate a good deal of course material into one exercise and also provide the students with an opportunity to puzzle over a difficult or perplexing situation, thereby discovering solutions for themselves without the direct intervention of the instructor. I present the students with a so-called problem statement and I ask them to address it through research on their own and by discussion in groups. I explain to them that there is no right or wrong answer to the questions in the statement and they are to formulate their response based upon the information from the course material and other sources. An example of a problem statement is found in Appendix 7.D. Such an approach, I feel, offers an indirect, yet effective way to lead students to learn through inquiry and their own investigation of a topic. Problem-based learning (PBL) is a powerful tool to assist students in acquiring problem-solving strategies that will be useful to them well beyond the context of my course.

Assessment of Student Work

The learning objectives and the course assignments lead naturally to the last of the three initial questions, namely, the assessment of students' work. In addition to the traditional means of course assessment, such as term papers, tests, and exams, I employ a variety of classroom assessment measures throughout the course of the semester to provide feedback to both myself and the students on an ongoing basis. The One-Minute Paper, for example, developed by Angelo and Cross (1993, pp. 148–149), in which students articulate a major point they learned in class that day and a point they still have a question about, is a useful tool for evaluating student learning in a casual and nonthreatening way. The Classroom Critical Incident Questionnaire developed by Brookfield (1995, pp. 114–139) is another effective means of measuring students' progress and their approach to the material during the course of the term. I have found that these frequent mini-assessments are helpful in gauging students' progress. I also make use of a writing rubric in the assessment of student papers, which I give to students early in the semester and have found to be particularly useful in letting students know exactly what is expected of them. The work of Bean (1996) and Walvoord and Anderson (1998) have provided a wealth of ideas to assist with student assessment in an IGL classroom. All in all, I have found in this course that the quality of students' work and their ability to think critically has greatly improved as evidenced by their thoughtful responses to classroom assignments, their investigation of important and complex topics for term papers, and their knowledge and understanding as demonstrated on in-class exams.

Learning about and using the principles of inquiry-guided learning in my French culture and civilization course has been an invigorating experience for me and has contributed in a significant way to my professional development. By teaching and transforming my course in this way, I feel that I am being a more effective instructor and providing students with a course that will have a powerful impact on their lives. Assisting young adults in the process of learning to reflect and think critically is a most exciting endeavor, and I am grateful for the opportunity to be part of the effort. As such, making use of the principles of IGL assists in empowering students to navigate in their world and play a large role in cultivating the life of the mind.

References

Angelo, T. A., & Cross, K. P. (1993). *Classroom assessment techniques: A handbook for college teachers* (2nd ed.). San Francisco: Jossey-Bass.

Bean, J. (1996). *Engaging ideas: The professor's guide to integrating writing, critical thinking, and active learning in the classroom.* San Francisco: Jossey-Bass.

Brookfield, S. D. (1995). *Becoming a critically reflective teacher.* San Francisco: Jossey-Bass.

Kramsch, C. (1993). *Context and culture in language teaching.* New York: Oxford University Press.

Walvoord, B., & Anderson, V. (1998). *Effective grading: A tool for learning and assessment.* San Francisco: Jossey-Bass.

INTENDED STUDENT LEARNING OUTCOMES

By the end of this course, students will have a good knowledge of historical facts of French civilization and a clearer understanding of how the French people live and work. In the process of doing so, they will be able to:

1. List and identify the principal historical facts in the evolution of French civilization

2. Describe major historical movements and events and their cultural significance

3. Compare and contrast various facets of French and American culture both orally and in writing in order to acquire guided practice in critical thinking

4. Develop the habit of inquiry in reading the French press and relevant research by analyzing and seeking solutions to important cultural themes and issues through problem-based learning scenarios

5. Design and compose a well-organized written research paper that demonstrates knowledge, analysis, and synthesis of a selected cultural thesis question

6. Evaluate and self-reflect upon your growing appreciation of French civilization and culture, the development of your cultural knowledge, and your ability to take responsibility for your own learning

OUTLINE FOR NEWSPAPER ARTICLE ANALYSIS

Please follow the following guidelines for preparing your oral presentation in class.

I. The presenter is requested to write the title, date, and source of the selected French newspaper article on a large card or half sheet of paper. On this card, write three major points that you wish to make concerning the contents of your article. After you have listed these three points, write a one- or two-sentence summary statement expressing what you have learned from the article and how it relates to the French historical context and to your increased understanding of French culture and civilization. When presenting your material in class, you may read from your notes, but do not read from the newspaper article itself (unless you are quoting someone). You are also asked to write on the blackboard the title, source, and date of the article, as well as any new vocabulary words or expressions that are important to an understanding of the news report. Plan on a presentation of 10 to 15 minutes. Also keep in mind the following guidelines for giving oral presentations:

a. Be well prepared and ready to present your work on the day assigned.

b. Be clear and precise and follow the guidelines for preparing the assignment.

c. Speak clearly and loudly enough using correct grammar and pronunciation.

d. Maintain eye contact with your audience and appeal to the interest of your listeners.

e. Stay within the time limit given for the oral report.
Hand the card in to me after you have completed your oral presentation in class. Your presentation will be evaluated according to how well you have followed the outline given above. Students will receive a grade for their work, noted on their cards, and returned to them by the instructor.

II. The students at their seats will listen to the oral report and then write a one- or two-sentence reaction to the presentation, focusing on what they learned that they didn't know before. Those slips of paper will be handed in and will serve as a daily participation grade for the students.

STUDY QUESTIONS TO PROMOTE CRITICAL THINKING

1. In what way is the Middle Ages a kind of bridge—as its name implies, "the middle"—between Antiquity and the Renaissance?

2. The year 1870 was particularly difficult for France, the date of the Franco-Prussian War and the defeat of Napoleon III at Sedan. What was happening in the other countries of Europe at the same time? What was happening in America? Compare and contrast the different situations.

3. What effect did the two world wars have on the arts and life in 20th-century France?

4. Given the importance of all aspects of cattle production in France as it has developed over the centuries, imagine how the French people have felt in light of two catastrophic events that have unfolded recently, mad cow disease and hoof and mouth disease, that are threatening their meat production. What would you say if you were writing a letter to a local French newspaper?

5. According to an article that appeared in the June 6, 2000, *Le Monde,* "France is in good health . . . ," France holds third place, just after Japan and Australia, for longevity with an average lifespan of 73.1 years according to the World Health Organization. How would you explain this high rating for the French nation?

6. On February 4, 2002, a public debate took place in Paris surrounding the topic of genetically modified organisms (GMOs) and the use of GMO crops on experimental terrain. The French people are taking sides for and against the propagation of GMOs with the militant José Bové, leader of the Farmers' Confederation, as one of its most vociferous opponents. How do aspects of this debate help you to understand the diversity of French public opinion toward GMO experimentation?

7. Imagine that you are a journalist for the *New Yorker Magazine* and you are starting a new column entitled, "The French Take." In it, you plan to discuss the French point of view on a number of key cultural issues, such as the French perspective on smoking, teenage drinking, capital punishment, and reckless driving. What would your first column be like?

8. Picture this: two elementary school classrooms on either side of the Atlantic—one in France, one in the United States. Both groups of students are studying about food and nutrition. In the American classroom, the teacher is explaining the Food Pyramid to the students and the importance of eating a balanced diet based on the model given. In the French classroom, the students are being visited by a French chef who is teaching the students about the subtle difference in taste between red and purple grapes and between Camembert and Brie. What do these two very different approaches to the study of nutrition tell us about the French and American attitudes toward food and eating?

PROBLEM STATEMENT

You have just obtained the position that you were hoping for: You've been promoted to the position of manager of a leading American fast-food European branch office in France. You will now have the opportunity to use all of the French language skills that you have learned at NCSU! The problem is this: The executive director in New York has given you instructions to investigate the feasibility of establishing a new franchise in Nice, France, on the Cote d'Azur. He understandably wants to be assured that such an undertaking will prove to be a financial success. Since you are very well informed about French cultural background and what is going on in France today, you are aware that the French are concerned about such things as environmental factors, globalization, and the quality of life. Conferring with your advisory board, develop a plan for how you would present your enterprise to the average French citizen so that he or she would be likely to become a regular customer at the French affiliate. What kinds of marketing strategies would you propose in order to appeal to the French public? What kinds of design (exterior and interior) features would you recommend? What modifications to the menu would you suggest? Where is the best location in the city? Devise a list of four strategies that you think will be effective and will ensure your high standing in the company. Write them on the overhead transparencies provided and be prepared to present your findings to the full board of trustees at their next meeting.

8

ENHANCING INQUIRY-GUIDED LEARNING WITH TECHNOLOGY IN HISTORY COURSES

By Richard W. Slatta

Over the past 10 years, I've added more and more technological tools to my courses. I've found that computer and multimedia technologies enhance student engagement and improve inquiry-guided learning activities. History 216 "Latin America since 1826," a course I've taught virtually every semester for the past 20 years, provides a good example of how I've done this. The course surveys the region's political, social, economic, and cultural developments since most of the countries gained their independence. Pulling anywhere between 20 and 50 students with 30 the norm, it fulfills our general education requirement for a humanities course in a non-English-speaking culture. In 1999, I taught HI 216 as the History Department's first online course and have since adapted much of the online material for use by classroom students as well.

The Old Didactic Versus the New IGL History

For the first 10 years, I taught the course in a traditional didactic, lecture style. That's how I had been taught as an undergraduate, and that's how most of my colleagues taught. That meant two or even three 75-minute lectures, often delivered back to back. I took pride in structuring tight, thematic lectures, making it easy for students to follow. I occasionally showed a documentary video and presented a slide-illustrated lecture. Students only participated when someone asked a question.

As a central goal, I wanted students to know the facts and "correct" interpretation (mine!) of Latin America's past. Students read an introductory textbook, supplemented by three or four additional monographs on more specialized topics. To assess student learning, I used four in-class examinations with multiple-choice questions and one or two essay questions. Students wrote a research paper, usually based entirely on secondary sources. Except for the occasional student in a technical discipline, who had never written a college research paper, most students left with no more skills than they brought to the class. They left with a certain quantity of information about Latin America that likely did not penetrate long-term memory.

Since the mid-1990s, I have gradually revised the course, making it more interactive and adding new technologies. I strive to give students the experience of doing what historians do. I use information from Latin America's past to guide students in how to think about history and how to construct their own interpretations of the past. By the end of the course, I hope that students will be able to do the following:

1. Analyze and explain the impact of major historical forces and events that shaped the region, with special attention to human rights abuses and issues
2. Evaluate and critique primary and secondary historical sources, including material on the Internet
3. Organize logical historical arguments, supported by specific evidence
4. Write logical, interpretative historical essays phrased in clear, logical, active-voice prose
5. Evidence growth in critical thinking (measured by the higher levels of Bloom's taxonomy) and in cognitive level (based on Perry's model)

I include descriptions of Bloom and Perry in the syllabus, and we discuss these goals, their measures and meaning, at the beginning of the semester. Indeed, the first assignment is to write a response to and then discuss my online essay, "Our Approach to History." I have additional goals beyond IGL that I've discussed elsewhere (Slatta, 2001).

I also draw upon the concept of "uncoverage," developed by Wiggins and McTighe (1998): ". . . inquiring into, around, and underneath content instead of simply covering it" (p. 98). "Beyond learning about a subject, students will need lessons that enable them to experience directly the inquiries, arguments, applications, and points of view underneath the facts and opinions they learn if they are to understand them. Students have to *do* the subject, not just learn its results" (p. 99). In a history course, students should get their hands "dirty," digging into the documents and extracting meaning.

Although a bit exaggerated, here's how I see history teaching and learning, past and present. Table 8.1 summarizes the differences, which are then discussed in greater detail in the chapter.

Table 8.1   The Old Didactic Versus New IGL History

Course element	Old didactic history	New IGL history
Definition of history	Rigid, static, linear, fixed, predetermined content.	Exciting process of exploration, discovery, problem-solving, seeking interconnections.
Core goal	Coverage of facts, coverage of the textbook.	Uncoverage of the means by which we discover, explore, and explain history.
Basis of pedagogy	Knowledge is transferred magically or through osmosis from faculty to students.	Knowledge is jointly constructed by students and faculty; interaction rules.
View of students	Students as passive learners, empty vessels needing to be filled with content.	Students as active learners, partners, teachers.
Instructor's role	Sage on the Stage, infallible source of knowledge.	Guide on the Side, fellow learner.
Type of inquiry	Almost completely deductive.	Primarily inductive.
Grading and assessment	Faculty classify and sort competencies; the normal grade curve rules.	Faculty help students develop their learning skills. Explicit rubrics guide performance.
Classroom atmosphere	Competitive classroom; zero-sum, The Lone Ranger, and Social Darwinism rule.	Cooperative classroom. Collaboration and dialogue rule.
Focal point	Instructor-, syllabus-, event-, textbook-centered.	Student-, learning-, evidence-, process-centered: "Think like a historian."
Nature of assignments	Limited number of formal written assignments.	Mix of many formal and informal writing and speaking assignments.

Nature of the Assignments

In rethinking assignments, I applied principles learned from our Campus Writing and Speaking Program. A semester-long workshop with Chris Anson and Deanna Dannels provided excellent advice for making many of the changes described here. Students engage in many formal and informal speaking assignments. They give oral presentations and news reports. "Salsa Day," a Latin American version of "show and tell," and "Gaucho Poetry Day" offer more informal speaking opportunities. Students also participate in a variety of discussion formats. Students write many informal assignments, notably brief (i.e., 250-word) papers that respond to specific "Thought Questions." In some assignments, students engage in role playing, taking on the character of a historical figure. Although I comment on these informal activities, they are not graded.

For formal writing, students use a four-part essay rubric, developed with assistance from Arlene Malinowski (Department of Foreign Languages and Literatures, NCSU) that explicitly lays out the competencies necessary for good historical writing. The very sound ideas of Walvoord and Anderson (2000) inform my approach to student assessment. Students also practice peer editing as well as peer and self-evaluations of their writing. I concur with historian McClymer (2003) of Assumption College, who calls his approach "structured access." "The first goal is to draw students into an ongoing scholarly conversation *as participants*" (p. 25).

Teaching Strategies and Activities

I've revised the course around the following principles.

1. Employ a constructivist approach that allows students to act as apprentice historians rather than merely reading and regurgitating what professional historians have written. Through IGL, history becomes a dialogue between students, historical sources, and other historians, rather than a closed, fixed set of dead facts. Creed (1998) summarizes well this approach: "The deepest, most usable kind of knowledge (knowing how to use the knowledge, when to use it, and why) is best attained by learners when they:
    *   have a shared cognitive set with the instructor,
    *   are motivated to learn,
    *   actively construct their knowledge."

2. Assign far more primary than secondary (i.e., textbook) sources. Now students do what historians do—examine and interpret historical documents. They engage the "raw materials" to construct their own interpretations of the past. Because no printed source book existed for my teaching, I've used the Internet to create one. History graduate

student assistants Carrie Collins and Daire Roebuck located potential sources in the library. We scanned the materials, and I created web documents. The resulting Online Primary Sources page now includes more than a hundred items. I also digitized many of my color slides for web use. After scanning Spanish language sources, I used Easy Translator 3 software to quickly create a rough but workable English language version and then cleaned up the translation. In fact, I now assign only two secondary sources: a brief 200-page textbook and my own monograph about 19th-century Argentina, *Gauchos and the Vanishing Frontier* (Slatta, 1983, 1992).

3. Assign less reading. I've reduced the total volume of reading, in hopes that students will read more closely and critically—quality over quantity. Instead of focusing on "covering" a vast amount of factual material, I want students to "uncover" and practice the method by which historians read and interpret primary sources. Furthermore, it takes far more time, concentration, and rereading to understand primary sources than it does to skim a textbook.

4. Cover fewer topics. I've dropped many topics in favor of covering fewer major themes in greater detail. This reflects my hope that students "uncover" interesting and relevant themes, trends, processes, and issues, rather than merely "covering" and regurgitating textbook material.

5. Do more evaluation of sources and interpretations. Students evaluate one another's interpretations, compare secondary source views with primary source documents, and take the roles of historical actors. We also explore ideas about critical pedagogy in Latin America, using the rich thought and life of Brazilian educator Paulo Freire.

6. Practice vital collaborative skills by working in groups and teaching one another. Students participate in teaching one another and me via news reports and other assignments. The Internet provides access to many Latin American newspapers, which students read and analyze to get Latin American perspectives.

7. Provide a richer audio and visual classroom. I've incorporated more documentary videos, music, maps, PowerPoint presentations, and other visuals into the course. This enriches the classroom experience and appeals especially to visual learners. I have a web-based essay on music and politics in Latin America, which I supplement by playing a variety of older and contemporary music. We listen to Mexican *corridos* (i.e., folksongs, often with political content), Bob Marley, and Selena, among others. Acquiring audio and visual materials costs money. A 2001 grant from NCSU's Faculty Center for Teaching and Learning allowed me to purchase a library of enrichment materials. I also develop concept maps, using Inspiration software.

8. Encourage students to take this course with the same seriousness they would a "real world" job. That means that students have to take responsibility for important skills and behaviors, such as submitting assignments on time, having the right equipment for the job (e.g., reliable computer storage media), gaining necessary research skills, and being honest.

I've also increased my availability and interaction with students. Technology allows me to hold virtual office hours during much of the day or night. While logged on to my computer, I respond immediately to student email. I use instant messaging to answer brief questions and "put out small fires" in real time. Many students have thanked me for being readily available day or night. In the course evaluation, a summer 2003 student wrote: "Dr. Slatta was always there to answer any questions I had. He offered a phone number, a screen name and an email address. Whenever I emailed him I received a quick response." Getting an instant response to a question at 10 P.M. seems very special to them. Students with hearing impairments especially welcome such ready access. The downside is that fewer students visit me personally during office hours, and I miss those face-to-face chats. I began these practices as a service to online students, but classroom students also communicate with me electronically.

Online communications can also "stretch" discussions beyond the classroom. In the early 1990s, I began using NetForum, then migrated to WebCT, and will explore the potential of Facilitate. I generally teach a Tuesday/Thursday schedule, which means that students have a five-day break from class over the weekend. I don't want them ignoring my course for such an extended period. Thus, I often assign asynchronous online discussion questions due over the weekend, so that they must engage the course materials a third time.

Following is an example, based on firsthand descriptions of conditions in a 19th-century Latin American countryside.

Lives of the Rural Masses

On your primary documents page, read items 58–64. You are a European natural scientist, exploring conditions in 19th-century Latin America. Like Alexander von Humboldt and Charles Darwin, you keep a journal of your observations.

> Last name A–G: Summarize the social and political problems faced by the rural masses.
>
> Last name H–N: Summarize the economic difficulties faced by the rural masses.

Above groups post by Saturday noon.

> Last name O–Z: By class on Tuesday, read the documents as well as the discussions by your colleagues. Who has identified the most serious problems, so serious that they might generate political unrest or even revolution?

The groups rotate responsibilities for initial or follow-up postings. We open Tuesday's class by viewing some of the discussion postings, projected onto a screen. When teaching in a classroom with Smartboard technology, I have a student volunteer write major points onto the Smartboard. Students love the touch-screen technology and colorful markers, and they get further involved on a rotating basis in distilling discussion ideas into brief, salient points. Most students voluntarily utilize websites or PowerPoint when making group presentations.

Changes in Student Behavior and Learning and Responses to IGL

Inquiry-guided learning brings a number of advantages to students. All students, except the tiny number who are truly antisocial, enjoy and thrive in an atmosphere of collaboration and communication. The greater variety of activities reaches a wider range of learning styles. They construct informal and formal learning groups. Most importantly, students function as apprentice historians: They don't just read other versions of history; they make it.

While many instructors report some student resistance to IGL, I have found little strong objection. More than 90% of students routinely answer yes to the question, "Would you recommend this course to other students?" (58 of 61 students for summer 2003). At this point, I can only hypothesize about the generally positive reactions. Prior boring high school history courses may predispose students to welcome a new approach. Or, more positively, students may welcome grappling with history as more than a mere set of dead facts to be memorized.

Web-based IGL courses, in particular, force students to be more proactive, and many value the experience. Student comments from a summer 2002 online course reflect this view: "I became much more disciplined. I also write papers better now." "Self-discipline to make sure all online work was completed and remembering to read since class attendance didn't come into play." "I learned to analyze readings on my own without having an explanation, and I also learned to use them effectively in essays." "I enjoyed the homework interpretations the most because you were allowed to use your own thought for them."

I see evidence of students learning from one another. For example, "Some of the readings were difficult to understand, but with the discussion postings, usually I was able to figure out what I didn't understand" and "The [online] discussions made me think more creatively than usual." A summer 2003 student noted, "I loved getting to read the other students' responses and thoughts posted for discussion. I think the Internet breaks down some of the barriers that are present in the classroom." I provide a safe place, an online virtual study hall, where students can post queries or gripes anonymously. They also do midterm self-assessments and a final course evaluation using WebCT-based evaluation forms.

.Finally, the higher level of engagement offered by IGL appeals to many students: "I enjoyed the way the assignments enabled us to become a part of the history." "Having a different role each discussion kept the assignments interesting and fun." In midsemester self-assessments, summer 2003 students often made invidious comparisons between old didactic history and the IGL approach: "Being able to incorporate my ideas into history allows me to analyze what happened and comprehend the facts much better. I enjoy having readings and a question to respond to that enables me to interpret the material on my own and draw my own conclusions from it." Another student noted, "I love that it is not just a textbook with definitions and dates, but that we are reading some actual primary sources and learning about how and why everything happened and not just what happened." A third opined, "This really forces you to formulate your own ideas about the material and to learn the information. I am very excited about this style of learning."

Instructor's Role

As a discussion facilitator, I still inject and teach key points, but in small chunks, inserted as the students need them. Instead of an hour-long lecture, I intersperse four to six five-minute mini-lectures to provide information and to stimulate further thought, questions, and discussion. Students engage in active thinking, interaction, and expression most of the time.

This change offers a number of tangible advantages. First, the entire burden of course development and performance does not fall on me alone. Students play vital, creative roles, and responsibilities become distributed among the entire class. I gain a much better knowledge of students, because I interact with and hear from them frequently. I get to model and mentor, doing what I like to do in the classroom, acting and thinking as a working historian, instead of as an anthropomorphized history textbook.

I also get to explore exciting innovations in pedagogy, in dialogue with dozens of colleagues on campus and far away. Participation in the Hewlett Continuation project offered an excellent means of further revising my courses. I've come to consider Bean (1996), McKeachie et al. (1998), Palmer (1998), Stratton (1999), and many other teaching advocates as friends and mentors, even though I know them only through their books.

Finally, I can integrate research with teaching and share what I do in archives, libraries, and historic sites with students. They get a more personal, tangible, and direct experience with history, instead of the stale kind encapsulated in textbook generalizations. Whenever I begin a new book, I teach a research seminar on the topic, so that students can share in the adventure of exploring new historical frontiers. Their discussions and work also add to my knowledge of the subject.

Future Directions

I am moving all of my courses, both classroom and online, toward an IGL approach enhanced with technology. In 2003, I added a second online course, this one covering U.S.–Latin American relations. Primary documents now form the evidentiary basis for all the courses that I teach. I will continue to explore new technologies to integrate into both classroom and online teaching. The existing literature, such as Jonassen, Peck, and Wilson (1999), Sandholtz, Ringstaff, and Dwyer (1997), White and Weight (2000), and Palloff and Pratt (1999), provides many models. "The Inquiry Page" (www.inquiry.uiuc.edu/) offers a convenient place for instructors to exchange ideas.

Inquiry-guided learning's special strength lies in the increased engagement and participation of students. "If we regard truth," wrote Palmer (1998, p. 51), "as something handed down from authorities on high, the classroom will look like a dictatorship. If we regard truth as a fiction determined by personal whim, the classroom will look like anarchy. If we regard truth as emerging from a complex process of mutual inquiry, the classroom will look like a resourceful and interdependent community."

Neither learning nor life is a spectator sport. Intellectual exchanges actively involving students and the instructor enrich learning for all. Real learning is not merely plug and chug exercises, memorizing facts, "covering" a textbook, or acquiring a set of skills. I believe that IGL, bolstered by today's technologies, offers an opportunity to revitalize the teaching of history and to impart the importance of a critical historical perspective, not just a bundle of facts, to the next generation of students.

Course Web Pages

HI 216, Latin America since 1826: courses.ncsu.edu/classes/hi300001/
HI 453, U.S.–Latin American Relations: www2.chass.ncsu.edu/slatta/hi453/
Latin American Press Links: courses.ncsu.edu/classes/hi300001/lapress.htm
Our Approach to History: courses.ncsu.edu/classes/hi300001/approach.htm
Primary Sources Page: courses.ncsu.edu/classes/hi300001/doclist.html
Thoughts by Paulo Freire: courses.ncsu.edu/classes/hi300001/documents/ freire.htm

References

Bean, J. C. (1996). *Engaging ideas: The professor's guide to integrating writing, critical thinking, and active learning in the classroom.* San Francisco: Jossey-Bass.

Creed, T. (1998). Effective pedagogy: Course structure that enhances learning. www.users.csbsju.edu/~tcreed/workshop/effped.html

Jonassen, D. H., Peck, K. L., & Wilson, B. G. (1999). *Learning with technology: A constructivist perspective.* Upper Saddle River, NJ: Prentice Hall.

McClymer, J. (2003). The internet: Coping with an embarrassment of riches. *Perspectives: Newsmagazine of the American Historical Association, 41*(5), 24–26.

McKeachie, W. J., et al. (1998). *McKeachie's teaching tips: Strategies, research and theory for college and university teachers* (10th ed.). New York: Houghton Mifflin.

Palloff, R. M., & Pratt, K. (1999). *Building learning communities in cyberspace: Effective strategies for the online classroom.* San Francisco: Jossey-Bass.

Palmer, P. J. (1998). *The courage to teach: Exploring the inner landscape of a teacher's life.* San Francisco: Jossey-Bass.

Sandholtz, J. H., Ringstaff, C., & Dwyer, D. C. (1997). *Teaching with technology: Creating student-centered classrooms.* New York: Teacher's College Press.

Slatta, R. W. (1983). *Gauchos and the vanishing frontier.* Lincoln: University of Nebraska Press, 1992 reprint.

Slatta, R. W. (2001). Connecting teaching goals with technology. *History Computer Review, 17*(1), 19–29. (Available online at *http://courses.ncsu.edu/ classes/hi300001/ HCRsp01.htm).*

Stratton, J. (1999). *Critical thinking for college students.* Lanham, MD: Rowman & Littlefield.

Walvoord, B. E., & Anderson, V. J. (2000). *Effective grading: A tool for learning and assessment.* San Francisco: Jossey-Bass.

White, K. W., & Weight, B. H. (2000). *The online teaching guide: A handbook of attitudes, strategies, and techniques for the virtual classroom.* Boston: Allyn & Bacon.

Wiggins, G., & McTighe, J. (1998). *Understanding by design.* Alexandria, VA: Association for Supervision and Curriculum Development.

9

INQUIRY-GUIDED LEARNING IN A FOOD SCIENCE CAPSTONE COURSE

By Lynn G. Turner
and Christopher R. Daubert

The primary focus of FS 475 "Problems and Design in Food Science," a required capstone course for senior students majoring in food science, is a major research project conducted in teams. We choose research topics based on their utilization of emerging technologies, timeliness to the industry, appeal to students, scope to fit time frame, and inclusion of multiple aspects of food science. Topics have included the development of a shelf-stable blue cheese dressing, survival and implications of *Lactobacillus acidophilus* in ice cream, assessing processing techniques for a fully cooked specialty meat product, extraction and purification of neurofactor II from milk, and improving whey protein isolate function and sensory characteristics in nutritional beverages. Data collected from the projects have resulted in one patent disclosure and provided the basis for the development of several research grant proposals.

In addition to the research project, students attend two lectures and one laboratory period per week. Lectures review basic food science knowledge including concepts from engineering, chemistry, nutrition, processing, microbiology, sensory, and marketing. Periodically, we present case studies of real-world industrial or regulatory problems to the students in small groups during the lecture period. The students must rapidly formulate solutions to these problems and defend their proposed solution. Faculty, teaching assistants, and other students critique their explanations. This activity assists with the development of both critical-thinking and problem-solving skills. The laboratory period is utilized for team meetings, specifically focused on group research project activities.

Because of the nature of both our curricular-level outcomes and the specific course objectives of FS 475 (see below), we have incorporated inquiry-guided learning very naturally. Students work in teams to collaboratively collect information and data, solve technical problems, critically analyze issues, and devise effective solutions. This process of active investigation provides an opportunity for students to master, learn, and apply basic principles of food science; increased classroom participation for less confident students; dramatically increased oral and written communication skills; and motivation for students to learn at a higher level. Students have transferred certain IGL practices to other departmental and nondepartmental courses by establishing informal workgroups outside the classroom, for example. In addition, the ability to work in teams, communication, critical-thinking and problem-solving abilities, information acquisition, and organizational skills have been enhanced in this type of learning environment.

The Role of Accrediting Bodies and Outcomes-based Assessment in the Development of FS 475

We developed the course initially in response to a requirement by the Institute of Food Technologists (IFT), the food science professional society, to provide a capstone experience to integrate all previous food science courses in the curriculum. Education standards developed by IFT assist colleges and universities in preparing undergraduate students for careers in the food industry and in evaluating the effectiveness of their programs in accomplishing this task. Recently the IFT revised the requirements for an IFT-approved curriculum from a list of courses offered in the degree program to outcomes-based competencies. Concurrently, NCSU implemented outcomes-based assessment for undergraduate program review.

Using the broad competencies (see Appendix 9.A) and success skills (see Appendix 9.B) developed by the IFT, the Department Undergraduate Committee defined the following curricular-level outcomes that fulfill the requirements of both the IFT and the university.

1. Engage in clear and careful scientific inquiry.
2. Apply critical thinking to solving problems and generating designs related to food science and technology.
3. Understand, manage, and communicate source materials related to food science and technology.
4. Work effectively in teams.
5. Give effective oral presentations.
6. Develop and utilize the personal and professional attributes that mark a successful food science graduate.

The outcomes of individual courses within the curriculum relate to these broader curricular-level outcomes, including FS 475 course objectives.

1. Work effectively in teams to solve technical problems.
2. Identify key factors influencing project success.
3. Integrate principles of food preservation, nutrition, sensory analysis, and statistics to project completion.
4. Evaluate processing options using recognized criteria and justify recommendations.
5. Critically analyze problems and devise effective solutions.
6. Develop a project management plan for the completion of each phase.
7. Describe end uses, competitive market analysis, and potential competitors for a product.
8. Analyze and explain safety concerns for a process using Hazard Analysis and Critical Control Point (HACCP) methodology.
9. Describe specific regulatory constraints and their impact on a process.
10. Communicate technical information through preparation of written and oral reports in a way that is appropriate to the audience.

Guidelines for the Research Project

The following project report guidelines set uniform expectations for team reports and successful project completion and ensure that teams will have a learning experience that satisfies key course objectives.

1. Project Mini-Proposal/Research Methodology (Report I) includes Executive Summary, problem description, literature review, overall project objective, project design and experimental plan, process flow diagram, benefits and deliverables to company, assumptions, raw materials cost, marketing information, organizational chart for experimentation, and team expectations.
2. Experimentation (Report II) includes Executive Summary, modified mini-proposal, unit processes and specific conditions, materials and conditions for experimentation, preliminary and anticipated results, corrections to preliminary experimental design, HACCP plan, and organizational chart for results and data interpretation.
3. Results and Data Interpretation, Environmental, Safety, Operability Review, and Preliminary Costs (Report III) includes Executive Summary, resubmission of mini-proposal and experimentation section, environmental concerns and recommendations for control, cleaning and sanitizing program, pertinent laws and regulations, labeling issues, equipment requirements, conclusion, results and benefits, and organizational chart for final report.
4. Final Report with Executive Summary and all previous project updates as a cumulative document.

In addition to the written reports, the student teams also do two oral presentations, one at the middle of the semester and one at the end. In both presentations we encourage students to use visual aids, preferably a PowerPoint presentation. Following both presentations, students respond to questions and defend their presentations as necessary. We also videotape and grade both presentations. However, in addition to the faculty, teaching assistants, and students in the class, the final presentation also includes an array of interested individuals, many from outside the course (e.g., graduate students, industry representatives). Consequently, there is a greater emphasis on presenting for a technically knowledgeable audience than in the midsemester presentation.

Each team also participates in the university's Undergraduate Research Symposium. They prepare a poster and present at the symposium, responding to questions as they would at a poster session at an academic conference.

The Formation and Responsibilities of Teams

Group research projects are the primary focus of this course, and teams provide the mechanism and environment for cooperative learning. We assign students to teams to maximize diversity (e.g., academic, gender, ethnicity) and to assure heterogeneity of academic ability. The determination of ability is based on previous grades in food science courses and cumulative academic averages. The team's primary responsibility is completing the research project during the semester according to the guidelines specified previously. An assigned technical advisor provides additional guidance to the groups. The advisor may be a faculty or staff member, a graduate student, or an industrial representative. We have designed the course to promote a great deal of interaction between team members, advisors/sponsors, and instructors.

Each team must do the following:

1. Develop a project plan for each phase of project completion. The plan should describe the deliverables of the phase, the projected time line for completion of each deliverable, and who within the team is responsible for the completion of each task.

2. Turn in project updates on time, recognizing that there may be a trade-off between on-time submission and level of detail accomplished. While a sloppy report turned in on time will get critiqued for its content, a meticulous report turned in a week late also misses the mark. Thus, project management skills are critical to producing the required deliverables in a timely fashion.

3. Ensure that names appearing on the report are those contributing to the work. If a team member fails to cooperate or contribute to the phase reports, his name should not be included on the report.

4. Review returned phases. Make sure everyone understands why points were lost and how to improve the report. Subsequent updates should reflect previous phase suggestions.

5. Complete and submit peer-rating sheets for all team members when required. We collect ratings periodically throughout the semester. The evaluations are confidential and used to adjust the final grade for each student.
6. Consult with the instructor to resolve interpersonal conflicts, but only when the team has been unable to resolve these conflicts itself.

Evaluating Team Performance

To assess the teams' performance, we utilize the rubrics in Tables 9.1, 9.2, and 9.3 for the oral and written reports as well as for team performance.

Table 9.1   Grading Rubric for Written Reports

	Possible Points	
Technical Content (60%)	60	
Topic mastery including technical correctness.		20
All requested deliverables included.		15
Appropriate level of detail and thoroughness of documentation.		15
Completeness of analysis and interpretation of data.		10
Organization (15%)	15	
Clearly identified purpose and approach.		5
Clearly organized content that supports the objective.		5
Transitions between topics.		5
Presentation (15%)	15	
Easy to read.		5
Grammatically and stylistically correct.		5
Uniform writing style.		5
Layout/Visuals (10%)	10	
Consistent presentation of graphics.		5
Uniform document design and layout.		5
Possible Total	100	

Source: Department of Chemical Engineering, NCSU, Raleigh, North Carolina.

Table 9.2 Grading Rubric for Oral Presentations

	Possible Points	
Technical Content (60%)	60	
Topic mastery including technical correctness.		20
All requested deliverables included.		15
Appropriate level of detail.		15
Completeness of analysis and interpretation of data.		10
Organization (15%)	15	
Introduction clearly identifies purpose, approach, and preview of main points.		3
Content is clearly organized and supports the objective.		2
Conclusion provides clear, memorable summary of design.		3
Introduction and conclusion are tailored appropriately to the audience.		3
Presenters respond to questions clearly, sufficiently, and succinctly.		2
Presentation includes logical transitions from one presenter to another.		2
Presentation (15%)	15	
Presenters are professional in their dress, language, and style.		3
Movement, eye contact, and gestures enhance presentation and do not distract from it.		3
Vocal quality is varied and illustrates interest in topic and design work.		3
Presenters speak with appropriate pace and volume.		3
Presenters make reference to other parts of the presentation and connect their part to the whole.		3

Layout/Visuals (10%)	10
Visuals are clear, consistent, readable, and understandable.	5
Visuals accurately follow the oral presentation and provide "visual map" of presentation.	5
Possible Total	100

Source: Department of Chemical Engineering, NCSU, Raleigh, North Carolina.

Table 9.3   Team Performance

I. Team Project Management

- Team set and followed collective goals and ground rules.
- Team set time lines for project completion and managed their work to meet critical path requirements.
- Entire team attended and participated in meetings with advisors, industry sponsors, and consultants.

II. Team Productivity

- Team delegated work among members responsibly and appropriately.
- Individual team members contributed an appropriate amount of effort and time.
- Team coordinated effective information exchange between all members.
- Team collaboratively addressed feedback from multiple sources and successfully incorporated it into successive deliverables.

III. Team Cohesiveness

- Team members made efforts to understand, include, and respect other team members, perspectives, and ideas.
- Team addressed personality problems and conflicts as a constructive whole.
- Team oral presentations and written reports reflected integration of different members' content into a coherent team voice.

Assessing the Effectiveness of FS 475

The primary impetus for assessment of FS 475 was the Hewlett Campus Challenge Project, Undergraduate Program Review (UAPR), and the discipline-accrediting agency (IFT) requirements. We have utilized course-based, program, and indirect assessment. Course-based assessment included homework, problems, examinations, and "break-out sessions" using small groups to identify and solve problems. Because FS 475 is the capstone course for the major, assessment of certain aspects of the course also functions as assessment for the program as a whole. In this regard, the various phases of the written report and the final presentation (see above) serve as both a course and program assessment tool. Senior surveys, student course evaluations, employer surveys for permanent employment and internships, and exit interviews conducted by the department head provide indirect assessment. Food industry representatives conducting student interviews for permanent and internship positions have cited the importance of success skills including teamwork and communication, computer, analytical, and critical-thinking skills as key outcomes and employment qualifications.

Student course evaluations ranged from 4.9 to 5.0 on a scale of 1.0 to 5.0. Peer evaluations provided honest appraisals of effort by all team members with additional support from individual student project logs. A survey submitted by the Food Science Undergraduate Assessment Committee indicated that this course was positively involved in all departmental curricular outcomes. Exit interviews with graduating students indicated that FS 475 provided fundamental knowledge and skills to be successful in graduate studies, internship experiences, and permanent employment. As a further indication of the success of this course, the department's program was one of three approved by IFT at the national level using outcomes-based assessment.

Based on results from the various assessments we have conducted over the past three years, we've made a number of adjustments to the course since its inception. A key change has been the introduction of multidisciplinary teams to force students to interact with students having different backgrounds from their own and to mimic the typical team atmosphere found throughout the food industry. For example, in 2000, the first year we offered the course, single discipline teams (i.e., food science) were utilized with one project. Various teams focused on different aspects of the project (microbiology, chemistry, engineering, regulations, and marketing). In the second year, we introduced one multidisciplinary team along with three single discipline teams, using four independent projects. In the third and fourth years (i.e., 2002, 2003) we scheduled a common laboratory period to accommodate multidisciplinary teams. We also assigned greater weight to the project in determining the final grade (75% versus 60%) in 2003. We also initiated videotaping of midsemester and final oral presentations in 2002 and continued this practice in 2003. The presentations have not been formally graded in the past, but will be graded in the future by those who attend.

Conclusion

We successfully utilized IGL in our capstone course, and it has proven to be beneficial for the professional development of our students. Benefits include an opportunity for students to master, learn, and apply basic principles of food science; increase oral and written communication skills; develop the ability to work in teams; improve critical-thinking and problem-solving ability; and enhance both information acquisition and organizational skills. We would encourage other faculty to consider this active learning process in the classroom.

Acknowledgements

The following individuals have made significant contributions to the development and implementation of IGL in food science: Steven Perretti, Lisa Bullard, Chris Anson, Paula Bernardinelli, Deanna Dannels, Amanda Granrud, Naomi Kleid, Addie Anderson, Michelle Leach, Matt Evans, Amanda Dees, Noel Pollen and Virginia Lee. This effort was partially funded by the Hewlett Campus Challenge Project.

IFT CORE COMPETENCIES/OUTCOMES

Content	By the completion of the food science program, the student should:
Integration and application of food science principles (food chemistry, microbiology and engineering/processing, etc.)	Be able to apply and incorporate the principles of food science in practical, real-world situations and problems.
Computer skills	Know how to use computers to solve food science problems.
Statistical skills	Be able to apply statistical principles to food science applications.
Quality assurance	Be able to apply the principles of food science to control and assure the quality of food products.
Analytical and affective methods of assessing sensory properties of food utilizing statistical methods	Understand the basic principles of sensory analysis.
Current issues in food science	Be aware of current topics of importance to the food industry.
Food laws and regulations	Understand government regulations required for the manufacture and sale of food products.

IFT SUCCESS SKILLS

Content	By the completion of the food science program, the student should be able to:
Communication skills (oral and written communication, listening, interviewing, etc.)	Demonstrate the use of oral and written communication skills. This includes such skills as writing technical reports, letters, and memos; communicating technical information to a nontechnical audience; and making formal and informal presentations.
Critical-thinking/problem-solving skills (creativity, common sense, resourcefulness, scientific reasoning, analytical thinking, etc.)	Define a problem, identify potential causes and possible solutions, and make thoughtful recommendations. Apply critical-thinking skills to new situations.
Professionalism skills (ethics, integrity, respect for diversity)	Commit to the highest standards of professional integrity and ethical values. Work and/or interact with individuals for diverse cultures.
Life-long learning skills	Explain the skill necessary to continually educate oneself.
Interaction skills (teamwork, mentoring, leadership, networking, interpersonal skills, etc.)	Work effectively with others. Provide leadership in a variety of situations. Deal with individual and/or group conflict.

(Continued)

Content	By the completion of the food science program, the student should be able to:
Information acquisition skills (written and electronic searches, databases, internet, etc.)	Independently research scientific and nonscientific information. Competently use library resources.
Organizational skills (time management, project management, etc.)	Manage time effectively. Facilitate group projects. Handle multiple tasks and pressures.

10

INQUIRY-GUIDED LEARNING THROUGH COLLABORATIVE RESEARCH IN A GRADUATE COURSE

By George R. Hess and C. Ashton Drew

Introduction

I (GRH) got involved in inquiry-guided learning for somewhat selfish reasons—it was a scheme to carry out collaborative research without funding and to gain simultaneous credit for teaching and research. At the time, I had no idea there was a name for this style of teaching, and I certainly didn't know it was something educators considered cutting-edge.

During my first semester as a newly minted landscape and conservation ecologist at NCSU, forest economist Bob Abt joined me to offer an elective graduate course called, "The Ecology and Economics of Clearcutting" (Hess et al., 1998). The course objective was to research the issues surrounding the forest clearcutting controversy and produce a written, publishable analysis and synthesis of the competing perspectives. The students would have a real-world collaborative research experience, learn along with us, and gain authorship on a peer-reviewed publication. In addition to the publication, Bob and I would obtain the information we needed to write proposals for further research without having to plow through all of the literature ourselves. Indeed, it seemed the epitome of a synergistic, win-win scenario (Covey, 1989). Things didn't work out quite as we expected, but more on that later.

Three attempts later, I have a much better idea of what I'm trying to do in these courses, how to market them, and how to make them work (see Table 10.1

Table 10.1   Six Key Ingredients for a Collaborative Research Course

The essence of the approach is on-the-job training: build a small team of advanced graduate students and treat them as peers in a collaborative research project. Think of the course and carry it out as you would a research project with fellow faculty, with your role being that of team leader. To make it work, mix six key ingredients and then get out of the way as the team takes ownership.

1. Technical and professional development objectives

2. Real-world, controversial topic

3. Real-world product

4. Strong collaborators

5. A common foundation

6. Open channels of communication

and Figure 10.1). In the range of inquiry-guided learning applications, from a single, brief activity during a course, my collaborative research courses are at the opposite extreme—completely built on inquiry. In what follows, I describe briefly the key ingredients for such a course and provide students' comments about the courses (indented, in italics).

> *I liked the approach of coming into the experience with a blank slate and creating something from the ground up. It is really helpful in stimulating original thinking on the subject. Many times, one is given so much background information on a subject or a textbook about the subject and this constrains the original thinking process. I liked the brainstorming aspects of the group and I thought it was good how the instructor acted more as a facilitator than as a dictator.*
> —"Measuring Suburban Sprawl"

> *I'm now looking forward to a lifetime of collaborative projects.*
> —"Surrogate Species Planning"

Ingredient 1: Technical and Professional Development Objectives

A collaborative research course has two types of objectives: technical and professional development (see Table 10.2). The technical objectives relate to the *subject* and intended *product* of the research, and are often what initially attract student interest. The professional development objectives relate to the *process* of carrying out collaborative research. Students must understand that they will be working on a research question for which the answer is unknown, and that they will become part of an interdependent, collaborative team seeking new knowledge. If they are looking for textbook answers, they should not sign up.

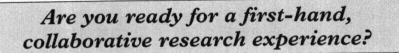

Are you ready for a first-hand, collaborative research experience?

Surrogate Species Planning (NR 595E)
George R. Hess, Forestry Department—3 credits S/U—Tu 4:10-7PM
george_hess@ncsu.edu   Phone: 515.7437

Surogate species approaches to planning wildlife conservation networks—including umbrella, flagship, keystone, and focal species—reduce date requirements by limiting conservation and landscape planning activities to a small number of species. The central concept is that habitat protected for surrogate species will support many other species.

Objectives

Carry out original research and co-author two peer-reviewed papers:

(1) *The Surrogate Species Conundrum—* a detailed literature review.

(2) *Pick a Card—* compare threee planning approaches in the Triangle: focal species, expert opinion, inventories.

Focal Species Richness

Forest Species
1
2
3
4

Agricultural Species
1
2

Major Lakes
Cities & Towns

10   0   10   20 Kilometers

Joining the Team

Enrollment is limited to 5 students, by application. For more information and to apply, please visit courses.ncsu.edu/nr595e/common
Apply by 2002 Dec. 6. Final decision on participants will be made by 2002 Dec 13.

Figure 10.1   Course Announcement for *Surrogate Species Planning.* Note how the announcement incorporates many of the key ingredients: technical objectives, a real-world topic, real-world products, and a method for selecting strong collaborators.

Table 10.2 Ingredient 1: Technical and Professional Development Objectives

---

A collaborative research course has technical (T) and professional development (P) objectives, both for the students and the instructor.

Objectives for students
In the natural resources, graduate work tends to be undertaken by individuals. Graduate students need more experience working collaboratively, which is how complex natural resources issues are approached in a professional environment.

- Learn the technical subject matter (T)
- Participate in collaborative research (P)
- Planning and organizing to perform collaborative research (P)
- Chance to work on a real-world problem (P, T)
- Exposure to diverse perspectives on a problem (P)
- Experience the publication peer review process (P)
- Develop publication or presentation other than thesis work (P, T)
- Improve writing skills (P)
- Improve presentation skills (P)
- Improve interpersonal communication skills (P)
- Develop leadership skills (P)

My objectives as an instructor
Use a teaching approach that allows one to simultaneously teach and perform useful research.

- Work with students on a research project in a team environment (P)
- Work with students from a variety of disciplines and backgrounds (P)
- Develop leadership skills (P)
- Broaden perspectives (P, T)
- Learn new technical material (T)
- Do research without writing grants (T)
- Publish new research (P, T)

The most attractive components of the course [Surrogate Species Planning] objectives were the opportunities to work on a collaborative project, to wrestle with a topic with direct applications in conservation ecology, and to produce a potentially significant and broad reaching publication in a short period of time. This course offered a chance to gain skills that will be important in my career, but are not provided through dissertation research or more traditional classes: skills in collaboration, cooperation, conflict resolution, compromise, and group responsibility. I knew next to nothing about the course topic when I began the course—it was the nature rather than the subject of the course that attracted me.
—*"Surrogate Species Planning"*

Ingredient 2: Real-world, Controversial Topic

The technical objective should relate to a real-world, controversial topic that will interest students and the instructor (see Table 10.3). By "real-world topic" I mean one that is making headlines, at least in the research community. The course topics I have chosen were all current, controversial topics that I wanted to learn more about and that interested students: "The Ecology and Economics of Clearcutting" (1996), "Measuring Suburban Sprawl" (2001), "Focal Species Conservation Planning" (2002), and "Surrogate Species Planning" (2003). Controversy is a key ingredient to attracting students and ensuring that there will be a diversity of stimulating perspectives. Controversy helps break the ice at the beginning of the course by making it easy to brainstorm various points of view, provides a starting point for quickly engaging the literature or

Table 10.3   Ingredients 2 and 3: Real-world Research Topic and Product

The research topic should be one:

- That the instructor wants to learn more about
- That will excite the interest of students
- Is complex and involves multiple disciplines
- Is current and in the headlines
- Is controversial
- For which data are readily available (unless collecting data is the objective)

The research product should be:

- Of value beyond the classroom
- Manageable within the time constraints of the course (although submitting and revising publications might take a bit longer)
- Flexible, to allow for modification based on discoveries during the course

splitting up the work, and ensures that the research product will be of interest to a broad audience.

"Surrogate Species Planning" was constructed around two technical objectives: (1) a detailed literature review of surrogate species planning approaches and (2) a comparison of surrogate to other conservation planning techniques. The effectiveness of surrogate species approaches is strongly debated in the conservation community, which ensured interest in the project among conservation ecologists and planners. The availability of comparative data from the region surrounding NCSU and the participation of people involved in local ongoing conservation efforts also gave this project a heightened sense of immediacy.

In "Measuring Suburban Sprawl," the technical objective was to develop quantitative measures of suburban sprawl. This objective required that we first define sprawl operationally, something that had not been done in a systematic manner despite the many opinions about sprawl and how it affects people and the environment. With this in mind, the team was able to enter the literature and controversy with a strong focus and sense of mission.

> *Because it was a real problem, it was much more complex and challenging than any simulated class exercise—but it also provided a much better motivation to put in the extra effort and it provided a much greater sense of accomplishment at the end.*
> —"Surrogate Species Planning"

> *It was great that the course dealt with a real-world problem and had the potential to offer new insights into that problem; this was much more fulfilling than the usual academic exercise.*
> —"Measuring Suburban Sprawl"

> *This was such a wonderful opportunity to work on a project that can cause some ripples not only in the research community and hopefully trickle down to practicing planners/managers, but also to work with real datasets for the surrounding area that can be directly applied to conservation efforts being presently made in the field.*
> —"Surrogate Species Planning"

> *Dealing with a real problem made the project have more purpose for me and also [led me] to be more concerned with doing a good job since others outside the class might actually be interested in the outcome.*
> —"Focal Species Conservation Planning"

Ingredient 3: Real-world Product

The technical and professional development objectives are inextricably linked with the product of the course. Collaborative research is about organizing the efforts of people with diverse skills to produce results. Technical objectives define the subject and nature of the product, while the process of creating the product determines professional development objectives.

A collaborative research course should have a well-defined, real-world product (Table 10.3). By "real-world product" I mean something that will be used or published well beyond the classroom. In the case of "Surrogate Species Planning," two peer-reviewed publications were defined as the products in the course announcement (Figure 10.1; Favreau et al., 2003; Hess et al., 2003). The "Focal Species Conservation" team produced a poster displayed at a professional meeting and data used by conservation planners (Hess et al., 2002). The "Measuring Suburban Sprawl" team produced a peer-edited publication in a planning journal (Hess et al., 2001). Other possible products might include a database needed by a nonprofit organization or government agency, a working simulation model for use in future analyses, or a detailed review of policy options for decision-makers. Depending on the product and the intended user of the product, the course might take on service-learning attributes (Eyler et al., 2001; NSLC, 2003).

The product can be established before the course begins, or by the students as the course progresses. For recruiting students, it seems best to have an enticing product defined at the outset. Flexibility is important, however, because findings along the way might require changes to the products.

> *The real-world product was important as an initial attraction to the course. Having that product well defined in the course description allowed me to evaluate the time commitment that would be required for this course and the skills that I would contribute and gain. However, the final product must also be flexible if we are truly equals. Our literature review turned into an essay publication as the nature of the controversy surrounding our topic became clear. Also, the well defined topic represented the instructor's vision for the class and as equal collaborators we had some different opinions. As a consequence, several new products were added (such as interviews of practitioners) and several were modified.*
>
> —"Surrogate Species Planning"

Ingredient 4: Strong Collaborators

Failure to select an appropriate mixture of students resulted in the failure of my first attempt at collaborative research in "The Ecology and Economics of Clearcutting." Bob Abt and I envisioned a group of experienced and highly motivated students, drawn from multiple disciplines, collaborating with us as peers. We needed students with solid technical skills and knowledge, whom we could organize into an effective, collaborative team. Unfortunately, we did little to ensure that the students who registered for the course met these criteria. Most of the students who registered did not have the technical background to contribute significantly to new research, nor were they ready for the kind of collaboration we envisioned. The course quickly acquired a traditional structure, with reading assignments and papers to be written for the instructors. Thus, although the students improved their technical knowledge, they did not advance research in the way Bob and I had envisioned, and we did not create the desired research products. The students also did not gain the collaborative research experience we intended.

Students must be prepared to work in an interdependent manner to hone the research question(s) and find solutions (see Table 10.4). I have found telephone or face-to-face conversation with interested students the most effective way to make this clear. Stating explicitly that I do not know the answer to the technical question being posed, but that we will work as a team to find it, often drives the point home.

I have raised the selection bar in each offering since the clearcutting course, and the results keep improving. For "Surrogate Species Planning" I required students to submit a written application describing their qualifications and interest. I also recruited specific students that I knew were capable and interested in the subject. One might ask faculty colleagues to recommend students and send course announcements (e.g., Figure 10.1) to appropriate departments. Selecting the right students is important enough to spend the time recruiting, and I am convinced that a combination of recruiting and written application is the right approach.

I have found that the best candidates are students who have completed at least a year of doctoral work. These students tend to have some well-developed technical skills and a good knowledge base on which to build. Doctoral students—at

Table 10.4   Ingredient 4: Strong Collaborators

When selecting students, think about building a strong research team. Some of these traits are hard to measure without prior experience with the student, which is why effective recruiting strategies are important.

- Well-developed technical skill in at least one subject area needed to address the research question(s)
- Self-starters—highly motivated
- Creativity
- Enthusiasm about the technical subject matter
- Willingness to speak out, even with minority opinions
- Willingness to hear out and consider diverse viewpoints
- Indications that the student will be a good collaborator, such as knowledge of how the student has done in past team assignments
- Indications of leadership ability

least from my experience—are also more likely than masters students to be considering careers in research and are thus more open to professional development activities aimed at improving their collaborative research skills. Students earlier in their careers tend to lack the knowledge base to make substantive and innovative contributions. Of course, there are always exceptions, which is one reason why a well-defined selection process is important.

> *The experience of planning and performing research with a fairly large group of people with only limited time was invaluable.*
>
> —"Measuring Suburban Sprawl"

> *Our group of students worked remarkably well together. Our skills complemented one another, so each naturally took leadership of a different area of the project. Also, from the first day when each arrived having completed all the reading and prepared for discussion, there was a high level of mutual trust. We each knew that the others were giving this project the highest priority and were giving an effort beyond expectations. Discussions were open and highly productive. Although our styles of working and organizing were frequently different, we were able to integrate the strengths from our diverse approaches to build a better product. At times, working together was frustrating as we sought to find a compromise among our diverse opinions and methods, but the resulting products were much stronger for having emerged out of this struggle.*
>
> —"Surrogate Species Planning"

Ingredient 5: A Common Foundation

A semester is not a very long time, so some structure is needed at the beginning of the course to quickly provide a common foundation and to ignite the collaborative process (see Table 10.5). There are a number of ways to accomplish this, including brainstorming sessions and assigned readings.

Table 10.5   Ingredient 5: A Common Foundation

A common foundation must be established early in the course. When establishing a common foundation, the team should:

- Develop a common knowledge base
- Define the framework of the controversy
- Become excited about the topic, product, and process
- Take ownership of the process and product
- Refine the vision of the product, considering the amount of work to be done and the time and resources available
- Reach consensus on an initial plan and time line for completing the work

In "Measuring Suburban Sprawl" I started with a brainstorming session in which each team member was given a pad of sticky notes and asked to write ideas about defining sprawl, one idea per sheet. We went around the room and posted the notes on the wall, attempting to group what seemed to be similar ideas. This proved a very effective way to get all the perspectives out into the open, and the students were surprised by the variety of ideas. This session invested the team in the process and provided the organizational spark for our efforts.

In both conservation planning courses, I assigned a sequence of readings with discussion questions to be completed for the first class meeting. These readings acquainted team members with the technical issues. Discussion revealed diverse perspectives and generated constructive controversy. These discussions led to a clearer definition of the research question, a plan of action crafted by the team, and consequent transfer of ownership to the team.

In "Surrogate Species Planning" I also did some "community building" before the course started, in addition to an initial reading assignment and brainstorming session. I established an electronic mail list server and asked the team members to introduce themselves by email with a brief description of their background and interests. There was some side chatter on the list server as well and team members began to get comfortable with one another. This relieved the anxiety some people feel when joining new research teams.

The readings provided a common foundation and introduction to the topic. Since most of us knew little about the topic (due to our interest in the process rather than the topic) this was important. The brainstorming sessions were very helpful to build community—all ideas were welcome and somehow fitted into the growing web of ideas on the whiteboard.

—"Surrogate Species Planning"

Ingredient 6: Open Channels of Communication

Team members must reach consensus on research direction, the nature of the final product, division of labor, schedules, milestones, and other issues that arise. Well-defined channels of communication among team members must be established, if the effort is to succeed. As team leader, the instructor must be prepared to facilitate communication and mediate conflict.

I make many methods of communication available to team members, and all are used heavily (see Table 10.6). Regular face-to-face meetings are perhaps most important. This is a lesson learned during the clearcutting course, which was initially to be conducted largely by Internet (Hess et al., 1998). After a few weeks, team members voiced a strong desire for personal contact to help them develop the sense of community critical to fruitful collaboration. Face-to-face interaction is also highly valued for brainstorming and bringing complex technical issues to closure. Since my experience in the clearcutting course, I have always scheduled weekly meetings.

Table 10.6 Ingredient 6: Open Channels of Communication

Communication among team members is critical. Multiple channels of communication should be available.

- Regular face-to-face meetings. Weekly is probably enough, with *adhoc* meetings as needed. Minutes should be taken and distributed to all team members—this can be a rotating assignment. At some points during the course, more or less frequent meetings might be appropriate.

- An email list or list server so that team members can send questions and ideas to all other team members.

- A contact page with email addresses and telephone numbers of all team members.

- A website with up-to-date work schedules, milestones, readings, drafts of documents in production, meeting agendas, meeting minutes, action items, and so forth.

Regular sit-down meetings are essential—I think that some people "collaborate" on projects with few meetings along the way. E-mail communication, electronic exchange of files, etc., is fine, but sitting down and hashing things out is just as important.

—"Surrogate Species Planning"

Having never participated in collaborative research before, it was helpful to have some direction in the process of planning the project.

—"Focal Species Conservation Planning"

Mix Well and Get Out of the Way!

As an instructor, one of the challenges to offering a course like this is that you never quite know what's going to happen. I start each course with a vision of how I expect things to go and resist the urge to push things in that direction. After all, a key goal is to get students to act as peers, which means you must treat them as peers and avoid the temptation to wield the power of an instructor by making unilateral decisions and manipulating the outcome. As long as the students have been selected carefully (Table 10.4), the role of facilitator is most appropriate for the instructor—someone who asks penetrating questions, removes obstacles, and creates opportunities. The team develops a very strong sense of ownership for the research and expects to have a say in its ultimate direction. The product is more than something to be submitted to the instructor at the end of the semester—it's *real* and the students care deeply about how it turns out.

Flexibility is essential. In "Surrogate Species Planning," my initial vision included publishing a literature review on the subject. As we became more familiar with the literature, the team decided that an essay describing the paralysis caused by the current debate, highlighting the lack of research data on the topic, and suggesting ways to move forward would be of more value to the conservation community than yet another literature review. So the team moved in that direction and began contacting other researchers by email and telephone to get their perspective on the issue. The excitement generated by this process fueled the team, especially as the outside researchers showed enthusiasm for the direction we were taking. It was a very empowering and enriching process for the entire team—far better than pulling rank and insisting on following my original vision. (Of course, pulling rank might be necessary from time to time with a team that is not as technically strong and eager to collaborate as this team was.)

> *Working on a controversial real-world problem gave our work an urgency and immediacy that is never encountered in regular classes. We were motivated to put in much more time and effort. When interacting with the broader conservation research and management community we were encouraged by the broad support and excitement prompted by our project.*
>
> *—"Surrogate Species Planning"*

> *There were three areas where your leadership and guidance were particularly important:*
>
> *(1) Frequently asking, "Is this feasible?" to help keep the project from growing beyond what we could accomplish.*
> *(2) Frequently asking, "Whom are we addressing?" to help ensure that our writing/product had a clear direction.*
> *(3) Facilitating communication with a broader audience by inviting people in, emailing introductions, and helping set up interviews that we as mere students might not have gained alone.*
>
> *Of course, as the work progressed, we each started doing these things on our own, which supplied good evidence that we were developing some important professional skills.*
>
> *—"Surrogate Species Planning"*

Is It Working?

In short, "Yes!" During the last session of "Surrogate Species Planning," the students and I participated in a focus group discussion about the course led by Dr. Douglas Wellman of NCSU's Faculty Center for Teaching and Learning. Students immediately focused on the professional development issues in answer to the first question of the discussion, "What was the most important thing you learned in this course?" They highlighted the value of working on a real problem, learning how to collaborate with peers, creating a tangible product, and beginning to network with other professionals beyond our university. One student commented that she joined the course for the professional development aspects and would not have participated had it been a lecture or readings course.

During the summer 2003, I surveyed students who participated in three of my collaborative research courses: "Measuring Suburban Sprawl," "Focal Species Conservation Planning," and "Surrogate Species Planning." The quantitative results and associated written comments (many of the quotes presented in this chapter) make it clear that students valued these courses primarily for the emphasis on collaborating to address a real-world problem. In written and verbal comments, students noted consequent increased levels of interest, motivation, ownership, and accomplishment. Written comments also revealed that students consciously focused on skills they were not able to hone in other courses—those dealing with collaboration and interdependence.

> *This course is one of the first times where I've sat down with a group of researchers and really examined the greater implications of the completed analysis/research. Since I am now working on a collaborative project with broad implications, I'm glad to have the preparation.*
> —"Surrogate Species Planning"

> *[Improving interpersonal communication skills] was one of the most positive aspects of the course. Most courses do not incorporate communication among students and that was what this course was about.*
> —"Focal Species Conservation Planning"

> *I especially valued the chance to collaborate with people from diverse backgrounds and disciplines. This type of class is how I expected all my doctoral level classes to be—but unfortunately it was the only one to offer this opportunity.*
> —"Surrogate Species Planning"

Future Plans

In "Surrogate Species Planning" I was more explicit about professional development than I had ever been before. I included several readings and assignments about collaboration and team development. This seems a good direction, as it spotlights concepts that might otherwise go unnoticed. In future offerings, I will tune the explicit focus on professional development to ensure that it is in concert with the technical objectives and products. I will experiment with different readings and perhaps assigning more team leadership roles to the students. Depending on the technical objectives, some attention to facilitation and conflict resolution might be appropriate. Yet, the focus on professional skills cannot become so intrusive as to dominate the hands-on collaborative research work, which is clearly what the students value most.

Acknowledgments

Thanks to Matha Groom and Doug Wellman for comments on an earlier version of this manuscript and to Doug Wellman for conducting the focus group for the "Surrogate Species Planning" course. Thanks also to the students who completed the collaborative research course survey—your quotes helped make this chapter come alive. GRH thanks Fred Cubbage and NCSU's Forestry Department for encouraging and supporting his interest in teaching.

References

Covey, S. R. (1989). *The seven habits of highly effective people.* New York: Simon and Schuster.

Eyler, J. S., Giles, Jr., D. E., Stenson, C. M., & Gray, C. J. (2001). *At a glance: What we know about the effects of service-learning on college students, faculty, institutions and communities, 1993–2000,* (3rd ed.)., Nashville, TN: Vanderbilt University. www.compact.org/resource/aag.pdf, visited 2003 July 31.

Favreau, J. M., Drew, C. A., Hess, G. R., Rubino, M. J., Koch, F. H., & Eschelbach, K. A. (2003). Short-cut or dead-end? A road map to resolving the surrogate species debate. *Conservation Biology,* in review.

Hess, G. R., Abt, R., & Serow, R. (1998). Reshaping expectations for web-based collaborative learning. *Natural Resources and Environmental Issues, 7,* 104–109.

Hess, G. R., Daley, S. S., Dennison, B. K., Lubkin, S. R., McGuinn, R. P., Morin, V. Z., Potter, K. M., Savage, R. E., Shelton, W. G., Snow, W. M., & Wrege, B. M. (2001). Just what is sprawl, anyway? *Carolina Planning, 26*(2), 11–26.

Hess, G. R., Bode, R. C., King, T. J., Rubino, M. J., Bailey, A., Norwalk, J., Potter, K., Scott, J., Shimps, B., Smith, M., & Summitt, K. (2002). Regional planning for wildlife using a focal species approach. Poster presented at the International Association of Landscape Ecology Conference, Lincoln, Nebraska.

Hess, G. R., Rubino, M. J., Koch, F. H., Eschelbach, K. A., Drew, C. A., & Favreau, J. M. (2003). Inventories, surrogate species, and simple plans: Choosing an approach to conservation planning. *Conservation Biology,* in review.

NSLC (2003). National Service-Learning Clearinghouse. www.servicelearning.org/, visited 2003 July 31.

II

INQUIRY-GUIDED LEARNING AND THE UNDERGRADUATE MAJOR IN THE DEPARTMENT OF MICROBIOLOGY

By Michael Hyman and Gerry Luginbuhl

Inquiry-guided learning is a promising approach to learning for a research-based scientific discipline like microbiology and directly addresses many of the limitations and shortcomings we had identified in our courses during a comprehensive appraisal of our undergraduate curriculum. The Hewlett Campus Challenge Project (see Chapter 2) provided a framework for working on course improvement and access to campus experts who could help us understand student learning styles, development of critical-thinking skills over time, assessment, and other issues. We placed particular emphasis on a sequence of courses that could serve as a solid base from which further IGL-based modifications could be made throughout the curriculum.

Background

The Department of Microbiology offered only graduate degrees for many years, and served undergraduates through service courses and through a microbiology concentration within the biology major. Departmental faculty's desire for more control over the curriculum led to the development of the undergraduate major 11 years ago. Since then we have expanded our undergraduate course offerings significantly, and enrollment has grown as well:

Table 11.1 Department of Microbiology Undergraduate Curriculum*

Yr1	Yr2	Yr3	Yr4	
			MB 414	E L E C T I V E S
	MB 351 +Lab MB 352	MB 411 +Lab 412	MB 409 +Lab	
MB103	Honors Lecture Honors/Majors Lab		Senior Seminar MB 490	

*Bold boxes indicate a significant inquiry-guided learning component.

from 58 majors in 1992 to over 200 today. In the process, we have devoted much time and thought to undergraduate teaching.

In 2001, in response to a university-wide mandate, the department developed curricular outcomes for our undergraduate major with the assistance of a skilled facilitator (see Appendix 11.A). The process of developing these learning outcomes spurred the faculty to think more carefully about the kinds of learning experiences we provide for the students. Our teaching approach at the time was almost entirely lecture based. We aimed to cover as much material as possible without providing opportunities for students to use the information in meaningful ways. The accompanying laboratory sections were also designed simply to expose students to the mechanics of various techniques. Although many of the faculty recognized the need to change the way our courses were taught to allow students to gain these competencies, we were generally unaware of the best approaches to take to achieve these changes.

It was at this point that we applied to participate in the Hewlett Campus Challenge Project. We decided to concentrate our efforts on four required courses that occurred in a clearly defined sequence: our First Year Seminar course, "Introductory Topics in Microbiology" (MB 103); "General Microbiology" (MB 351), a large enrollment course with accompanying lab; "Medical Microbiology" (MB 411); and our capstone course, "Microbiology Senior Seminar" (MB 490). See Table 11.1.

Integration of Inquiry-guided Learning into the Course Sequence

Table 11.2 summarizes the changes we made in the core course sequence.

Table 11.2 Attributes of Microbiology Required Courses Before and After IGL

Course	Pre-IGL	Post-IGL
MB 103 First Year Introductory Course 1 credit, 1 hour/week	College-wide 150/section Presentations by different disciplines, presentations and assignments on computer and library use	Department's own course 25/section Mostly guided discussion Assigned reading/ writing assignments to assess and develop critical thinking
MB 351 General Microbiology Over 250/semester	Large lecture—all lecture Graded work: multiple-choice exams	Large lecture—mostly lecture, minute papers, in-class challenge questions Graded work: 4 homework assignments (total equal to one exam), 4 exams: combination multiple choice and essay
MB 411 Medical Microbiology 80/year in 1 semester	Mostly lecture, occasional case studies Graded work: exams combination of multiple choice, short answer, and essay	2/3: mostly lectures, in-class challenge questions and discussions 1/3 (one day/week) group work on discussion questions: total group work grade equal to one exam
MB 352 General Microbiology Lab 25 students/section	Techniques described and then practiced by students	Same for nonmajors New labs for majors and honors students: Learning basic techniques and scientific reasoning through 2 experimentation modules

(Continued)

Table 11.2 Continued

Course	Pre-IGL	Post-IGL
MB 412 Medical Microbiology Lab 25 students/section	Techniques described and then practiced by students	New laboratory modules: virology and bacteriology experiments designed by students within limited parameters
MB 490 Senior Seminar	25/section Discussion and student presentations Several writing assignments	Not changed

"Introductory Topics in Microbiology" (MB 103)

We teach this course, required of all freshmen and transfer students, in sections of approximately 20 students in the fall semester. The instructor provides appropriate readings on topics of interest in microbiology. Students list the main points of the readings, generate questions stimulated by the readings, and identify underlying hypotheses and assumptions in the articles. Students bring their individual work to class, discuss the material in small groups, and then submit both their individual work and their group answers to the assignment. The objective of these assignments is to stimulate the students' critical-thinking skills. We also challenge students to take responsibility for their learning through several assignments, including developing a plan of study for their four years at NCSU. We encourage them to include volunteer work, internships, research experiences, and other learning opportunities in their plan of study. The students also take a learning style inventory and discuss learning styles and strategies to enhance their awareness of the learning process.

"General Microbiology" (MB 351) Lecture

"General Microbiology" is a required course in many of the biological and agricultural curricula on our campus. It is a large class (approximately 270 students per semester), and Microbiology majors make up about 10% of the enrollment. The major changes we have instituted in this class are the addition of four major homework assignments during the semester, the introduction of essay questions as part of the comprehensive written final exam, and the opportunity for honors students to make in-class presentations. The aim of the homework assignments is for students to apply their knowledge through analysis and interpretation of data. These assignments require a significant time commitment from students, typically a five- to six-page typed response per assignment. Grading these assignments also requires a large time commitment from faculty responsible for teaching the course. We originally offered these assignments on a voluntary basis and provided an opportunity for students to drop their lowest conventional exam score. About 90% of the students participated under these conditions. More recently, we have made these assignments a required element of the course. Many students have commented that the homework assignments help them learn the material and that the assignments are very worthwhile. We have begun asking more application questions on the exams and finding that the students are successful with these questions. We have felt free to require a deeper level of reasoning on the exams because the students have had an opportunity to practice using their knowledge on the homework assignments.

We introduced other modifications as well. We originally created an essay-based written comprehensive final exam to provide a much needed opportunity for students to practice their writing skills. Grading of this exam was again something that required a large time commitment from the teaching faculty. Recent modifications to relieve or redistribute this commitment include adding essay components in other midterm exams and correspondingly decreasing the number of essays required in the final exam. The other modification we introduced into the class, presentations by honors students, has had a more checkered history. Before we formally introduced an Honors section in MB 351, there were a relatively small number of students who enrolled in a Student Initiated Honors version of the class. These students were required to write a detailed research report and make an in-class presentation on the same subject. Opening an Honors section in the class led to a dramatic increase in the number of honors students, and it became impossible to accommodate all of these students' presentations in class. The latest incarnation of this requirement is the preparation of case study–based learning modules. These case studies are designed to illustrate broader issues that are only briefly touched upon in class. The case studies typically direct students to web-based resources and contain a series of questions that can be answered for credit by all students enrolled in the class.

"General Microbiology Laboratory" (MB 352)

Probably the most visible IGL-based changes we have made in our curriculum have been in the Laboratory course (MB 352) that accompanies "General Microbiology" (MB 351). This course was originally taught as a series of largely stand-alone modules that introduced students to individual basic techniques widely used in microbiology laboratories. Although this course remains extremely popular with nonmajors, it failed to serve our own undergraduate needs, not only from the IGL perspective but also from a basic training perspective. We tackled this problem by introducing an Honors section in which students participate in two modules that are designed as experiments. The first of these experiments examines one of the core concepts of microbiology, the issue of pure cultures and the notion of cause and effect in disease (Koch's postulates). The second experiment involves the isolation and characterization of antibiotic-producing strains from soil samples. After completing these two experiments the students write a comprehensive report describing their hypotheses, their work, and their conclusions. They also make a presentation to their peers, either orally or as a poster. This course now emphasizes the testing of hypotheses and the collection and interpretation of scientific data as the key activities, and the techniques are merely the methods needed to support these activities. Again, the modifications to this class are more demanding on both faculty and TAs in terms of their time commitment. However, the benefits of this revised approach include the opportunity for students to practice techniques on numerous occasions, rather than just once, and an understanding that a particular technique is relevant in a particular situation, but there are limitations to each technique that must be considered during the interpretation of results.

The impact of these modifications has been very encouraging. Faculty teaching higher level courses have noted a general improvement in the core skill sets of students passing through this course and have modified their own courses accordingly. The challenge we now face is how to expand this experimental approach and develop new materials for this class. This is another area where honors students have been successfully engaged, and their contribution has been allowed to flow back to the class as a whole. Currently we offer this laboratory as Honors and majors sections of the "General Microbiology Laboratory" course. Two sections, each with approximately 10 majors and 10 honors students, enroll in this course each semester.

"Medical Microbiology" (MB 411) and Laboratory (MB 412)

"Medical Microbiology" (MB 411) had been taught as a lecture course with occasional case studies. Although the instructor was already moving slowly toward incorporating more case studies into the course, the Hewlett Project provided an opportunity to rethink the student experience with this course. As a result, the instructor now lectures two out of three meetings per week and utilizes group discussion work one class meeting per week. The students interpret research papers or work through extensive case studies. Some examples of group discussion starters are: interpret a table from an article in *The Lancet* (requiring application of statistics and virology knowledge); describe key findings of an article in *Science* and discuss the implications for polio eradication; and propose a vaccine formulation for gonorrhea and use knowledge of immunology and pathogenic microbiology to explain why this formulation would work. The groups write their reports and the sum of their report grades count the same as one exam.

The laboratory course, MB 412, has also been modified. From teaching a series of techniques for techniques' sake, students now work on three major experiments through the semester: one experiment on virology, one on pathogenic bacteriology, and one on immunology. The pathogenic bacteriology experiment, for example, begins with the students reading a recent article from the *Journal of Clinical Microbiology*. The students discuss the article in the laboratory before developing experiments that would follow up on the research findings. The students work in groups of four to develop and do such experiments. Poster presentations, oral presentations, and research papers are now a significant part of the graded work for the laboratory.

"Microbiology Senior Seminar" (MB 490)

The Senior Seminar is a one-credit capstone course that has always involved IGL. Class size varies from 10 to 25 students per semester and is restricted to students majoring or minoring in Microbiology. The class chooses an umbrella topic at the beginning of the semester. Recent topics have included extreme microbes, prions, and HIV. Students choose individual topics, research the latest findings or issues, and complete two oral and three written assignments. The first oral report is on general information about their topic and the second is a report on one research paper they have read on their topic. The writing assignments are a one-page article for the general public, an annotated bibliography, and a research paper critique.

Evaluating and Extending IGL Throughout the Microbiology Curriculum

Roughly midway through the funding period for the Hewlett program, the department's team planned a retreat for the rest of the undergraduate teaching faculty and for any other departmental faculty who wished to attend. The purpose of the retreat was to discuss the results we were seeing in our courses and explore how this process supported the department's undergraduate curriculum learning outcomes and program assessment.

The most useful exercise at the retreat was a mapping of curricular outcomes to courses. To do this, we discussed each of the undergraduate courses in our curriculum, the types of assignments given to the students, the types of exams, and the overall mixture of lecture, class discussion, and group work. The faculty agreed that the learning experiences provided by the IGL courses were what we wanted for our students, and all of the faculty teaching undergraduate courses agreed to incorporate IGL into their courses. We then attempted to determine how well the course was preparing the students to achieve our intended learning outcomes. This discussion highlighted the sense of ownership the whole faculty felt toward the curriculum, and the importance of seeing the courses as part of a larger learning experience rather than stand-alone faculty domains. The IGL courses had a rich array of student learning measurements. We discussed the need to develop portfolios to collect representative samples of student work from each course.

A second important question addressed at our retreat was how well our current curriculum addressed the needs of our student population in terms of academic rigor and student performance. By examining the GPA distribution of our current undergraduates as well as other factors, we decided that our more gifted and motivated students needed more intensive courses and other enrichment opportunities. To respond to this need we expanded the number of seats available in the Honors section of "General Microbiology" (MB 351H) and the "Honors General Microbiology Laboratories" (MB 352H), as discussed above. As an extension of this approach we are now also developing a "research-intensive" Honors curriculum in Microbiology. This curriculum requires several more challenging general education courses as well as a four-semester-long research program in a faculty member's laboratory in the Microbiology Department. This program was offered for the first time in Fall 2003.

As we have become more comfortable with the different demands required in IGL-based courses, we have begun to investigate new directions in which we can take them. One realization is that IGL-based approaches often place greater demands on resources than do conventional lecture-based approaches. One temporary solution to the increased time commitment associated with some of our IGL-based modifications has been to hire an additional instructor using faculty funds previously allocated to a recently retired full faculty member. Our original justification for this change is that position would enable us to offer high-quality Honors-level courses to both our own majors and nonmajors. The important contribution made by the instructor in this position has allowed us to significantly expand the honors student enrollment in both MB 351 and MB 352. This expansion has also led us to realize that we could also make the IGL-based MB 352 Laboratory course a requirement rather than an option for our majors. This policy came into effect in Fall 2004.

As indicated, honors students have played an important role piloting the IGL-based modifications we have instituted in our curriculum. In general we believe this is a sound approach. These students are typically some of the brightest students in our classes and as such are more prepared to participate in novel or alternative approaches and tend to be more forgiving when unexpected deviations occur. We further believe we have demonstrated that investment in the needs of our best students can also raise the quality of the education provided to all of our students and that this is a compelling argument for continued institutional support for the instructor's position that has made this possible. We are fortunate to have college-level administrators who can see this as money well spent, even in the hard economic times currently facing many academic institutions.

As a final direction we have also taken steps to introduce IGL-based principles into graduate-level courses. Two of our faculty, including our Hewlett team leader, Dr. Hyman, received funding from the Sloan Foundation to establish a professional master's degree program in Microbial Biotechnology. This program is designed to prepare master's level students for positions in the local biotechnology industry centered in the Research Triangle Park. This multidisciplinary degree program involves required courses in Microbiology, Biotechnology, and Business Administration. Perhaps most significant from an IGL perspective, this 72-credit-hour program is centered around a 12-credit-hour (3 credits/semester) case studies course. In this course students will be required to solve real-life problems posed to them by industry executives and experts. This will involve required teamwork, extensive self-initiated research, extensive writing, and effective live presentation of results and their interpretation.

Reasons for Successful Integration of Inquiry-guided Learning and Summary

Although the department has always had a strong research focus, historically it has also valued undergraduate teaching. Further we have also received strong support from our own college, the College of Agriculture and Life Sciences. The college has been very supportive of infrastructure modifications to teaching laboratories: for example, the provision of projection equipment and the funding of an additional instructor position. Hired in 1974 with undergraduate instruction as her focus, Dr. Luginbuhl has provided ongoing support for the undergraduate curriculum. The involvement of senior faculty who are committed to undergraduate teaching has conveyed to the junior faculty that their efforts toward improving undergraduate teaching will not go unnoticed or unappreciated by the department. This is a reassuring message that there is a valued role for good undergraduate instruction in research-intensive institutions like NCSU. Senior faculty members also provide a wealth of experience and institutional wisdom that can be used to direct team or individual efforts into productive channels. The challenge for the senior faculty within our group has been to balance that wisdom with the need to allow room for experimentation.

We have been fortunate to have virtually all of the undergraduate teaching faculty involved in the Hewlett Project. Moreover, we are also involved in a discipline that does not provide much latitude for disagreement over core subject matter and values. The small size of our group has certainly facilitated easy communication and coordination of effort, allowing us to quickly establish a united front when presented with questions and concerns addressing undergraduate education. We have therefore been able to spend our time trying to arrive at solutions to problems rather than spending valuable time getting no further than defining the problem.

Another feature that has helped stimulate interaction is that several of the junior faculty are teaching the same course and are therefore facing essentially the same problems. The rotation system for a course like MB 351 is enabling us to become a learning organization where the successes and failures of different approaches are rapidly disseminated among the group, and we are therefore able to avoid having to relearn the lessons from history. The collegiality of this group also rests on the fact that many of the participants are junior faculty who have had little or no prior teaching experience. These faculty members tend to have a strong motivation to do well in these early pretenure teaching assignments. Yet the entire process is still new enough that they retain flexibility and enthusiasm and are keen to swap ideas, notes, and approaches. It is also an encouraging sign that the benefits of IGL do not appear to be simply skin deep or short lived. As junior faculty have gone on to develop other new courses, it is apparent that cooperative and interactive habits initially established during the Hewlett Project are reappearing and flourishing. This suggests to us that good habits that are established early may serve faculty well throughout their subsequent teaching careers.

The department has been sufficiently open to new ideas and influences that it has heard, and has acted upon the fresh perspectives of new faculty. Rather than regarding new faculty as inexperienced and not ready to influence the curricular decisions in the department, department leadership and senior faculty have welcomed the insights of new faculty and have been willing to make significant changes based on their insights and recommendations.

Finally, as microbiologists, we are fortunate to have a very well-organized and progressive national association, The American Society for Microbiology. The society strongly supports undergraduate teaching and runs a specific annual conference on this subject each year just prior to the much larger annual general meeting. The society has also provided clearly defined expectations for the well-rounded and comprehensive training of microbiologists. We continue to ensure that our modified laboratory courses adhere closely to these recommendations.

The conditions described herein represent a state of readiness that was highly conducive to a change intervention like the Hewlett Campus Challenge Project. Before the Hewlett Project, the development of curricular-level student learning outcomes provided a vision of undergraduate learning for the department that focused subsequent change efforts including the introduction and dissemination of inquiry-guided learning. The realization of student learning outcomes through inquiry-guided learning also stimulated a broader strategic decision-making process within the department. We began to assess more deliberately our strengths, values, and opportunities and how we might capitalize on these in the area of teaching and learning. As a result over the past few years we have continued to develop the department's capacity to further learning at all levels in the curriculum—undergraduate, graduate, and even postdoctoral work—and aspire to make this capacity a hallmark of the Department of Microbiology at NCSU, in addition to our already established research capability. Other modifications consistent with this emphasis include hiring junior faculty who are sympathetic with and interested in our teaching mission, allocation of resources in support of teaching, and recognition of the value of alternate paths of career development in promotion and tenure decisions. In addition, the retreat, with its focus on undergraduate teaching, provided another venue for discussion and decision making that had not existed previously. While establishing a research agenda remains important, increasingly the department recognizes teaching as an area of excellence warranting recognition in the tenure process.

DEPARTMENT
OF MICROBIOLOGY
LEARNING OUTCOMES

1. Demonstrate a sound working knowledge of the field of Microbiology.
   (a) to show that they have acquired a foundational knowledge of microbiology that allows them to continue to grow in the field.
   (b) to show that they can apply their foundational knowledge in microbiology when challenged with new situations by asking intelligent questions that lead to an understanding of the new situations.
   (c) to show that they can synthesize from the answers to those questions new knowledge about microbiology.
2. Demonstrate a command of the skills necessary to perform effectively and safely in a microbiology laboratory.
   (a) to show that they have mastered the techniques essential to sound laboratory practice.
   (b) to show that they can ask pertinent questions about microbiology, formulate hypotheses based on those questions, and design experiments to test those hypotheses.
   (c) to show that they can apply deliberate and thorough observational skills to conduct experiments and collect data.
   (d) to show that they can organize and summarize data and present them in a way that is accurate and comprehensible in both verbal and graphical modes.
   (e) to show that they can interpret data and draw conclusions that allow the students to support or refute hypotheses and make a case for alternative hypotheses.
3. Understand, manage, and apply information about microbiology from both scholarly and popular sources and to communicate their understanding clearly and coherently for different audiences.
   (a) to show that they can effectively explain information related to microbiology in the popular press to nonscientific audiences.
   (b) to show that they can summarize the important information from scientific articles.

(c) to show that they can make a critical judgment of scientific material, using as support their analysis of its research questions and hypotheses, the appropriateness and precision of its research methods, the effectiveness of its presentation of results, and the interpretation and conclusions it draws from the results insofar as they answer the research questions.

(d) to show that they can effectively organize and make sense of scientific information from multiple sources, raise pertinent questions about that information, and draw appropriate and useful conclusions from it.

(e) to show that they can find suitable scientific sources for answering questions about microbiology, evaluate the pertinence, value, and credibility of those sources, and make a convincing case for their answers using evidence from the sources.

12

THE CHALLENGE OF IMPLEMENTING AN INQUIRY-GUIDED APPROACH IN A HIGHLY TECHNICAL CURRICULUM

By Adrianna G. Kirkman, Medwick V. Byrd,
Hasan Jameel, and John A. Heitmann

The Paper Science and Engineering Program is a multidisciplinary program that applies the principles of chemistry, physics, engineering, and material science to the paper industry. Graduates of the program must be able to integrate and apply the theory of these different disciplines to the complex systems that produce pulp, paper, and paper products. Many of the graduates will be process engineers and technical service or consulting engineers responsible for problem solving and management at mill sites. Others will be engaged in the research and development of innovative paper-based products that will move the industry forward into new markets.

The Paper Science and Engineering Program is one of only eight such programs in the United States. As such, it is less well known in the general population than other engineering disciplines, and it relies heavily on a vigorous recruiting and scholarship program to make prospective students aware of the major and its career opportunities. As a relatively small program, most of the courses have about 25 to 40 students.

A summary of the Paper Science Program's curricular outcomes, as developed by the faculty, students, and industry constituents, is shown in Table 12.1. Many of the characteristics and skills desired in our graduates follow naturally from the more general outcomes of inquiry-guided learning: foster critical thinking, promote inquiry, and develop students' taking responsibility for their learning.

Table 12.1 Abbreviated Paper Science and Engineering Curricular Outcomes

Graduates of this program should be able to:

1. Apply critical-thinking skills and knowledge to solving problems related to the paper science and engineering field	Define and analyze a problem, identify pertinent information and apply effective search procedures, apply fundamental understanding of basic sciences, synthesize and critically evaluate information to generate a solution, communicate their solution appropriate to the audience
2. Apply a broad perspective to the paper industry and its relationship to society and to the environment	Accurately and objectively describe role of paper industry in society, apply a strong sense of ethics to issues associated with the industry
3. Develop their skills for being successful professionals	Communicate effectively as professionals, capably use computer technology; articulate their worth as professionals, work effectively in teams, seek out educational opportunities for professional and personal growth

Because of the complexity of the processes involved in the paper industry and the diverse career paths open to paper science graduates, the skill set defined by these outcomes is critical to producing students who will be accomplished in problem solving and who will be able to continue to learn and adapt as their careers evolve.

We believe that implementing inquiry-guided learning early in the curriculum and reinforcing it regularly throughout the academic program by using in-class exercises and outside assignments that require inquiry and critical thinking is the best approach. However, using IGL techniques in an engineering/technology-based curriculum is often difficult to envision for many people, faculty and students alike. There is a lot of terminology, process/equipment descriptions, and problem-solving methodologies to cover in this multidisciplinary field. Traditionally it has been thought that this kind of content must be covered, usually in lecture format, before a student can begin to practice critical thinking and independent inquiry. On the other hand, some of the freshest ideas can come from people who do not already have the mindset of how the process currently works. Through a shift in our approach to teaching and learning, we need to require students to take responsibility for learning terminology and process descriptions through independent inquiry, while we use class time and project assignments to foster critical thinking and team-building skills that are so important in today's workplace.

Implementing IGL in the Curriculum

The schematics shown in Figures 12.1 and 12.2 represent the flow of students through the Paper Science Program, the desired changes that should occur during their academic career, and the course array for the curriculum, arranged by subject area.

We chose three courses required in the major, highlighted in Figure 12.2, for the initial implementation of IGL methodologies during the Hewlett Campus Challenge Project (see Chapter 2).

- WPS 100 "Introduction to Pulping and Papermaking"—1 credit hour, orientation course for first-semester freshmen
- WPS 201 "Pulp and Paper Technology"—3 credit hours, gateway survey course for second-semester freshmen
- WPS 415 "Senior Research Problems"—3 credit hours, capstone course in experimental research design and analysis

WPS 100 and 201 were selected in part because they are critical to engagement and retention of the freshmen in the program. Previous versions of these courses had been presented primarily in lecture format. WPS 100 utilized several faculty members to introduce various topic areas that are discussed in later courses, resulting in a "talking heads" effect. Feedback from the students, both by direct comments and by attrition numbers, indicated that the material had no life when presented in this passive format. WPS 201 had previously been two three-credit survey courses; in order to compress the material to one course, clearly we had to change the mode of content delivery. WPS 415 is a new senior capstone course in the curriculum, and was selected because its essence is inquiry based. Student teams, working with a faculty advisor, design and carry out an experimental project similar to one that they might be assigned in their first job following graduation. This course also provides an opportunity for assessing the extent of development of the key IGL characteristics across the major.

CURRICULUM

FRESHMEN

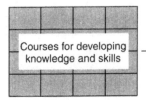

GRADUATES

• Basic capabilities
• Basic concepts
• No applications
• Unfamiliar with engineering
• Unsure of self and future role
• "Thinks like a student"
• No knowledge of raw material science, process technology, products

• Advanced capabilities
• Advanced concepts
• Knows applications
• Familiar with engineering
• Secure, self-confident
• "Thinks like a professional"
• Knows raw material science, process technology, products

Figure 12.1 Flow of Students Through the Program with Desired Changes.

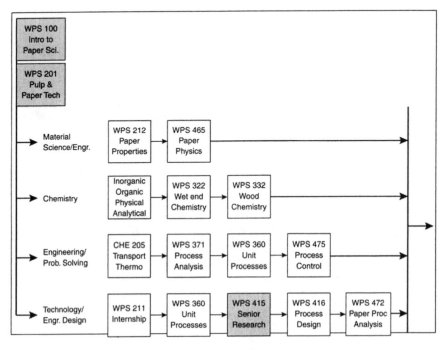

Figure 12.2 Course Array in Paper Science and Engineering Curriculum.

IGL in WPS 100 "Introduction to Pulping and Papermaking"

WPS 100 is a critical component in the PSE curriculum. Students get their first view of the industry and of the major in this course. If we don't capture their interest, the work that went into recruiting them can be wasted if they transfer out. A brief summary of the course prior to implementing IGL is shown in Table 12.2a. Notice that the course structure is mainly based on passive teaching/learning strategies. The reliance on lectures given by several different faculty members did not seem to be intellectually engaging.

Following the implementation of IGL strategies, the course includes exercises that challenge the students to find out about the industry and processes on their own, and to use that information to propose new ways of doing things within the industry. The course structure is shown in Table 12.2b.

Changes and Techniques Used

- The number of lectures has been reduced and some of those are organized as guided discussions.
- One of the professional development sessions involves a role play by a faculty member with an industry personnel agent; the students analyze several different interviews as a class exercise. This is followed by a practice interview session with pairs of students interviewing each other.

Table 12.2a WPS 100 Before IGL

Learning objectives Student should be able to:	• Describe the pulp and paper industry and careers • Identify key academic resources on campus • Write an effective resumé • Interview properly • Describe an example of a mill/converting/ supplier operation • Know several classmates by first name
Course structure	• 9 lectures on process areas, professional development, academics; handouts given • 3 mill tours • 2 laboratory exercises
Assignments/testing	• Resumé • Quizzes on trips and labs • 1 leadership development module • Oral final exam

Table 12.2b WPS 100 After IGL

Course outcomes Student should be able to:	• Introduction to the paper industry • Develop professional skills • Develop skills for good academic planning • Create excitement and enthusiasm for the engineering profession • Create excitement about challenges and opportunities within the paper industry • Create a positive work ethic and a desire to learn new things
Course structure	• 6 sessions on process areas and academics; handouts given • 3 sessions on professional development • 6 mill tours: forest, paper plants, converters, suppliers
Assignments/testing	• Resumé • 2 projects • Quizzes on trips • Oral final exam—performed like a job interview

- The projects required are done in teams with a goal of developing planning and execution skills in teams. The first project leads students into the literature of the field through a simple question to be researched.
- The second project is designed to encourage nontraditional thinking through an open-ended assignment and to continue practice of team skills.

  Project statement: *Teams of 3 students are to design a new process (from trees to end product) that satisfies customers' needs, is environmentally clean, increases the industry's profitability, and satisfies employees' needs for good wages, safe working environment, and job security.*

  Although the project is done outside of class and requires students to investigate paper products and markets, the teams are given a time limit since the project is not intended to be a research project. The results are submitted via the Internet.

- Finally we formalized a rubric for different faculty examiners to use to assess the oral final exam/interview.

Assessments and Challenges

Because we had no formal rubrics in the first year of this revised course, assessments of student performance and critical thinking were mainly anecdotal (e.g., student attitude, engagement in the program/industry, retention in the program). These methods indicate that the changes have improved overall student attitude, engagement, and willingness to think critically. However, we need to develop more formal assessment tools. In the next version of the course, rubrics will be developed to assess the students' critical thinking and group interaction skills in the second project and in the final oral exam.

IGL in WPS 201 "Pulp and Paper Technology"

WPS 201 is the first and only technology "survey" course, in which we introduce the students to the basic terminology, technology, and concepts for the complex process that converts wood into a finished paper product. In initially offering the course in the standard lecture mode but with compression of the material, we found that the students did not respond well to the fast-paced delivery of detailed information about the process. Testing and post-course performance seemed to show that their retention of and ability to use the information was not at the desired level. We decided that an inquiry-guided approach might help in this regard and that a departure from a traditional lecture-only approach might improve student engagement and retention.

Changes and Techniques Used

Critical changes are outlined in Tables 12.3a and 12.3b.

At the heart of the new IGL approach was a heretical concept: Take the bulk of precious lecture time and devote it to group-based problem solving, in an effort to teach the students how to think critically. Since a technology survey course requires that a certain amount of material be delivered in one form or another, the new format mandated that the students review much information in their own time instead of hearing it in lecture. Lecture material was put into PowerPoint format and placed into "lockers" which students could access via the Internet. Students were told that they had to take responsibility for this material. They were tested on this, using five-question quizzes at the start of nearly each lecture period.

After one or two traditional lectures, students spent the remaining class sessions in each module in their randomly assigned four- or five-member groups. We gave the students challenging problems that might confront a typical process engineer. The problems were advanced in nature, similar to those being

Table 12.3a WPS 201 Before IGL

Learning objectives Student should be able to:	• Know key terms and phrases for the industry • Recognize and be able to explain the purpose of key equipment in the industry • Walk into a typical mill and explain the process flow
Course structure	• 42 lectures, using projected slides and PowerPoint presentations, working through the process
Assignments/testing	• Three tests, each covering material in one section (no comprehensive final exam) • Occasional homework problems

posed to seniors in the curriculum. In struggling with trying to solve these problems, students tended to discuss basic material at a much more advanced level than they would if simply presented with the material in lecture.

As an exercise in integrating all their learning, each student conducted a semester-long project that asked them to identify a pressing industry challenge, research "evolutionary" solutions proposed to date, and propose a "revolutionary" solution.

Assessments and Challenges

We assessed student critical-thinking skills by using formal rubrics to evaluate their performance on the in-class problems and on the semester-long project. Assessment of their learning and retention of the basic information was done using these same methods and also by standard grading of tests and quick quizzes. We will assess the longer-term effectiveness of the new IGL approach by interviewing instructors of the students in their sophomore-level classes to see if they exhibit improved critical-thinking skills relative to students from the previous WPS 201 approach.

The main challenge for the new format was the constant feeling that not enough material was being covered, and the fear that students would take the path of least resistance and not review the material parked in their Internet lockers (material not covered in class). However, the use of the quick quizzes (which made up a substantial portion of their grade) seemed to encourage the students to invest due diligence in their out-of-class study.

As expected, there have been mixed reviews from the students. Most students did like the "non-lecture" approach for its energy and ability to engage,

Table 12.3b WPS 201 After IGL

Learning objectives Student should be able to:	• Know key terms and phrases for the industry • Recognize and be able to explain the purpose of key equipment in the industry • Walk into a typical mill and explain the process flow • Analyze and solve typical problems confronting a process engineer • Think like a paper scientist/engineer
Course structure	• Material broken down into 6 modules • 1–2 lectures for each module, covering main concepts • Remaining material delivered to student via Internet in PowerPoint modules • Remaining class time in each module devoted to group-based problem solving or interactive activities
Assignments/testing	• 1–2 quick quizzes per module to ensure students are reviewing Internet-delivered materials; test is administered first individually, then in preassigned groups • In-class group assignments/projects • Individual homework • 3 tests, each covering material in one section (no comprehensive final exam) • One individual semester-long project, in which students must identify one critical industry problem, research "evolutionary" solutions to date, and propose a "revolutionary" solution

but many indicated that too much out-of-class time was required and that more material should have been covered in class. An anonymous survey was administered twice during the semester. Table 12.4 lists the results.

These results tended to show that the students thought that they had learned critical-thinking skills without sacrificing significant learning of content. This self-assessment was confirmed by test and quiz scores; average student test scores after the IGL changes were similar to those before the treatment.

Table 12.4   Survey of Student Perceptions of WPS 201 After IGL

Question	Avg. response early in semester	Avg. response late in semester
Compared to a traditional lecture-based format, did you learn the basic required information . . .	3.2	2.9
Compared to a traditional lecture-based format, did you learn how to think critically and solve problems . . .	4.3	4.4

1 = significantly less well, 3 = about the same, 5 = significantly better than a traditional lecture

IGL in WPS 415 "Senior Research Problems"

The objective of WPS 415 is to give students a learning experience in which they will work as a group on a multitask problem, similar to the problems that they will face in their first job, such as a mill trial. The course requires the students to work closely with a faculty mentor to select a problem, and to develop and complete a set of laboratory experiments to solve that problem. This course was included in the curriculum to help the students better define a problem, and develop solutions through experimentation and data analysis. We also envisioned that the students would have sufficient leeway to develop their own experimental plan for a given problem. As a result, this course exemplifies inquiry-guided learning and was designed to use IGL concepts. Because this is a new course we have tried to incorporate IGL concepts from the beginning (see Table 12.5).

Changes and Techniques Used

The lecture periods have been kept to a minimum and the main emphasis is on the students meeting as a group and with the advisor to develop a meaningful research project. At the beginning of the course all the faculty members present ideas on possible research areas to the class. The student groups (randomly formed) submit their top three choices for research areas. The course coordinator assigns each group a faculty advisor matching the students' interest and making sure that each faculty member has a group. Most faculty members have one group to work with so that they would not be overburdened with too many groups. Once the research areas have been assigned most of the responsibility for the project is with the students. The students do

Table 12.5   WPS 415 with IGL

Course outcomes	• Clearly define a technical problem • Perform a literature search on a problem • Develop an experimental design • Collect a consistent set of experimental data • Analyze the experimental data • Make oral and written presentation of results
Course structure	• One 2-hour lecture period per week for presenting lecture material, group discussions, and student presentations. When no lecture or presentations are scheduled, the class time will be used for group meetings or project work.
Assignments/testing	• Written Reports 　1. Project proposal including the literature search 　2. Progress report 　3. Final report 　4. Project logbook with EXCEL summary 　5. Disk with proposal, progress and final report, and EXCEL summary • Oral Presentations 　1. Project proposal by Member 1 　2. Progress report by Member 2 　3. Final report by Member 3 • Homework Assignments 　1. Scientific Method 　2. Literature Search Methods 　3. Experimental Design 　4. Data Analysis

their own literature search, develop the experimental plan, conduct the experiments, and analyze the data. Progress reports, presentations, and meetings with the advisor at scheduled intervals ensure that the students are making sufficient progress.

Assessment and Challenges

We have taught and assessed the course twice. We used a uniform rubric to evaluate the proposal and final report documents for all seven student groups (23 students total) with the results shown in Table 12.6.

For both outcomes, the majority of students did not obtain the desired level of performance, although it was fairly close for the first component. This shortcoming was manifested in the following ways.

- The students did not define the variables and levels in a way that was clear to the reader.
- In the analysis of their data and observations, the students did not relate their findings to those obtained by other investigators.
- In the analysis of their data and observations, the students did not relate their findings back to the problem being addressed, and there was minimal effort to come up with solutions to the problem, based on the findings.
- The conclusions drawn from the data were cursory and were not related back to the problem being addressed.
- There was minimal effort to use the findings to recommend future work.

Some of the challenges we faced in the implementation of this course with IGL included the following:

- Consistency of using the IGL concept among the various advisors: some of the advisors were more comfortable in outlining the experimental plan instead of letting the students develop their own plans and, thus, learning from their mistakes

Table 12.6   Results of Assessment of Student Performance on Proposal and Final Report

Component	Needs improvement	Competent	Proficient	Exemplary
The student can design and conduct experiments for gathering necessary data.	14.2%	42.9%	42.9%	0%
The student can synthesize, analyze, and critically evaluate information to generate a solution that is effective and efficient.	42.9%	42.9%	14.2%	0%

- Reluctance of the students to use the literature search: some groups did not spend the time necessary to do a proper literature search so that they could develop the right experiments

We decided that a major reason for these shortcomings was that we had not given the students detailed expectations for their proposal and reports, in the form of a rubric with the specific required elements. In preparation for fall 2003, we are designing a detailed course rubric that defines the expectations for each deliverable item in WPS 415 (i.e., proposal, notebook, progress report, final report, final presentation). This rubric will be supplied to the students on the first day of class.

Summary and Challenges for IGL in the Major

The approach to IGL within the Paper Science and Engineering Program has been to begin in the freshman year to use active learning techniques that will foster critical thinking and the habit of inquiry. Reinforcement of these principles will occur across the curriculum and will build to the senior year, culminating in senior capstone courses that require open-ended problem solving and analysis of complex systems. For example, Table 12.7 shows the progress

Table 12.7   Progression of Skills in Paper Science and Engineering Curriculum

Curricular outcomes/ Course	Apply critical-thinking skills and knowledge to solving problems of their professional fields
WPS 100	• Provide an overview of paper industry processes • Begin to synthesize, analyze, and critically evaluate information in a series of introductory projects
WPS 201	• Identify and label major processes/equipment in pulping and papermaking • Define basic terms and elements in paper processes and products • Learn how to extract information from literature • Approach, critically evaluate, and solve complex process engineering problems • Identify examples of process interactions
WPS 415	• Clearly define a technical problem • Perform a literature search on a problem • Develop an experimental design • Collect a consistent set of experimental data • Synthesize, analyze, and critically evaluate the experimental results

across the major of desired competencies in critical thinking based on the three courses discussed here. It is too early to determine the success of this approach across the entire curriculum.

At a recent department retreat we reviewed all of the courses in the curriculum to determine the extent of IGL techniques already being used by the faculty. Nearly all of the courses already include one or more elements that instructors have been using or have recently introduced. The exchange of ideas for other opportunities in each course was very enlightening. Most of the PSE faculty recognize the value of a more active teaching approach, but implementing more IGL activities requires rethinking courses and retooling to meet the learning objectives. This can be a daunting task if undertaken all at one time. Rather, the approach to implementing IGL should be to introduce new approaches and activities gradually—a few new things each year.

13

ENGINEERING COMPUTING AS AN ESSENTIAL COMPONENT OF INQUIRY-GUIDED LEARNING

By Roger P. Rohrbach, Joni E. Spurlin,
Kathy Mayberry, and Sarah A. Rajala

Introduction

Over the past 10 years there have been three important drivers of change in undergraduate education in the College of Engineering at NCSU. The first driver has been the growing awareness at the university of the role that inquiry-guided learning can play in engineering education. In engineering the properties of matter and the sources of energy in nature are used to solve problems confronting people by the creation of new or improved machines, structures, products, processes, or products. In the practice of modern engineering, today's students will draw upon two important resources: the human brain and the computer. The education of engineering students requires that they be trained in problem-solving skills and understand the significant contribution that computers can play in extending the ability of the brain to define, investigate, and solve engineering problems. In summary, meaningful learning demands involvement.

In the late 1980s, then dean of College of Engineering, Dr. Larry Monteith, recognized the important role of computing in engineering education, a second key driver of change, and gathered a committee of representatives from each engineering department in the college. His message was simple: As a faculty we were spending far too much time in various departments teaching the students only how to operate and interface divergent variations of the computing systems. His charge was equally simple: Configure a computing environment for the entire college in which the students can move from department to department accessing identical computing resources each time.

By the late 1990s it was clear that this model was no longer robust, and changes in personal computing options were becoming more plentiful and economically attractive. Engineering students were arriving on campus with a multitude of personal computing devices. Surveys of incoming freshmen students have shown that more and more students are bringing their own computers to campus. In 1998, 75% of NCSU engineering freshmen said they were bringing their own computers. By 2003, 98% of the engineering freshmen said they were bringing their own computers and of these students, 52% said they were bringing laptops. The engineering faculty began to realize that this student-owned computing resource was significant and could form an exciting new mechanism to enhance student learning and achievement. Meaningful learning demands involvement of not only students but also the faculty and a dedicated support staff who are willing to champion and sustain the effort.

The final driver of change has been the new emphasis on outcomes-based education by the Accreditation Board for Engineering and Technology, Inc. (ABET) and the Southern Association of Colleges and Schools Commission on Colleges (SACS-COC), the two principal accreditation agencies for the undergraduate engineering programs in the College of Engineering. Our faculty, individually and collectively, has had to give greater attention to structuring course learning objectives to be relevant, deliverable, and assessable.

In this chapter we will describe how the College of Engineering is attempting to integrate mobile wireless computing and inquiry-guided learning into the curriculum for the students. We will begin by providing the details of the Mobile Computing Pilot Program, provide several instructors' experiences with integrating laptops into their courses, and summarize our current assessment of the program related to inquiry-guided learning.

College of Engineering Mobile Computing Pilot Program

The College of Engineering Mobile Computing Pilot Program is designed to allow faculty and students to collaborate on how to use the flexibility provided by wireless Internet access to enrich the classroom experience and improve learning. The goal of the Mobile Computing Pilot Program is to determine how the use of laptop computers and wireless connectivity enhance the undergraduate academic experience in engineering. Students are able to collaborate on class projects, explore web resources, and use software in the classroom through wireless connectivity (Rajala et al., 2001).

We implemented three successive phases of the pilot programs in the fall semesters of 2001, 2002, and 2003. The first two phases were volunteer honor students, with 37 and 45 students respectively. The third phase has 200 student volunteers who are not necessarily honor students. In each phase, students have purchased a powerful computer (e.g., IBM ThinkPad A22m or T22, Dell C610, Dell C840) at a special price. Faculty in turn have used the resulting capacity for mobile computing to facilitate collaboration and interactive learning in their classrooms.

The first year in engineering is a common first year (see Table 13.1) for which the students must take required general education courses. For those students bringing credit for the required general education courses, they may begin taking elective general education courses their first year. The Student Owned Computing Coordinator has worked with the faculty in many of these courses to produce at least one section for the Mobile Computing Pilot Program. The program enjoys campus-wide faculty support and involvement by virtue of having focused the initial year of the pilot on freshmen engineering students whose course enrollment is largely outside the College of Engineering.

The participating students in the pilot program from each fall semester have been scheduled in a block of courses, so that they are taking mostly the same courses together. Upper-division engineering courses are now beginning to be offered to early participants in subsequent years. As an incentive for faculty teaching upper-division courses to participate in the pilot, the college purchased two carts of 30 laptops each. Interested faculty members submit a proposal to teach a laptop course and the carts are available so that all students have immediate access to suitable equipment in a wireless classroom. So far a variety of course sections have been developed and offered. As the program expands and as our pilot project students reach more of the upper-division courses, we will be able to continue to provide students the opportunity to utilize their computers in class.

Table 13.2 lists courses that have been offered during the past two years or are to be offered in the fall 2003 and illustrate the broad faculty support of the pilot. Each course has one or more specific sections in which faculty will require the use of the wireless laptops in the classroom and is considered part of the Mobile Computing Pilot Program run by Student Owned Computing. These courses incorporate various IGL methods as briefly shown in Table 13.2 and more extensively in the following section. All courses listed have at least one section taught using IGL and the wireless laptop computers. These are for illustrative purposes and do not include all the courses in the pilot program.

The adoption of sound IGL principles by the faculty is influenced by a number of factors. As can be seen by the courses listed above, the more advanced the course, the more advanced the use of computer technology and IGL principles. Clearly, the early innovators, a small percentage at best, are always looking for something new to try. But the majority of the faculty will generally only try one or two new things at a time, if they see evidence that it might work and if it doesn't require large amounts of effort (and time) to implement. Following are in-depth examples of using IGL with the laptop wireless technology in the classroom that show some of the techniques used by faculty teaching engineering students.

Table 13.1 Common First Year for Engineering Students

All engineering students take the same courses in the first year. The # beside the course number (**and bolded**) indicates that at least one section has been modified to fit the Mobile Laptop Computing Pilot Program.

Fall Semester
CH 101 General Chemistry I (3cr.)
CH 102 General Chemistry Lab. I (1cr.)
#E 101 Introduction to Engineering & Problem Solving (1cr.)
#E 115 Introduction to Computing Environments (1cr.)
#ENG 101 English (4cr.) (was ENG 111 or ENG 112)
#ENG 113H for honors students
#MA 141 Calculus I (4cr.)*
#EC 205 Introduction to Economics (3cr.)
PE 1xx Physical Education Fitness & Wellness (1cr.)

Spring Semester
CH 201 General Chemistry II (3cr.) **and**
CH 202 General Chemistry Lab. II (1cr.)*
OR
CSC 110 Introduction to PASCAL (3cr.)**
OR
CSC 112 Introduction to FORTRAN (3cr.)**
OR
CSC 114 Introduction to C++ (3cr.)**
OR
#CSC 116 Introduction to Java (3cr.)**
#MA 241 Calculus II (4cr.)
PY 205 Physics for Engineers and Scientists I (4cr.)
PE xxx Physical Education Elective (1cr.)

*Students take a second semester of chemistry or the first computer science course, depending on their intended major.

**Exact requirements for individual degree programs differ.

Table 13.2   Annotated List of Selected Courses with Special Wireless Laptop Sections and Specific Applications of Laptops and Inquiry-guided Learning

Required General Education Courses for Freshmen Engineering Students

E101 Introduction to Engineering and Problem Solving. To enhance teamwork, to provide individual access to resource material on the web, and to share results with classmates.

E115 Introduction to Computing Environments. To interactively access software and services available on the system, network hardware configurations, online help and communication, file and directory manipulation, and software applications such as email, publishing packages, spreadsheets, mathematical and CAD packages.

ENG 113H Composition, Rhetoric, and Reading. To read texts online and to incorporate technology as a focus of critical reading and writings of course.

ENG 101 Academic Writing and Research. To interactively research library holdings and other materials on the Internet, to share research processes, to critique and assess resources found.

Elective General Education Courses for Freshmen Engineering Students

ENG 331 Communication for Engineering and Technology. (Required by some disciplines.) To increase class discussion of sample professional documents, to peer review and edit others' documents.

HON 101 Honors Colloquium I. In the context of discussions about issues of concern in higher education and relationships between education, personal development, and community involvement, to conduct web searches for class discussion, PowerPoint presentations, and interaction with other courses synchronously with web connection.

HON 293E Like Romeo and Juliet. To use multimedia, online resources and to enhance interaction among students and faculty and with the course material.

HON 296M Spanish for Engineers: Language, Culture and Technology. To enhance foreign language acquisition and understanding of global culture through an interactive website, to permit online submission of projects and course work, and to increase availability of course materials.

HON 296N Making and Using Maps in a Digital Age. To utilize "Ask the Audience" classroom assessment software and StatView® for interactive classroom exercises.

(Continued)

Table 13.2 Continued

Upper-Division Engineering Courses

BME 200 Introduction to Biomedical Engineering. To directly execute sample computer code and immediately evaluate the results.

BAE 473 Introduction to Water Quality Modeling. To provide direct hands-on access to water quality modeling software in an interactive mode and to weigh the effects of alternative "what-if" strategies.

CHE 205 Chemical Process Principles. To access information and physical property tables on the web related to case studies, to discuss equipment types in the Visual Encyclopedia, and to run a virtual experiment.

Comprehensive Examples of IGL Principles in Laptop Courses

- CSC 116 "Introduction to Computing: JAVA." The emphasis of this course (required by some engineering disciplines) is on algorithm development and problem solving. Sections are usually taught in two 50-minute lectures per week plus one 1-hour and 50-minute laboratory. The lectures are usually taught in large (~180 student) sections. The new laptop section used an inquiry-guided learning approach by pairing the lecture and lab experience within the same two-hour period and with the same ratio of teaching assistants to students as the regular sections. There was less formal lecture and more hands-on guided problem solving by students working in pairs at the computer during the class. Students work with each other, asking and getting answers to questions, clarifying concepts and sharing excitement over getting their JAVA programs to work. Having the laptop in the classroom allowed students to immediately practice programming skills directly after lecture and gave the instructor immediate feedback on what the students did not understand.
- MA 241H "Calculus II" and MA 242 H "Calculus III." Required by all engineering disciplines, these courses are the second and third of three semesters in the calculus sequence for science and engineering majors. They incorporate laptops with Maple®, a modern engineering tool for visualizing concepts in calculus used to solve real-world problems. In a typical problem the students sketch curves and surfaces in space in order to identify the boundaries of a three-dimensional region. The analytic description of the boundaries of the region is the crucial and difficult part of these types of problems. Without laptops instructors describe the process by sketching curves and surfaces on the blackboard. Now the students "let Maple® do the sketching." As a result students sketch many more surfaces

than they could sketch by hand, and they have the advantage of seeing the surfaces immediately in front of them as the instructor discusses the process. The students become quite involved in the discussion and seem much more interested in the entire subject because of this interactive process of learning. Based on course exams, the laptop class learned the traditional calculus content at least as well as the traditional class and the graphical material much better than the traditional class.

- GC 120 "Computer Graphics, Foundations of Graphics." In contrast to the regular section in which students meet in a computer lab every third and fourth class period, in the laptop section (a general education elective course), students bring and use their computer every day. As a result faculty can move seamlessly between lectures, discussion, and activities that include sketching and computer-based modeling. The sharing of files between students aids instruction and allows for intimate student teamwork in the classroom. The faculty can immediately detect student misconceptions and provide just-in-time instruction. Because of the daily use of the computer, the instructor in the laptop section is more demanding about the complexity and sophistication of models, and in the final project the student teams develop and design a working model of a product.

- MAE 206 "Engineering Statics." This class is required by some engineering disciplines. Students use Matlab® for in-class problem solving. Using the "Ask the Audience" software, the instructor can interactively provide the students with sample homework problems to solve during class, and they can then receive immediate feedback on their answers. The students work in teams of two or three for the class work problems, mainly with the same partner(s) all semester. For the students who seriously participated in the class problem sessions, the team sessions aid their understanding. The laptops facilitate more team interactions by enabling the instructor to present lecture material faster and allowing prompt interactive feedback to the students on the problems completed in class.

All of the laptop sections above are designated with the suffix LT by the registrar. It is interesting to note that students who are not participating in the pilot, but own a laptop, have figured this out and are now asking to be registered in laptop sections.

Assessment of the Mobile Computing Pilot Program

The goal of the Mobile Computing Pilot Program is to determine how the use of laptop computers and wireless connectivity enhances the undergraduate academic experience in engineering. The assessment of the program focused on evaluating the impact of teaching with wireless technology in a collaborative setting on student performance, specifically in the areas of problem solving and on faculty workload, pedagogy, and amount of material delivered. We also measured the satisfaction of students, faculty, and technical staff with the use of this technology in academic settings. For the purposes of this chapter, we will discuss assessment results that show an impact on student learning and the ability of faculty to conduct classes interactively using inquiry-guided techniques. This assessment discussion will fall into three categories: classroom assessment, assessment by the students, and assessment by the faculty.

Classroom Assessment

Students in the Computer Science Department Senior Design course developed classroom assessment software in the fall semester 2001, currently dubbed "Ask the Audience." The software allows faculty to engage in classroom assessment electronically. Angelo and Cross (1993) developed classroom assessment techniques, many of which are based on asking the students one or two questions to assess their level of knowledge and understanding of the material. For example, using "Ask the Audience" software, the faculty can display a question on the screen, and all students can respond in either a multiple-choice format or a short written response. The faculty can then immediately receive a display that shows both the instructor and students how the question was answered, how many students responded correctly, and the exact written responses. This technique allows the faculty to immediately identify material that needs more attention, to display correct and incorrect answers, and to explain why answers and thought processes were incorrect. This process allows the faculty to increase the depth and breadth of material taught based on students' current level of knowledge, with greater student comprehension and retention. The students are transferred from passive listeners to active learners. It increases student participation and thereby increases their retention, cooperation, and involvement with the material.

Assessment results have shown that faculty used the software between once a month and once a week. The faculty indicated the following effects on teaching and learning.

- Influence faculty pedagogy as the faculty design questions prior to each class period
- Influence student learning, because faculty continually review what students do and do not understand
- Increase student learning, since questions and correct answers are posted as study guides for the students after the class
- Speed up interaction between faculty and students, since faculty get information from all students in the class simultaneously
- Allow students to solve more challenging problems in the classroom
- Influence classroom activity, since students can respond to questions singly, in pairs or larger groups

Assessment of the Pilot Program by the Students

Students in the fall 2001 and 2002 phases of the laptop programs as well as two matching groups of students (one honors/scholars students, the others not) were asked to complete surveys about their experiences with computers in the classroom. In fall 2001, 28 students in the laptop program versus 48 students not in the program completed a survey. In fall 2002, 45 students in the laptop program completed a survey versus 69 students not in the program. All the laptop students are honors or scholar students. Survey results are shown in Table 13.3.

Comparison of the laptop students, who are honors students, to a selection of students who were not in the laptop program, but were honors students, showed that the students in the laptop group had higher agreement that the technology facilitated teamwork and made learning more enjoyable and stimulating. In contrast, there was little difference between groups of students concerning the enhancement of learning *outside* of class, where all students should be equal. The comparison to regular students not in the laptop program shows that on most questions, the laptop students agreed that laptops enhanced their learning and skills. Several questions were asked of the laptop students only, and these indicate that most of the laptop students agreed that the laptop improved their communication with their classmates, helped with classroom discussions, and gave them the freedom to work anyplace, anytime.

The students were also asked to respond to two open-ended questions about the strengths and weaknesses of the wireless laptop technology in the classroom. A summary of the findings indicated that the majority of students said that the ability to use Internet and sophisticated tools in class was the strength of the wireless laptop technology. Another strength students indicated was in their ability to communicate and interact with others. Students also said it made learning more fun or engaging and said it helped with the "ease of use" or organizational issues. The weaknesses focused on some faculty's inability to use the IGL methodology with technology in the classroom. The faculty's ability affected how students felt about the program. When the technology failed, then the students felt that the class period was wasted. Students who had Maple® on their laptop in the mathematics courses could find positive things to say about how the software and its use had affected their learning, while those who used it only in a lab felt it was not useful, disliked it, and felt it was a waste of time.

Assessment of the Pilot Program by the Faculty

The faculty members who teach the laptop sections are self-selecting. Many have benefited from exposure to a number of inquiry-guided learning initiatives in recent years at NCSU. Faculty reflections on teaching with wireless laptops are varied and provide important clues on how the faculty members

Table 13.3 Summary of Laptop Survey Results (in percentage of students who "strongly agree" or "agree")

	Laptop students		Non-laptop honors/scholars		Non-laptop regular	
	Fall 2001 N=28	Fall 2002 N=45	Fall 2001 N=33	Fall 2002 N=28	Fall 2001 N=18	Fall 2002 N=41
Use of laptop/computers in class significantly enhance my learning	64%	64%		70%		59%
Use of the laptop/computer this semester enhanced my computing skills	89%	84%	67%	90%	84%	83%
Use of the laptop/computer facilitated teamwork	86%	62%		44%		39%
The benefits of using technology outweighed the hassles or difficulties	75%	80%	51%		62%	
Laptop/computers make learning more enjoyable	80%	82%		64%		73%
Use of instructional technology made learning more stimulating	82%	84%		68%		73%

Use of the laptop/computer outside of class significantly enhanced my learning	82%	78%		75%		61%
I felt I had a voice in the classroom	61%	71%	73%	50%	59%	51%
Use of the laptop/computer improved my communications with my classmates		78%		75%		66%
Use of the laptop/computer improved my communication with my instructor		44%		54%		56%
I use the laptop to check email and other users when I am bored in class	82%	73%				
I used the Internet in class to help with in-class discussions		93%				
I share files with other students in my courses		60%				
The laptop gives me freedom to work anyplace, anytime		100%				

Note. "Blank cells" indicate that this group of students was not given this statement on their survey.

are integrating laptops into the undergraduate experience at the university. During 2001–2002 faculty met in a group to discuss the impact of the technology in the classroom and wrote an essay at the end of the semester about their experiences. During 2002–2003, faculty members answered a series of open-ended questions throughout the semester and then wrote an essay at the end of the semester. The following is a summary of the findings from these assessments.

On the technical side, most faculty members (73%) felt they had received their laptop in time and had received necessary software in time to prepare for the course. Although many of the faculty had technical problems, the faculty felt this had minimal impact due to the responsiveness of the technical staff.

Faculty who are teaching for the first time using wireless laptops acknowledge that the preparation time has increased enormously. The second time they teach the course, they feel that the preparation time is equal to any other course preparation time. The preparation that takes the time includes transforming the method, content, and direction of the course; developing a greater variety of IGL activities that either the instructor or the student must perform in class; integrating interactive learning activities; and writing new homework/lab assignments. Most faculty comment that there has been increased quality of teaching and learning. It takes time to develop "Ask the Audience" classroom assessment questions.

The faculty addressed many pedagogical issues through their assessment. One important consideration was how to integrate the use of the computer into the class time. Some faculty thought about what the computer could bring to the course that could not have been included in the course otherwise (e.g., readings from the web, passing of files between faculty and among students, doing lab-type work in the classroom, using graphic tools in the classroom). Other faculty considered how to make use of the laptop as an alternative to what they normally would do (i.e., lecture, demonstrate, have students draw on paper, take notes on paper). Several of the courses tended to interactively use more resources from the web during class. This meant that the faculty had to know which resources to use or had to have the students search for relevant resources during the class. For example, the faculty of the ENG 113H course had the students read a hypertext novel on the computer, not in paper form. Several of the faculty had the students share their homework during class by either electronically sharing the file or by electronically projecting it. The entire class could then critique the work during class time. Several faculty members said that next time, they would use more computer simulation or web-based information to illustrate concepts.

One of the most significant findings was the use of the computer for communal and interactive learning. The students could easily share information and files as well as coordinate schedules for team activities and peer study groups. It improved and facilitated teamwork. Teams can use the World Wide Web to meet without all being in the same room. As most of the courses had a large component of the class work as team efforts, the laptop proved itself in making the teamwork more effective and efficient.

To encourage creativity and student problem-solving ability, faculty listed a number of techniques they employed.

* Cooperative learning within the classroom
* Problem-solving activities in class, including inviting offbeat/creative solutions to problems
* Group activities
* Use of faculty and engineers to participate in projects
* Techniques that ask the students to think and brainstorm aloud
* Systems that allow students to assume responsibility for their own learning
* Homework that requires students to develop websites related to coursework
* Classroom assessment techniques with "Ask the Audience" questions
* Hands-on activities to complement textbook

The faculty felt that the laptop was a valuable tool for the following reasons.

* Helps students visualize many concepts that are hard to understand
* Helps students solve more challenging problems during class time
* Gives web accessibility in class
* Allows e-labs, e-workbooks, and simulation software to be used in class
* Allows faculty to see where students are having difficulty and help students understand issues at the time of difficulty

Improvements to the Program Based on Assessment Results

All of the results gathered on the Mobile Pilot Program were analyzed in the summer 2001 and modifications to the program were made based on all the findings. The preliminary data were very encouraging and showed that the honors students were fairly satisfied with the technology, and they wanted more courses taught this way. As related to IGL and the technology, most of the improvements were made to individual courses. In addition, what the faculty learned in 2001–2002 was shared with all the faculty teaching during 2002–2003, including those who used the "cart" of laptops to teach upper-division engineering courses. In addition, as part of the pilot, a College of Engineering Faculty Forum was organized, beginning in fall 2002, to provide an opportunity for faculty to share their experiences with each other on the IGL strategies including in-class activities that work and do not work.

Another improvement was to enhance how the assessment was to be done in 2002–2003. It was decided that the assessment of student learning for 2002–2003 should be done with courses that had two sections: one of these sections should be taught with the wireless laptop and at least one section should not use this technology. In addition, it was clear that the impact on the faculty was greater than anticipated. The main focus of the assessment for 2002–2003 was for faculty to keep a "journal" during the semester in which they teach the course to determine, among other issues, how the technology affected their teaching, the differences in time needed to prepare lectures, what were useful and nonuseful techniques, and overall changes made to the course.

The findings from 2002–2003 indicate that the program is effective in helping students enhance their learning, especially in courses that use the laptop for problem solving. Several courses were implemented with comparative sections with and without the technology and showed ways in which students improved their learning. It created from day one a happy unifier in the class; while studying a skill, a course used technology to enhance and to maintain student interest in the content areas. Engineering students arrived on campus predisposed to this learning tool, and the faculty made the most of it. Classes flowed, learning was optimum, and students were engaged.

The next step, to be implemented fall 2003, is to see how the technology and the new IGL pedagogy affects "regular," non-honors students and their learning, and how well this program can be increased from 50 students to over 200 students. More training of faculty in technology and pedagogy is being planned, and the Faculty Forum will continue to meet several times during each semester. As the program moves into the third year of the pilot, engineering students and faculty expectations to fully integrate mobile computing into the academic life are beginning to materialize. Engineering faculty who teach upper-division courses are being offered opportunities to continue to fully integrate mobile computing into more and more courses.

Conclusions

Inquiry-guided learning principles are being successfully incorporated into many courses being offered in the College of Engineering. The Engineering Mobile Computing Pilot Program has established a direction that serves to encourage both students and faculty throughout the university to elevate their expectations of how computing can enhance the learning environment and the learning experience. The success of this effort is due in part to the growing awareness at NCSU of the role inquiry-guided learning can play in engineering education, and the campus-wide access by the faculty to resources for integration of IGL principles into their instructional efforts. The fact that engineering students are willing to bring their own personal computing devices to campus as freshman has underscored, for the faculty, the increasingly important role of computing in engineering education. The engineering faculty is beginning to address the new emphasis on outcomes-based education by the Accreditation Board for Engineering and Technology, Inc. (ABET) and the Southern Association of Colleges and Schools Commission on Colleges (SACS-COC). Within the

College of Engineering, student-owned computing will likely support the development of e-portfolios and outcome-based assessment. Finally, this pilot program has enjoyed campus-wide exposure and involved many faculty from several colleges.

Acknowledgments

We gratefully acknowledge the direct and indirect support of the NSF-SUCCEED Coalition, William and Flora Hewlett Foundation, IBM, and Dell. Thanks to all the NCSU faculty members who have boldly extended the student-owned computing effort and contributed to this chapter.

References

Angelo, T. A., & Cross, P. K. (1993). *Classroom assessment techniques. A handbook for college teachers* (2nd ed.). San Francisco: Jossey-Bass.

Rajala, S. A., Spurlin, J. E., Mayberry, K., & Lavelle, J. P. (2001). *Assessing the impact of mobile computing on teaching and learning.* A white paper submitted to IBM, August 29.

14

INQUIRY BY DESIGN

LEARNING IN THE STUDIO SETTING

By Meredith Davis and Paul Tesar

British professor Bruce Lawson gave two groups of college seniors the same problem: to determine certain unknown rules for combining variously colored wooden blocks. Students majoring in the sciences comprised one group, while architecture majors made up the other. The scientists approached the problem by generating as many combinations as possible; the architects proposed rules and tested the resulting configurations of blocks. Lawson then assigned the same problem to college freshmen in the same two majors. There was no difference in the freshman problem solving strategies of the two disciplines, leading Lawson to conclude that how the advanced students solved problems was the direct result of curriculum and instructional pedagogy. The scientists were problem-focused, while the architects were solution-focused.

—Lawson, 1990

It is probably fair to say that many members of our university community look upon the College of Design with a strange mix of admiration, envy, and skepticism. The admiration may be due to the national reputation and academic excellence of our students, the envy to the college's privileged small size, its introverted setting, and the high-level selectivity maintained through a separate and unique admissions process. The skepticism, however, seems to arise from an uneasiness about the academic legitimacy of the various design disciplines in the context of a university (as opposed to a trade school or art academy). They seem to lack the rationality and quantitative rigor of the sciences and engineering, as well as the traditional modes of inquiry and scholarship that characterize the social sciences and humanities. Design, many people think, is simply a mixture of manual and perceptual skills combined with subjective, artistic sensibilities: a multidisciplinary field of somewhat questionable provenance focused on inconsequential problems of style, technical skill, and personal expression.

A good part of this skepticism is directed at a unique course type called the "studio," a 6-credit-hour lab/seminar focused on projects in conceiving and making places and things. Students work in small classroom settings of 15 to 20 students to make sketches, models, prototypes, and digital presentations, which embody the values and performances demanded by the problems and their contexts. At NCSU and most other design schools students have permanent work spaces with 24-hour access. These studios are filled with physical artifacts, visible traces of their inquiry, as omnipresent references for later work as well as for their co-learners and faculty who visit these spaces for instruction. Student learning is also documented over time in *portfolios,* collections of artifacts that can be studied and evaluated as evidence of what students know and are able to do. The evaluation process includes ongoing critical response from the student group and periodic presentations by peers, as well as one-on-one discussions between students and faculty who are collaborators in the learning process.

Although the design studio has been around for more than 50 years on this campus and others as an effective alternative to more conventional models of learning, few seem to have noticed or cared until recently. The very "academic impurities" that have made the pedagogy of the studio somewhat suspect—the fact that it is project centered, inquiry guided, cross disciplinary, action oriented, and broadly inclusive of types of cognitive behavior—now emerge as its particular strengths as a model of student-centered learning for the real world.

In 1992 the U.S. Department of Labor secretary's *Commission on Achieving Necessary Skills (SCANS)* defined the competencies that will describe productive adults well into the 21st century. The six "thinking skills" (creative thinking, decision making, problem solving, seeing things in the mind's eye, knowing how to learn, and reasoning) are abundantly evident in successful graduates of college design programs. Although the content to which adults apply SCANS "competencies for productive work" (use of resources, use of information, using systems, using technology, and interpersonal skills) varies, it is impossible for design students to complete their curricula without daily practice of these competencies in studio work (U.S. Department of Labor, 1992).

Therefore, the learning outcomes of a design education clearly map closely to the demands of the contemporary world of work, as well as to life in general. Design students are comfortable with high levels of ambiguity in the nature of problems and the increasing complexity of problem contexts that demand systems thinking. The "content" of their education resides less in the specific facts with which we expect them to be familiar or the current skill set or theory to be mastered, and more in the enduring understanding that transcends time or place and allows them to adapt to changing circumstances.

These are among the main reasons why design education has proven to be an effective foundation for many career paths that may have little or nothing to do with *design* in the conventional use of the term. Being quite the opposite of job training or vocational education, it prepares students for virtually all occupations that rely on intellectual flexibility, a balance of analytical and intuitive faculties, and entrepreneurial self-reliance. While mainstream education has recently adopted features of this unique education (smaller class sizes, project-based learning, peer evaluation, portfolio assessment), the pedagogical tradition of design has produced generations of innovative thinkers who follow ideas with action.

The Nature of Design Inquiry

In the university setting, it is easy to forget that learning is not an activity confined to institutions. Learning, in its most basic form, is one of the natural consequences of living and survival. This predisposition to learn from what we do, and to project what we have learned from experience into future action, is natural and fundamental to life.

In contrast, one of the justifications for the existence of institutions of learning is that they facilitate increased efficiency in the acquisition of knowledge. They do that by separating learning from the necessity of direct, personal experience, in favor of learning from the thoughts and experiences of others.

If we accept the view of humans propagated by the German school of philosophical anthropology as not just the being that thinks, but as the being that thinks and knows in and through action, then all learning focused by a possibility for action would tend to connect more profoundly with who we are or aspire to be. Perhaps it is recognition of this fact that lies at the root of the proverb: "What I read I forget, what I see I remember, what I do I know." More than commenting on the strength and reliability of various sources of memory, it seems to identify three sources of knowledge: knowledge acquired through abstract means (I know the diameter of the earth), knowledge from sensory perception (I know that face or melody), and knowledge from doing (I know how to ride a bike). In contrast with conventional notions of what constitutes "higher" and "lower" order thinking, it assigns the highest cognitive status to a type of knowledge we tend to regard as the most basic, knowledge of the body.

This—mostly Western—prejudice is perhaps due to the fact that the "lower" cognitive levels probably are referred to as such because they occur developmentally earlier in life and because so-called "higher" levels, which enable us to think abstractly and symbolically, distinguish humans most clearly from other forms of life. What this ranking overlooks, however, is that lower cognitive levels are not *primitive* as much as they are *fundamental,* literally forming the foundation from which higher levels grow. Intellectual knowledge that is not integrated with our bodily and emotional being leads to the *cold intellectual,* the *head without a heart,* a notion that seems equally far from a truly human ideal as the *heart without a head,* an overly emotional person oblivious to any rational construct.

Building on the work of Kolb, learning theorist McCarthy (1981) reinforces the notion that, for some students, *learning by doing* is essential. Their research measures two dimensions of learning preference: information perception and information processing. Most schools and methods of instruction are designed to accommodate learners who prefer to perceive the world abstractly (through theories and concepts) and process it reflectively. Traditional lectures, textbooks, and evaluation methods classify and sequence information in ways that favor these learners. Other learners prefer to perceive the world concretely (through sensory experiences) and process it actively (by making or doing). Schools are far less accommodating to these learners, especially at the more advanced levels.

More specifically, University of London researcher Kimball (1991) studies how designers think and describes the fluency with which designers move from hand to mind. Hazy impressions in designers' minds become diagrams and sketches through which they speculate and then elaborate through physical models that represent a possible reality. These models are judged and validated before moving to prototypes that pose solutions to a particular design problem for critical appraisal.

The typical inquiry in our design studios draws and builds on all of these cognitive levels more or less equally; designing means to think, to feel, and to act, calling on capabilities of the whole human being. Thus design inquiry tends to avoid the academic artificiality that comes from the reduction and separation of knowledge into discrete units of study that may be necessary in other academic disciplines. The modes of representation used in design thinking—diagrams, sketches, and sketch models—virtually force designers to think in and through things, things they make and remake, things that integrate all ways of knowing.

Designers know from experience that ideas do not precede their realizations. Instead they emerge in an interactive process with the thing being made and have existence only in the thing. Thus, effective designers tend to act first and then think about whether what they have done makes sense in light of the task at hand. This reversal of the customary "think before you act" principle not only encourages the use of our intuitive faculties but also prevents the "blind" gathering of information at the beginning of an inquiry; our first intuitive realizations filter for relevance and focus the search. The cycle of iterations, also characteristic of design, loops back to consider what might have been overlooked or what surfaces as important in a critique. As a result, inquiry in the studio is imbued with a heightened sense of urgency, relevance, and personal responsibility. Students feel that they "own" the problem in ways not found in many disciplines.

Imagination and insight are also critical in design inquiry. Bohm (in Sloan, 1983) describes insight as "an act of perception, permeated with intense energy and passion" (p. 143) that penetrates and removes barriers in existing thought and liberates the mind to serve in new ways and directions. Similarly design researcher Cross (1999) tells us that designers leap forward in the problem-solving process, experiencing moments of insight about possible solutions. They then return to a more deliberate process for filling in the gaps and confirming intuition. "Intuition" in this sense comprises accumulated perceptions from numerous trial-and-error experiences that precede the specific assignment and help to direct the designer's attention in the new context. For this reason, it is difficult to teach design students a step-by-step process of inquiry that, when followed, guarantees innovation.

The Nature of Design Problems

Design problems must provide the raw material for "sensing" the solution. While studio assignments may foreground specific skills, principles, or applications as the focus of study, they generally embed these issues within larger problems in which all the components and conditions of an "experience" are present. Dewey (1934) described experiences as events in which "every successive part flows freely, without seam and without unfilled blanks, into what ensues. At the same time there is no sacrifice of the self-identity of the parts" (p. 37). Dewey went on to discuss conditions to be met for something to constitute an "experience," which include pattern, structure, the perception of relationships, and the limitations imposed by causes. If we taught design simply as the acquisition of discrete skills and facts, removed from the richness of context, or as the execution of a predetermined process, these conditions would not exist, and we would lose the power of "experiences" in learning.

The notion of design inquiry taking place through "learning experiences" may also account for design students so frequently being in "flow," described by Csikszentmihalyi (1990) as "optimal experience" or total creative joy and involvement in work as an end in itself. University faculty and administrators frequently ask design faculty how we get students to work such long hours. In fact, such hours are usually self-imposed. Students recognize that they can view design inquiry in many ways and that they can foreground different issues in the same problem with alternative results. The more advanced the student, presumably the wider the array of perspectives. For this reason, a sophomore and a senior can tackle the same problem on varying levels of resolution in an afternoon, a week, or a month.

Design, therefore, is a goal-oriented activity that conducts its inquiry through project-based problems that are open ended with many right answers. As design faculty we engage with students as collaborators in this process of inquiry. Neither teacher nor learner knows in advance what the solution to the problem will be, although how it must be performed is often negotiated before the work begins or as the inquiry process unfolds. It is our task as faculty to direct inquiry by the structure and scope of the project and by questions posed as the student proceeds to solution. Our *authority* lies in these questions, not in answers, with the objective of developing students' ability to pose their own questions as they mature as designers.

Chief among those questions is the definition of the problem. We encourage students to find their own problem within each assignment: a learning goal that focuses on personal strengths and weaknesses and that leads to inquiry that is specific and builds on previous work. For this reason, it is difficult for us to quantify a particular studio performance as a part of an overall student grade. Recently a university curriculum committee that approves new courses asked design faculty to indicate the relative percentages assigned toward the final grade for each skill and unit of knowledge mastered. The design faculty response was that within a single class, students may need to focus on different things and that, depending on how individual students refine the problem statement, one skill or concept may be more important than another. The design studio is able to accommodate individual learners while addressing the larger set of learning outcomes.

In addition, design problems typically exist within specific settings and involve users or audiences with definable characteristics and patterns of behavior. Architectural methodologist Alexander (1964) describes design as the "goodness of fit between form and context" (p. 15). Among the factors that make up the problem context for design are social, cultural, and personal values that are frequently in competition with one another. Determining those values, often in the absence of one-on-one discussions with those who hold them, and resolving conflicts are inherent tasks of the designer. Design students must learn to mine the contexts of a problem for information that guides problem solving, much as they do in their interactions with the world outside of school. In this case, "information" takes the form of observations, conversations, images, and other resources in the physical world, not only what comes from books and the work of experts.

Imagine, for example, four existing cups: a plastic Dixie cup; my grandmother's bone china teacup; a wide-bottomed, stoneware driving mug; and a plastic mug with a recessed bottom that nests in the top of other cups to form a stack of perfect cylinders. The first cup design reflects disposability as a high priority; the second values elegance and social tradition; the third is stable and retains heat; and the fourth conserves horizontal space in the cupboard. In privileging each of these values, the designers ignored others; my grandmother's teacup has a tiny bottom and wide top in an effort to achieve a delicate shape and refined gesture for its use, however, it is tipsy and allows heat to dissipate quickly. Now imagine designing a fifth cup: one that is both elegant and disposable, or one that is both stackable and retains heat. The problem of the fifth cup demands that students resolve competing priorities. The clarity of values, apparent in the first four cups, is compromised by the requirement of two equally desirable traits.

Such is the nature of design, in which the complexity of problems and the diversity of users demand designers' critical judgments about the reconciliation of competing values. While the cup problem is relatively simple in its juxtaposition of physical attributes within an acceptable range of risk, most design problems are more complex and have constituencies that demand to be satisfied. Students must examine the physical, psychological, social, cultural, technological, and economic dimensions of the problem in a complex system of relationships. In marked contrast, many disciplines isolate content in discrete units of investigation focused almost entirely on *explanation and description*. By forcing the issue of competing values through problem definitions, we require students to *interpret* and *hold a perspective* on knowledge and skills acquired through inquiry.

Assessing Student Inquiry in Design

The project-based inquiry of design allows students and faculty to assess understanding through authentic performance. Students practice the same behaviors as experts in the field. Unlike other disciplines in which the amassing of facts, concepts, and theories precedes application, students of design inquire by *doing*. The quality of the inquiry process is made visible through carefully sequenced representations (analytical diagrams, sketches, models, prototypes, etc.), as well as through the final artifact in use. This visibility allows for peer review and adjustment of the inquiry strategy as the work proceeds.

The typical design studio employs interim and final critiques as an ongoing evaluation strategy. Students make individual presentations of work to faculty and peers through the artifacts appropriate to the stage of inquiry (problem identification/definition, analysis, generation of multiple solutions, refinement of solution, modeling or prototyping). Criteria for the evaluation are derived from the problem statement and negotiated publicly. Peer and faculty comments not only assess the quality of the work but also identify missed opportunities for investigation, alternative perspectives that could guide inquiry, and resources that might inform further work. Early in their education, design students learn to separate criticism of the work from criticism of the self; comments on the NCSU end-of-semester course evaluations reflect genuine student interest in rigorous criticism.

The value of such criticism is evident in a 1970s intra-institutional study by education professor Noonan at Virginia Commonwealth University of all evaluation methods used by disciplines in the university. Among his conclusions was that design majors, through the critique process, were the most confident of all students in determining what their next move would be following failure, and therefore, in their comfort with failure as part of the learning process. Unlike students who took paper-and-pencil tests, the design majors could retrace steps in their behavior to account for outcomes and were able to adjust inquiry behaviors in subsequent problem solving. Failure was seen as a natural part of the learning process.

Conclusions

In spite of this long tradition of inadvertent inquiry-guided learning in design studios, many of these principles have not always found their way into other design lecture and seminar classes, particularly those dealing with technical subject matter and design history. There we still find a prevalence of linear teaching methods in the typical "layers from the bottom up" model, accumulating first fundamental and then increasingly more complex facts and principles largely disembodied from their applications and contexts. As a result, students who have been exposed to "prerequisite knowledge" in this way often seem unable to use it in design projects. The tradition of teaching design history only as the chronological unfolding of events also presents challenges. Complementing the traditional historical survey with thematically organized investigations would expand students' understanding of how ideas connect across time. It is reasonable to conclude that all learners might benefit from encountering knowledge that is not "pure" but as it exists impurely in things. The use of various kinds of informal "case studies" in which students look for guidance from relevant precedents has proven to be highly effective in the action-oriented studio and is likely to be equally effective as a teaching method in more typical, large lecture classes.

While the design disciplines certainly have a history of inquiry-guided learning, they have practiced it inadvertently, simply because design arises from man's identity as a culture-making being. Design education only makes formal what cultures have done for millennia: create artifacts that reflect necessity as well as individual or collective aspirations that are instruments as well as symbols. We were simply lucky to have inherited these real-life ways of doing and making things, and have resisted, in an act of self-preservation, more conventional academic models of teaching and learning. Only in the past few decades have we become self-reflective, analyzing our own largely taken-for-granted methods and behaviors, which are by definition and necessity less academic, less linear, less artificial, and less one dimensional than other disciplines. As a consequence, design has become more articulate about itself, reaching certain conclusions about the nature of learning from practice rather than theory. These conclusions parallel what is now called inquiry-guided learning, which in many ways is a return to a more natural way of acquiring knowledge from and for life. Practices that initially created suspicion in academia may actually be a cure. Design is ready and willing to share it.

References

Alexander, C. (1964). *Notes on the synthesis of form*. Cambridge, MA: Harvard University Press.

Bohm, D., as quoted by Sloan, D. (1983). *Insight-imagination: The emancipation of thought and the modern world* (p. 143). Westport, CT: Greenwood Press.

Cross, N. (1999). Presentation to doctoral students in the College of Design at North Carolina State University.

Csikszentmihalyi, M. (1990). *Flow: The psychology of optimal experience*. New York: Harper and Row Publishers, Inc.

Dewey, John. (1934). *Art as experience*. New York: Penguin Putnam, Inc.

Kimball, R. et al. (1991). *The assessment of performance in design and technology*. London, England: School Examinations and Assessment Council.

Lawson, B. (1990). *How designers think: The design process demystified* (2nd ed.). Oxford, England: Butterworth Architecture.

McCarthy, B. (1981). *4MAT system: Teaching to learning styles with right/left mode techniques*. Oak Brook, IL: EXCEL.

United States Department of Labor. (1992). *Skills and tasks for jobs, A SCANS report for America 2000*. Washington, DC: United States Department of Labor.

15

INQUIRY-GUIDED LEARNING AND THE UNDERGRADUATE CURRICULUM

GENERAL EDUCATION AND THE MAJOR

*By Susan Blanchard, Marilee Bresciani,
Michael Carter, Virginia S. Lee,
and Gerry Luginbuhl*

Introduction

A variety of forces, initiatives, projects, and individuals have contributed to undergraduate education reform through inquiry-guided learning at NCSU. The initiative for reform has originated at the grassroots level through the efforts and initiative of small groups of faculty and staff, and it has been supported and encouraged by administration. Two major IGL projects on this campus explicitly linked IGL to General Education and the departmental major. As a result, examples of inquiry-guided learning and its associated outcomes (i.e., critical thinking, independent inquiry, responsibility for one's own learning, intellectual growth and maturity) now reside at all levels of the university (e.g., individual course, program). But now, due to the articulation of general education objectives by the Council on Undergraduate Education (CUE) and of curricular-level objectives and outcomes in connection with the Undergraduate Academic Program Review (UAPR) process by academic programs, the possibility for the more widespread integration of IGL throughout the undergraduate curriculum is even greater. Meta-analyses of curricular-level objectives and outcomes reveal overarching outcomes that parallel the IGL outcomes of critical thinking, independent inquiry, and responsibility for one's own learning. Other campus initiatives related to assessment and technology are also creating opportunities for more widespread dissemination of inquiry-guided learning. Taken together these efforts are contributing to inquiry-guided learning becoming more pervasive throughout the undergraduate curriculum.

Explicit Linkages Between Inquiry-guided Learning, General Education, and the Majors

Two major projects on our campus, funded by the William and Flora Hewlett Foundation, explicitly related inquiry-guided learning to the undergraduate curriculum, the first through general education and the second through the departmental major. The first inquiry-guided learning project on this campus grew out of a conversation about critical thinking and how deliberately instructors teaching general education courses were helping students develop the ability to think critically. During the spring 1996, CUE, charged by the Provost to oversee the general education of all the students in all curricula of the university, discussed the futility of general education requirements if students satisfied the requirements by taking unwanted courses and forgot their content as quickly as possible. So long as students saw their education as solely the faculty's responsibility, education was not going to happen. CUE drew up and passed a position paper on students' responsibility for and commitment to their education (see Appendix 15.A). It also charged faculty to help students to take responsibility for their own education by offering them "guided practice in critical thinking" in the classroom.

Following the approval of the position paper, the Provost received an invitation from the Hewlett Foundation in December 1996 to apply for a grant to "improve general education at a Research I University." This challenge was passed along to the council's chair, who worked with a small committee and a grant writer on a proposal that put the themes of guided practice in critical thinking and improvement of general education together under the banner of "inquiry-guided instruction" as we called it then. The proposal made the case that with Hewlett funding we could create a continuum of inquiry running from entering-level general education courses to individual or group research projects in the student's final semester that would also develop students' ability to thinking critically. The foundation funded our proposal.

In addition to establishing a critical mass of faculty and staff versed in inquiry-guided instruction, two additional outcomes emerged from the project. Participants identified three principles that characterized the outcomes of a general education course that provided opportunities for inquiry-guided learning: a sense of independent inquiry, the ability to think critically, and the capacity to take responsibility for one's own learning. Together these capacities encourage intellectual growth toward maturity, understood in the terms of the Perry model of intellectual development. The project also spawned a pilot First Year Inquiry Program, small seminars that would provide an expectation for learning at the university different from students' high school experience and explicit instruction in critical thinking. Consequently, the inquiry-guided learning initiative established a direct linkage with general education at its inception. And like future IGL projects the linkage occurred through an articulation of broad student learning outcomes that the undergraduate curriculum—both general education and the major—would further.

In January 2000 we were awarded a second grant from the Hewlett Foundation titled "Hewlett Campus Challenge: General Education and the Major." The proposal extended inquiry-guided learning into the departmental major. Participating departments identified a sequence of three to four courses in the major and transformed them through the integration of inquiry-guided learning. In addition to the 10 departmental teams chosen for the project, the project represented a collaboration among four administrative and support units—Faculty Center for Teaching and Learning, Campus Writing and Speaking Program, University Planning and Analysis, and Undergraduate Affairs (see Chapter 2 for more details). The basis for the collaboration was a common focus on student learning outcomes, although with a slightly different emphasis depending on the unit. By coordinating the efforts of these four units, we hoped that departments would recognize these efforts as related and complementary. We wanted the work of the four units to support and reinforce one another in the interest of undergraduate education reform.

Of particular interest for this discussion was the work of the Campus Writing and Speaking Program. It assisted individual departments in articulating curricular-level outcomes in response to changes in the general education requirements regarding writing and speaking. More than writing and speaking outcomes, the outcomes described what a graduating senior in the major would know and be able to do. Many of these outcomes emphasized students' ability to utilize the modes of inquiry in the discipline that could be assessed using writing and speaking assignments. Two sample sets of outcomes follow.

Department of Mathematics

1. Read, understand, and make informed judgments about mathematical arguments.
2. Generate clearly reasoned, convincing proofs.
3. Apply mathematics and mathematical reasoning to solving real-world problems.
4. Explain mathematics intelligibly to a variety of audiences.

Department of Food Science

1. Engage in clear and careful scientific inquiry.
2. Apply critical thinking to solving problems and generating designs related to food science and technology.
3. Understand, manage, and communicate source materials related to food science and technology.

4. Work effectively in teams.

5. Give effective oral presentations.

Like the two sample sets of outcomes, many other departments' curricular-level outcomes reflected the modes of inquiry of their respective disciplines. In essence, these outcomes described what it means to inquire and think critically in a particular discipline and so were quite consistent with inquiry-guided learning.

We also realized that the development of these curricular-level writing and speaking outcomes related to the unfolding undergraduate academic program review process, which in turn related to the requirements for reaccreditation. The portion of undergraduate academic program review related to teaching requires departmental programs to articulate student learning outcomes that describe what a graduating senior will know and be able to do. If not completely satisfying that requirement, the curricular level writing and speaking outcomes at the very least represent a starting point, and in some cases, significant progress toward that requirement. And once again, knowing the nature of these outcomes with their inclusion of the modes of inquiry of the disciplines, we recognized an opportunity to embed inquiry-guided learning more deeply into the undergraduate curriculum. Outcomes of this type also had implications for pedagogy, the types of teaching strategies instructors would use to bring them about and how they assessed students. And all were consistent with inquiry-guided learning.

As a result, in selecting departments for inclusion in the second Hewlett Project, we tried to recruit departments that already had curricular-level writing and speaking outcomes in place. As departments planned their sequence of courses, we tried to emphasize the importance of explicitly linking them to the curricular-level outcomes and how that exercise related to the requirements of the undergraduate academic program review process. Now at the end of the project, the most successful teams have successfully linked their IGL work with the program review process in some very exciting and fruitful ways. By leveraging the inquiry-guided learning project with three other initiatives on campus—the development of writing and speaking outcomes, Undergraduate Academic Program and Review, and accreditation—we hoped to provide a stronger foothold for inquiry-guided learning in the undergraduate curriculum and, more specifically, in the departmental major.

Further Developments in General Education

Over the past several years CUE has been engaged in articulating the learning objectives of our General Education program. CUE first developed the following overall objectives of the General Education program.

1. Provide instruction that enables students to master basic concepts of a broad array of the intellectual disciplines.

2. Help students develop versatility of mind, an ability to examine problems individually and collaboratively from multiple perspectives, including ethical and aesthetic perspectives.

3. Provide students the guidance and skills necessary to become intellectually disciplined, to be able to construct arguments that are clear, precise, accurate, and of relevant depth and breadth.

4. Encourage students to take personal responsibility for their education, including the ability to find, evaluate, and communicate new information, setting the stage for life-long learning.

These objectives clearly reflect the university's commitment to inquiry-guided learning, as they emphasize the development of critical thinking, inquiry, and student responsibility for learning.

Students at NCSU are required to select a specific number of courses from each of eight categories in order to fulfill their general education requirements. There are additional requirements in writing and speaking and communication and information technology that span the curriculum. The process of developing learning objectives for each general education category involved subcommittees of CUE working on initial drafts, seeking input from representatives of the affected disciplines, and making recommendations back to the CUE, where final revisions and approvals were voted on. For example, when the subcommittee met to discuss the requirement in Mathematics, the subcommittee's proposed revisions were distributed to representative faculty in Mathematics, Statistics, and Logic (Philosophy) for their comments. Final recommendations were made by CUE. Each of the individual categories within the General Education program emphasizes inquiry, critical thinking, and in many cases communication. For example, courses in the Natural Sciences will provide instruction and guidance that will help students to do the following:

1. Use the methods and processes of science in testing hypotheses, solving problems, and making decisions

2. Articulate, make inferences from, and apply to problem solving, scientific concepts, principles, laws, and theories

CUE has also adopted a plan that implements assessment of general education on two levels: (1) At the university level, CUE would generate objectives and apply those objectives as criteria to courses seeking to be included in particular categories of the GERs; and (2) at the academic program level, each program with courses in the GERs would assess those courses according to whether students were attaining learning outcomes that meet the objectives. This approach to assessment will allow faculty teaching the courses to develop learning outcomes and to assess the attainment of those outcomes. CUE believes that the departmental faculty are in the best position to make meaningful assessments and improvements in their courses. The council also endorsed the immediate implementation of a pilot assessment project to help inform future additional revisions in learning objectives and to obtain feedback from faculty teaching GER courses on the relative value versus burden of developing and teaching to learning outcomes. Hopefully this process will ensure that NCSU faculty will continue to grow in their ability to utilize instructional practices that promote inquiry and critical thinking.

Further Developments in Undergraduate Academic Program Review: Links with Departmental Programs and the Major

The university's Undergraduate Academic Program Review process has also provided a mechanism for disseminating inquiry-guided learning more broadly throughout the institution. The process has required departments to articulate curricular-level outcomes that describe what graduating seniors will know and be able to do as a result of their learning experiences in the major. Collectively these outcomes show how thoroughly critical thinking, independent inquiry, and responsibility for one's own learning, as well as other common outcomes, permeate the undergraduate curriculum as an expectation for learning.

In 1994 we began to evaluate the way we approached undergraduate academic program review. The discussions were framed by the institution's desire to improve its effectiveness and the quality of undergraduate education. An ad hoc Committee on Undergraduate Academic Program Development and Review Process Improvement (CUAPDRPI) was created from two already existing faculty-led committees. Over a three-year period the committee formulated the following recommendations.

- The creation of a faculty-led, college-represented task force to implement a new program review process
- The replacement of the existing 10-year cycle of mandatory reviews of undergraduate academic programs by continuous portfolio-based monitoring by departments of undergraduate programs
- The establishment of departmental program review teams so as not to "burden" any individual and to ensure faculty involvement in the formation of objectives and outcomes
- The establishment of a program review process that would simultaneously enhance the self-assessment activities of departments as well as program (departmental) autonomy

The Committee on Undergraduate Program Review (CUPR), the task force charged with developing the assessment-based program review process, was created in the fall 1999 with some committee members who served on CUAPDRPI. Using the Accreditation Board for Engineering and Technology, Inc. (ABET) process as a model, over the next two years CUPR worked on developing flexible program review guidelines and a recommended timetable for outcomes-based program review. In essence, the guidelines request descriptive information of the program and encourage faculty to engage in assessment-based program review by addressing the following questions about their programs.

- What are we trying to do and why are we doing it?
- What do we expect the student to know or do as a result of our program?
- How well are we doing in preparing them to know and do those things?
- How do we know?
- How do we use the information to improve?
- Do the improvements we make actually work?

The Undergraduate Academic Program Review (UAPR) process developed by this task force allows each program to determine objectives, outcomes, and measures appropriate for the individual discipline that meet student outcomes assessment, institutional effectiveness, and accreditation requirements. The UAPR process developed parallels and is similar to ABET in that both call for an outcomes-based review process. Appendixes 15.B and 15.C include two representative sets of department curricular-level objectives and outcomes— one from the Department of Biomedical Engineering, the other from Foreign Languages and Literature. Both sets of outcomes clearly reflect the IGL outcomes of inquiry, critical thinking, and responsibility for one's own learning in terms that make sense in those disciplines.

As indicated by the questions just presented, articulating curricular objectives and outcomes is only part of the program review process. Programs also need to develop ways of assessing how well they are doing in preparing students to know and do the things they value and then using evidence of student learning from those assessments to improve instruction. We refer to this as "closing the loop," and currently we are in the process of reviewing programs' "closing the loop" reports. Appendix 15.D provides an example of one of these reports from the Department of Foreign Languages and Literatures using an outcome related to inquiry-guided learning: the demonstration of skills in critical interpretation of texts. The report demonstrates how the program has systematically gathered evidence about student performance with respect to the outcome, noted discrepancies between actual and desired student performance, and devised a strategy to address the discrepancy in the interests of enhanced student learning. The example also illustrates the potential of the UAPR process to support inquiry-guided learning.

Meta-analyses of Curricular-level Outcomes: Inquiry Pervades the Undergraduate Curriculum

Two meta-analyses of curricular-level outcomes, performed independently and using different methodologies, also demonstrate the pervasiveness of the ability to think critically and inquire in ways appropriate to the discipline throughout the undergraduate curriculum. The first meta-analysis was conducted in the fall 2002 by one of us who has worked extensively with departments in the development of their program objectives and outcomes. Because these outcomes were created by faculty in each discipline, they reflect the forms of inquiry specific to that discipline. By analyzing these outcomes, we tried to identify the general modes of inquiry that characterize undergraduate study. In the process we discovered certain themes (e.g., identifying and analyzing a problem; asking pertinent questions, identifying hypotheses, and designing experiments) in these forms of inquiry that crossed disciplines. These common themes provided the four categories of inquiry—problem solving, empirical inquiry, research based on sources, and performance—that pervade the undergraduate curriculum at NCSU (see Appendix 15.E).

In order to better understand what outcomes academic programs were assessing, the Office of Undergraduate Assessment conducted a second meta-analysis of curricular objectives and outcomes submitted to CUPR in the fall 2002, utilizing grounded theory analysis (Strauss & Corbin, 1990). A total of 68 plans were analyzed in the spring 2003. The grounded theory analysis of objectives and outcomes revealed that academic programs were assessing similar values. The primary categories that emerged from this analysis included communication (e.g., writing and speaking); professional, ethical, and societal responsibility; critical evaluation (e.g., critical thinking); understanding group dynamics; lifelong learning (e.g., also including responsibility for pursuing learning beyond the academic career); technological competence; graduate competitiveness; research (e.g., inquiry); and cultural competence. A detailed summary of these categories can be found in Appendix 15.F. As mentioned, the IGL themes of critical thinking, inquiry, and responsibility for learning are present throughout more than one of these common outcome categories.

Summary

Throughout its seven-year history on our campus, inquiry-guided learning has woven in and out of broader discussions about the undergraduate curriculum. Sometimes the connections between inquiry-guided learning and curricular-level discussions have been explicit; for example, in earlier discussions about the importance of direct instruction in critical thinking and general education and in later discussions about the relationship between UAPR and the major in the Hewlett Campus Challenge Project. More frequently, the connections have been implicit as programs have articulated the kinds of learning outcomes they value for their graduates. In a research university is it surprising that faculty value critical thinking, the skills of independent inquiry, and the pursuit of lifelong learning—three of the defining outcomes of inquiry-guided learning as defined on this campus? And is it any wonder that the outcomes they articulate for their graduates would reflect these values?

Reference

Strauss, A., & Corbin, J. (1990). *Basics of qualitative research: Grounded theory procedures and techniques.* Newbury Park, CA: Sage.

POSITION STATEMENT ON INCREASING STUDENT RESPONSIBILITY FOR, INVOLVEMENT IN AND COMMITMENT TO LEARNING

NORTH CAROLINA STATE UNIVERSITY COUNCIL ON UNDERGRADUATE EDUCATION ADOPTED JANUARY 19, 1996

Education involves more than taking or offering courses that satisfy the requirements of a major and that meet general education requirements. In addition, it is important that students develop a sense of responsibility for, involvement in and commitment to their learning.

The Council on Undergraduate Education (C.U.E.) takes the position that both students and faculty have a role in this process. The students' role is to become actively involved in their education; to cultivate effective attitudes, behaviors, and skills for thinking and learning; and to engage fully in academic discourse. The faculty's role is to provide learning opportunities that stimulate and deepen students' desire for and abilities in learning and that help students to become lifelong learners.

Implications for Students

The C.U.E. position on the role of students can be expanded in the following way. Students who take an active role in their learning are those who:

1. cultivate curiosity;
2. recognize that struggle is a requisite for learning, for learning requires students to spend time in areas where they are not yet sure of themselves, and they have to spend time following leads that may turn out to go nowhere;

3. realize that accepting responsibility for their own learning entails spending the requisite hours preparing for classes and examinations, doing homework and writing papers, asking questions, finding help from faculty, seeking opportunities for learning, and using available resources;

4. tolerate the discomfort that sometimes accompanies contact with new ideas; this discomfort involves not rushing to judgment, but being open-minded and considering different views and frames of reference; and

5. recognize that thinking critically about ideas and problems and making mature judgments can take place only if they cultivate certain habits of mind, such as a readiness to gather information, to develop reasoning skills, and, when relevant, to learn methods of specific disciplines.

Implications for Faculty

Although students' sense of responsibility for their learning is the foundation of a university education, it is also, paradoxically, a primary goal of education. An important criterion of well-designed curricula and well-taught courses is how effectively they serve this goal. This position enjoins faculty members to think explicitly about how to help students become more involved in their education. Believing that efforts to this end can be deepened and widened, the C.U.E. suggests the following:

1. Encourage good teaching practice. There are several ways to identify the principles of teaching. The following list (derived from "Seven Principles of Good Practice in Teaching," Chickering and Gamson, 1987) is typical, not exhaustive. Good teaching
   a. encourages contacts between faculty and students,
   b. develops reciprocity and cooperation among students,
   c. gives prompt feedback,
   d. emphasizes persistent focus on the material to be learned and efficient use of time (i.e., "time on task"),
   e. communicates high expectations,
   f. respects diverse talents and ways of learning, and
   g. uses active learning techniques, which are those in which the student does not passively take notes but is asked and allowed to do something, and in the doing learn something. Examples are: i) cooperative learning; ii) experiential learning; iii) writing for learning, and iv) critical thinking initiatives.

2. Provides students with guided practice in critical thinking (e and f below). The operative term here is "guided practice." The following list of learning situations shows a range that varies from those that have no guided practice in critical thinking to those that include a significant amount:

a. Information is dispensed and learned, but students do not learn the thought processes involved in gathering or organizing it.

b. The teacher describes the thought processes involved in gathering, validating and organizing the information, and students are examined only on the information itself.

c. The teacher describes the thought processes involved in gathering, validating and organizing the information, and students are required to replicate the thought processes on examinations.

d. Students are examined on their ability to think critically, though they have not been given guided practice.

e. Students are required to practice good thinking, and the teacher guides and evaluates the practice, applying appropriate standards of clarity, accuracy, relevance and depth.

f. Students learn how to think about thinking. They learn concepts for describing and monitoring the processes, including the standards of critical thinking, and they practice thinking about thinking, guided by the teacher.

Although the learning situations described in a) through d) above may be necessary preconditions for effective thinking, the C.U.E. takes the position that it is important for students to have *guided practice* in critical thinking every semester.

3. Learns from what is already being done to provide guided practice in critical thinking to our students. By discussing how critical thinking is being guided in another's class, a faculty member can develop additional ways to guide the practice of critical thinking in his or her own classes.

Reference

Chickering, A. U., & Gamson, Z. F. (1987, March). Seven principles of good practice in teaching. *AAHE Bulletin*. Washington, DC: American Association of Higher Education.

APPENDIX 15.B

CURRICULAR-LEVEL OBJECTIVES AND OUTCOMES

DEPARTMENT OF BIOMEDICAL ENGINEERING

1. To educate students to be successful in Biomedical Engineering by emphasizing engineering and biology as related to basic medical sciences and human health.

    After completing the B. S. in Biomedical Engineering, graduates will be able to:

    a. Draw on knowledge of mathematics, science, and engineering to critically evaluate, analyze and solve problems at the interface of engineering and biology by using appropriate tools.
    b. Identify contemporary clinical issues and be able to discuss potential biomedical engineering solutions.
    c. Design and model biomedical materials, systems, and/or devices.
    d. Explain basic concepts of systems and cellular physiology.
    e. Design and conduct experiments to test hypotheses and to make measurements on and interpret data from living systems.
    f. Discuss the problems associated with the interaction between living and non-living materials.

2. To produce Biomedical Engineers able to communicate effectively with diverse audiences and prepared to work in multidisciplinary teams.

    After completing the B. S. in Biomedical Engineering, graduates will be able to:

    a. Deliver effective oral presentations to multiple audiences, including health care and engineering professionals.
    b. Prepare effective written materials.
    c. Use modern engineering tools to communicate ideas with others within the engineering discipline.
    d. Work effectively in multidisciplinary teams to complete projects.

3. To develop in students professional, ethical, and societal responsibility in Biomedical Engineering practices.

After completing the B. S. in Biomedical Engineering, graduates will be able to:

a. Demonstrate understanding of formalized ethical codes in engineering and medicine.

b. Articulate, identify, and evaluate contemporary ethical issues in biomedical engineering and their impact on society.

c. Demonstrate professional behavior.

4. To introduce students to advances in Biomedical Engineering practice and research and to instill in them a lifelong thirst for knowledge.

After completing the B. S. in Biomedical Engineering, graduates will be able to:

a. Assess, evaluate, and reference peer-reviewed technical literature.

b. Demonstrate a desire for learning through postgraduate career plans.

CURRICULAR-LEVEL OBJECTIVES AND OUTCOMES

DEPARTMENT OF FOREIGN LANGUAGES AND LITERATURES

Speaking:

- Outcome #4: Communicate in French and Spanish with fluency at the Advanced level in the interpersonal, interpretive and presentational modes so as to be readily understood by native speakers.
- Outcome #6: Produce the basic linguistic components of French or Spanish using appropriate behaviors and registers.

Writing:

- Outcome #6: Produce the basic linguistic components of French or Spanish using appropriate behaviors and registers.
- Outcome #12: With the aid of appropriate technologies, write coherent, well-organized routine social correspondence as well as essays demonstrating clearly the skills of critical interpretation.

Critical Thinking:

- Outcome #3: Read on the literal, interpretive and critical levels unedited French or Spanish works from various genres, periods, and regions involving literary, historical and cultural themes (such as novels, plays, essays, poems, newspapers, magazines, realia, etc.).
- Outcome #13: Report and discuss in French or Spanish a research project on a literary or cultural topic.

The following outcomes may also be included here:

- Outcome #14: Justify in French or Spanish a polemical issue involving literature or culture.
- Outcome #15: Evaluate a historical or contemporary work of art or literature using appropriate terminology in French or Spanish.

Cultural Competence:

- Outcome #9: Analyze, compare and contrast the ways in which the target language cultures and civilizations have evolved, and the products, practices and perspectives that constitute these cultures.
- Outcome #14: Justify in French or Spanish a polemical issue involving literature or culture.
- Outcome #15: Evaluate a historical or contemporary work of art or literature using appropriate terminology in French or Spanish.

CLOSING THE LOOP REPORT

DEPARTMENT OF FOREIGN LANGUAGES AND LITERATURES

Objective

To produce students with the advanced skills in French and Spanish essential to communicate effectively as global citizens in the workplace and beyond.

Outcomes

With the aid of appropriate technologies, students will write coherent, grammatically correct, well-organized routine social correspondence as well as essays demonstrating clearly the skills of critical interpretation.

Assessment Methods

Beginning in 1994, graduating seniors in the department are asked by the assistant head at the time of graduation clearance during their final semester to submit an essay that they have written for an upper-level major course (preferably, but not restricted to, the senior capstone course, FLF/S 492). This paper is to present a "best-case" portfolio containing a writing sample of at least five pages in length, treating a topic relating to a literary period or genre. At the end of fall and spring semesters, the coordinator of advising gathers the individual student portfolios, removes all identification (such as students' names, professors' names, course numbers, grades, etc.) and assigns their evaluation to a group of faculty assessors who read the student papers and rate them on fluency, grammaticality, organization, and level of sophistication in analytic and interpretive skills. These ratings are based in part on the ACTFL Proficiency Guidelines produced by a national organization, the American Council on the Teaching of Foreign Languages. More recently, all students are also asked to include a short, one- or two-paragraph "reflective piece" which is submitted by the student along with the written paper. This addition affords the students an opportunity for reflection and self-assessment, a part of the portfolio writing process, and it also affords the faculty some insight into students' approaches and attitudes towards writing. It is expected that at least 85% of the papers of the graduating seniors will be rated at the Advanced or Superior levels on the ACTFL scale.

Summary of Data, Process, Findings, and Decisions

Over the past eight years, a total of 101 student papers were collected and evaluated by faculty assessors, using the ACTFL Guidelines as a reference point. In addition, a faculty committee in French and Spanish also convened in the spring 2002 semester to read, analyze and discuss a random sample of these student papers and they made important suggestions and recommendations about the quality of the student's writing in the target language major. The findings show that overall, the majority of the French and Spanish majors are writing papers at the Advanced level or above according to the ACTFL scale and are also demonstrating critical thinking skills in literary interpretation (83 out of the 101 papers were rated at the Advanced or Superior levels). It was found, however, and generally agreed upon that there are several areas in need of improvement. Some graduating students are still making basic grammatical and orthographic errors and some tend to translate directly from English into the target language resulting in awkward and incorrect usage. Some students are not using the proper format for bibliographical information, quotations, and footnotes. Other students are having difficulty going beyond only plot summaries and cannot present and defend an argument or provide a critical literary analysis.

A number of recommendations and suggestions are being considered by the faculty in light of these important findings and results. While we are heartened to confirm that most students are writing at the advanced level when they exit from our French and Spanish major programs, we are likewise eager to address the identified areas of concern. A departmental faculty task force on student writing was created in fall 2002 resulting in the establishment of a set of general writing guidelines (addressing all of the problem areas) that can be used in all the upper-level courses in order to improve student writing. The faculty task force on student writing met again in January 2003 to further discuss the findings from the student data that we have collected since 1994 and the ways to address the problem areas that were identified. In addition to establishing a common set of general writing guidelines and a scoring rubric for assessing students' work, the task force members recommend that attention be placed on the content of the advanced grammar and composition courses, FLF 310, FLS 310, FLS 311, so that there can be agreement about some of the elements that these courses need to contain. It was also suggested that the French and Spanish faculty come to a common agreement about writing and research expectations for the students in the upper-level courses, and that attention also be focused on the importance of writing throughout the curriculum, beginning in the elementary courses through the advanced. It was agreed that future faculty discussion of these topics would be beneficial to all: instructors would be able to share ideas and expectations, and faculty could perhaps agree on some common course-level specific activities and assignments.

Also, in addition to the ACTFL Guidelines, a more specific scoring rubric has now been cooperatively developed in the department for use in the assessment of student papers for the purposes of program review. The rubric was tested by several colleagues in early spring 2003 semester in order to make adjustments and to gauge its effectiveness. A group of 13 faculty would like to begin assessing student papers using this rubric at the end of spring 2003 semester and will be able to do so with the assistance of an Undergraduate Affairs Mini-Grant in support of the UAPR. Thanks to this award, the group of 13 faculty members will receive a modest stipend to meet as a group this April 2003 to assess and reflect upon a number of student papers using the newly designed rubric. The information and insights that we gain from this endeavor will assist us in continuing to identify the areas of strengths and weaknesses in our undergraduate majors and to decide upon more ways in which we can respond to our findings. Such a continued dialogue would surely enhance the kind of academic quality that we wish to see in our French and Spanish majors.

Submitted by Arlene Malinowski
March 2003

STUDENT LEARNING OUTCOMES

FOUR MODES OF INQUIRY ACROSS THE CURRICULUM

1. Problem Solving
   Example from Food Science: Majors should be able to:

   - identify, define, and analyze a problem: what it is that generates the problem, what is given, what is unknown, and what are the criteria for viable solutions to the problem.

   - determine what information is appropriate to solving the problem and then find it, assess its authority and validity, and use it effectively.

   - integrate and apply basic science and mathematics as well as food sciences to the solution of problems in food systems.

   - offer a range of potential viable solutions to the problem.

   - evaluate the solutions according to the established criteria, choose the most viable solution, and make a convincing case for that solution.

   Programs that emphasize problem solving: agricultural and resources economics, accounting, animal science, business management, engineering, forestry management, mathematics, pulp and paper science, and zoology.

2. Empirical Inquiry
   Example from Microbiology: Majors should be able to:

   - Ask pertinent questions about microbiology, formulate hypotheses based on those questions, and design experiments to test those hypotheses.

   - Apply deliberate and thorough observational skills to conduct experiments and collect data.

   - Organize and summarize data and present them in a way that is accurate and comprehensible in both verbal and graphical forms.

- Interpret data and draw conclusions that allow the students to support or refute hypotheses and make a case for alternative hypotheses.

Programs that emphasize empirical inquiry: anthropology, biology, chemistry, geology, psychology, political science, sociology, etc.

3. Research from Sources
   Example from History: Majors should be able to:

- Pose an interesting research question about history.

- Locate relevant primary and secondary sources for investigating a research question.

- Critically evaluate primary and secondary sources in terms of credibility, authenticity, interpretive stance, audience, potential biases, and value for answering the research question.

- Marshall the evidence from the research to support a historical argument for an answer to a research question.

Programs that emphasize research from sources: literature, women and gender studies, philosophy, religious studies, and multi-disciplinary studies.

4. Performance
   Example from Art and Design: Majors should be able to:

- Understand basic design principles, concepts, media, and formats in various fine arts disciplines.

- Master basic foundation techniques, particularly as related to specific fine arts fields.

- Conceive, design, and create works in one or more specific fine arts fields.

- Demonstrate a working knowledge of various production methods and their relationship to conceptualization, development, and completion of works of art.

- Understand the similarities, differences, and relationships among the various fine arts areas.

Programs that emphasize performance: architecture, graphic design, industrial design, landscape architecture, and rhetoric, writing and language.

OUTLINE OF COMMON OUTCOMES FROM UNDERGRADUATE ASSESSMENT PLANS

SUBMITTED TO CUPR, FALL 2002

I. Communication
   A. Oral communication
   B. Written communication
   C. Visual/graphic communication
   D. Interpersonal communication

II. Professional, ethical and social responsibility
   A. Knowledge and application of professional code of conduct
   B. Knowledge and application of ethical implications of profession
   C. Knowledge of contemporary issues

III. Critical evaluation
   A. Problem analysis
   B. Problem solving
   C. Informed decisionmaking

IV. Cooperative learning (team/group work experiences)
   A. Comprehension and negotiation of group dynamics
   B. Working with interdisciplinary/multidisciplinary teams
   C. Working with disciplinary teams

V. Lifelong learning
   A. Participation in professional development activities
   B. Participation in professional improvement activities
   C. Participation in professional organizations

VI. Technological competence
   A. Information gathering
   B. Information sharing

    C. Problem solving

    D. Data management

    E. General skills for employment/graduate studies

VII. Graduate competitiveness

    A. Demonstrating professional activities/behavior

    B. Competing for entry-level jobs

    C. Competing for graduate school admission

    D. Advertising/stating professional skills and abilities

    E. Demonstrating leadership

VIII. Research skills

    A. Identification of credible research resources

    B. Location of credible and valid research resources

    C. Critical review of professional literature

    D. Conducting research

IX. Cultural competence (diversity)

    A. Recognition of diverse ideas and cultural context

    B. Recognition of diverse ability and learning styles

    C. Recognition of diverse people

PART III

INQUIRY-GUIDED LEARNING PROGRAMS AND RELATED INITIATIVES

Part III first describes, in Chapter 16, two inquiry-guided learning programs for first-year students—the university-wide First Year Inquiry Program and the First Year Seminar Program in the College of Humanities and Social Sciences. In Chapters 17 and 18 we explain how other campus-wide programs—the Campus Writing and Speaking Program and the Service Learning Program—support inquiry-guided learning in significant ways.

16

INQUIRY, CRITICAL THINKING, AND FIRST YEAR PROGRAMS

By David B. Greene,
Janice Odom, and Arlene Malinowski

Introduction

As emphasized in the 1999 Boyer Commission Report, *Reinventing Under-graduate Education: A Blueprint for America's Research Universities,* the first year is critical for establishing expectations for learning and for engaging students in the life of the university. One of the report's major recommendations is, "The first year of a university experience needs to provide new stimulation for intellectual growth and a firm grounding in inquiry-based learning and communication of information and ideas" (Boyer Commission, 1999, p.19). In response to that challenge, the campus-wide First Year Inquiry (FYI) Program and the First Year Seminar Program in the College of Humanities and Social Sciences (CHASS FYS) were initiated at NCSU to provide structure and support to students' growing ability to inquire, to think critically, and to take responsibility for their own learning. By promoting active engagement and interaction among faculty and students, the FYI and the CHASS FYS programs nurture community for both students and faculty and establish expectations for learning that students can apply to other classes. In these programs, by promoting learning through the active investigation of complex questions and problems, inquiry-guided learning capitalizes on the strengths of the research faculty and draws stronger connections between teaching and research.

The First Year Inquiry Program

Every educational initiative begins with real people and quite often, an interesting story. Tracing the history and the outcomes of the First Year Inquiry Program at NCSU not only tells a good story, but also reveals a great deal about the institutional structure and particular challenges faced by this institution and how it has been affected by inquiry-guided learning. In the early 1990s two different task forces urged that a first-year seminar program be established at NCSU. Although neither of these recommendations was fruitful, a group of seven faculty members began a bold experiment in the fall of 1999 anyway. It involved seven classes, each counting toward a general education requirement, each limited to 22 students, and each restricted to first-year students. By 2002–2003, the experiment had become the NCSU First Year Inquiry Program with 59 sections, offering courses to 1,300 of the 3,200 first-year students across the university. The growth and success of the program is due to several key factors: a sustained community of faculty with a passion for student learning; adopting a *pedagogical* (i.e., inquiry-guided) rather than a content approach to defining first-year seminars; and administrative support of a faculty-led initiative.

Steps Leading to the 1999 Pilot of FYI Classes

The Recommendations That Didn't Take

In summer 1994 in response to the Provost's concerns with matriculation and graduation rates of first-year students, a task force was appointed. Among its recommendations was a first-year seminar; not a seminar focused on learning skills or the nuts and bolts of the university, which were already in existence on campus, but a first experience in reading, discussing, and questioning, or what it means to learn at the university level. The Provost scaled back plans for implementing first-year interventions, and the first-year seminar was one of the casualties. The operation was seen as top-down and too hastily patched together. In response, the Faculty Senate assembled the Committee on Undergraduate Student Success (CUSS) that worked for the next two years on defining indices of student success. CUSS proposed, among other recommendations, a first-year seminar based on empirical evidence from other universities that a small-class experience in the first year had positive effects on student persistence at the university and their performance in sophomore courses. However, no faculty group offered to figure out how to recruit and train faculty or where to place the course in the curriculum, and no administrator offered to fund it. It was easy to conclude that a first-year seminar would never be established at this university. Either the first-year seminar was a top-down proposal that had no grass roots support, or it was a faculty idea that the administration couldn't fund. Yet, it was also possible to imagine that people were getting used to the idea and that maybe the right time was imminent.

Hewlett I

In fall 1996 NCSU received an invitation from the William and Flora Hewlett Foundation to submit a proposal for improving general education at a Research Extensive (or Research I, as it was then called) institution. At this point, faculty initiative and administrative support began, for the first time, to work together. The Provost's office sent the invitation to the Council for Undergraduate Education (CUE), comprising 30 faculty with concerns about learning and pedagogy as well as curricular issues. Having just completed a position statement on student's responsibility for their education and the faculty's role in helping develop this responsibility (see Appendix 15.A), the council was eager to take up the challenge, and the Provost's office provided funding for a grant writer.

The full story of the Hewlett grant has been told earlier (see Chapter 2). However, one of the subcommittees formed under the grant is particularly relevant to the inception of the FYI Program. The group considered pedagogical questions such as, "What is the difference between a general education course in, for example, history and a first course in history for prospective history majors?" "What might students learn in one general education course that they can use in other general education courses and in their major courses?" "What pedagogy is likely to help students grow beyond dualistic thinking (as defined in the Perry model of intellectual development)?" "What can we do to help students understand that worthwhile learning requires hard work and serious commitment?" "What can we do to help students retain what they learn?" "What can we do to see that general education courses are deeply relevant to quality of life and individual responsibility issues?"

As the two years of Hewlett I were coming to a close, members of this committee asked each other, "Would a course restricted to a small number of first-year students be a suitable place to work on these questions?" They realized the only way to find out was to give it a try. They each agreed to transform a course they were regularly teaching into a First Year Inquiry course and deliberately address these issues while still helping students achieve the same content objectives as their original courses. Thus, the seven initial FYI courses were born.

In developing and populating these courses, the group had to mobilize several administrative branches of the university quickly. Looking back, we are astonished that so many people were willing to be so cooperative: registration officers, scheduling officers, advisers, deans of academic affairs, and the people who do summer orientation. It began to look as though faculty and administration were no longer out of synch!

What made things finally come together? For one thing there was the prestige of the Hewlett grant: Recognition by an outside agency added considerable legitimacy to what the faculty were trying to do. Also, people had grown to see the importance and positive outcomes of interventions for first-year students and had gotten used to the idea of a first-year seminar. Perhaps most importantly was the passion and commitment of the seven faculty.[1] The respect they already carried on campus enabled the projects' acceptance. Finally, the project made sense. It was minimally disruptive: no new courses to approve or to work up; no new cost to anybody except the faculty doing it; and nobody's curriculum to be changed, for the courses all met existing requirements.

From the 1999 Pilot to 55 Sections in 2003

The seven faculty met monthly to share stories, and as they did they gradually honed the list of program objectives to four:

- Offer students guided practice in critical thinking.
- Enable students to take responsibility for their own education.
- Help students grow away from dualistic thinking and toward intellectual maturity.
- Develop a sense for and skill in inquiry.

(These program objectives have also become the shared outcomes of all IGL programs, projects, and courses at the university.)

Despite the struggles of a new venture, the first run of FYI courses deepened the commitment of the seven faculty as they struggled to sharpen teaching strategies and handle student reaction to the demands of inquiry-guided learning. Meanwhile, the Provost expressed an interest in supporting the program from tuition-increase funds. This funding made it possible to give participating faculty members a $1,000 stipend for the increased effort of reworking their course to integrate FYI objectives into the course's cognitive objectives and for the increased time for attending program workshops in inquiry-guided learning strategies and the monthly faculty team meetings. Ongoing funding and administrative support from the Division of Undergraduate Affairs has provided program advocacy, while encouraging and allowing faculty leadership of the program has been key to its sustained energy.

Expanding the program raised a number of questions beyond funding: Where were the additional faculty members to come from? How were they to be trained? Should part-time faculty teach FYI sections? How was the program to be assessed? How would students be recruited? Who would tend to course listings and enrollments? Can we pursue FYI objectives only at the expense of the course's content objectives? The timing was evidently right, for a number of these questions were more easily answered than expected. We

---

[1] The original group included Sarah Ash (Animal Science), Alton Banks (Chemistry), David Greene (Multidisciplinary Studies), Nancy Gustke (History), Erin Malloy-Hanley (Multidisciplinary Studies), Janice Odom (First Year College), and Samuel Pond (Psychology).

approached the 50-plus faculty who participated in Hewlett I about teaching an FYI class. And every Hewlett Fellow in turn had a friend who also cared about teaching As a result of this commitment, we've been able to increase in number of sections by 10 a year.

First Year Inquiry faculty members represent an array of disciplines: physics, biology, mathematics, chemistry, English, history, music, philosophy, religion, communication, sociology, political science, psychology, foreign languages, and multidisciplinary studies. While other first-year programs in the United States are typically orientation and skills courses or special topics courses, FYI courses are not special in their *content,* but in their overall learning outcomes and resulting *pedagogy.*

The shift of faculty focus from content to method has not been without concern and protracted conversation. For some FYI faculty members, it was intuitively obvious that pursuing the FYI objectives necessarily meant covering less material, and they worried that their students would not be adequately prepared for the next course in the sequence. One response to this worry was that if they exposed students to only 80% of the material, but students actually mastered and retained 90% of it, they were in better shape than if they had exposed students to 100%, and the students retained only 60% of it. Another response was that pursuing the FYI objectives need not diminish the amount of material presented, but had to do with *how* one presented the material. The small class size, the FYI faculty have agreed, enables them to use strategies that encourage inquiry-guided learning to present the same amount of material. A slogan that has gained acceptance is "Move from strategies in which the teacher *covers* the material to strategies in which the students *uncover* it."

Whatever their content, the FYI courses have four objectives in common. Working on this pedagogy and these objectives has been a bonding activity for the faculty. Literally all the faculty involved report that the monthly meetings in which they share ideas and approaches with colleagues from very different disciplines are among the most energizing sessions they have enjoyed at the university. One faculty member remarked, "In over 34 years at NC State, these are the first truly productive conversations about teaching and learning that I have had." Another faculty member has credited the FYI Program through its impact on faculty, and subsequently on students, with "deepening the intellectual climate at NC State."

Topics of discussion at FYI faculty meetings include characteristics of writing assignments that encourage demonstration of critical-thinking skills, rubrics for evaluating written work, classroom strategies for encouraging student discussion, designing experiential learning components, and meeting the particular needs and challenges of first-year students. Focusing on teaching and learning has been a shared challenge that has allowed cross-curricular discussion. The pursuit of weighty questions about teaching and learning has honed the teaching practice. Like their students, FYI faculty members have had an inquiry-driven, enriched learning experience.

The CHASS First Year Seminar Program

On a campus with a first-year class of approximately 3,200 students each fall, there exists the opportunity and need for multiple, complementary programs aimed at creating smaller communities of learning. With the addition of the CHASS FYS program, commitment at NCSU to inquiry-guided learning with first-year students took another step forward.

The CHASS First Year Seminar was initiated in the 2000–2001 academic year following the recommendations of a faculty committee that was committed to the success of CHASS first-year students. One perceived key to success was the creation of a sense of identity for students within the College of Humanities and Social Sciences. We envisioned a first-year seminar unique to CHASS as a way to ensure that, from the start, the new CHASS student interacts closely with members of the full-time CHASS faculty who are committed to developing the skills of critical thinking and inquiry in small introductory courses. CHASS faculty offer courses from their own disciplines in anthropology, communication, English, history, multidisciplinary studies, philosophy, political science, psychology, religion, and sociology.

Similar to FYI courses, a central feature of CHASS First Year Seminars is an emphasis on inquiry-guided learning and the development of critical-thinking skills regardless of disciplinary approach. In addition, CHASS has drawn upon the opportunities of common mission and centralized administration to add distinctive features to the seminars. First, CHASS FYS classes are scheduled in the same time block to facilitate coordinated common learning events involving all students. Second, CHASS FYS courses are annually organized around a common theme, such as "The World, the Nation and the Self" or "Ethics and Justice in Global Perspective." The same time block and shared themes have allowed for common learning events, such as an interactive session that focused on indigenous rights and globalization led by a faculty member in the History department. This session consisted of film clips, historical documents, and small group discussion questions designed to engage students in critical thinking and inquiry within and across a large group. Another event consisted of a midterm colloquium where students heard an address on "The World, the Nation and the Self: Building a Culture of Trust in the 21st Century." At yet another event, students discussed common reading selections read by several of the CHASS FYS classes. At the conclusion of each event, students wrote a short reaction statement addressing the following questions.

- What did you learn from the session that you did not know before?
- What questions did it answer for you?
- What new questions did it raise for you?
- How did this session relate to what you are learning in your seminar this semester?

The solicitation and selection of the proposed courses and biannual themes for the seminars is coordinated through a CHASS First Year Seminar Committee, made up of faculty representing all the departments in the college. We offer approximately 20 seminars each year, to accommodate the approximate 500 first-year students in CHASS. The CHASS dean's office funds a $1,000 stipend for faculty that parallels the FYI stipend and compensates for the additional expectations of attending IGL seminars and discussion meetings. A small discretionary fund is also available to the director of the program for related program expenses during the year.

As the CHASS FYS program has evolved, it has focused increasingly on faculty development and assessment of student learning. Workshops offer the instructors an opportunity to explore, discuss, and review the advantages of inquiry-guided learning so that they can enhance the use of cooperative learning, problem-based learning, and case studies in their seminar courses for first-year students, and hopefully in their other courses as well. The workshops are useful as a forum for sharing ideas; discussing readings, such as excerpts from *Understanding by Design* (Wiggins & J. McTighe, 1998); and constructing goals and objectives consonant with inquiry-guided learning that are appropriate for young adult learners. Faculty have also worked together to identify the following student learning outcomes, that is, the competencies that students should possess upon completion of the CHASS First Year Seminars:

- Demonstrate in writing an ability to articulate and critically evaluate a problem or issue relating to the common theme of "Ethics and Justice in Global Perspective."
- Inquire about, reflect upon, and discuss with others a series of complex problems or questions related to the common theme.
- Compare and contrast different approaches and perspectives with respect to the theme within the context of each course.
- Demonstrate taking responsibility for one's learning by developing a personal code of behavior that is consistent with intellectual growth and maturity.

Assessment of Inquiry-guided Learning in the FYI and CHASS First Year Seminars

From the inception of NCSU'S inquiry-guided seminars, faculty have paralleled students' content-specific inquiry with their own significant questions regarding teaching and assessment: How do we know what impact this learning environment is having on our students? Are we indeed meeting our program objectives? How does one recognize when and to what extent a student is thinking critically? The pursuit of these questions has honed faculty understanding and teaching practice as well as solidified the faculty through the shared challenge and significance of this undertaking.

Assessing inquiry-guided seminars at NCSU has been an iterative process. We assign students in each FYI or CHASS seminar a course-related essay early and late in the semester, and faculty review a sample of these pairs to gauge any progress in critical thinking. Faculty struggled over the scoring rubric before settling on use of the *Facione & Facione Holistic Critical Thinking Scoring Rubric* (available online at www.insightassessment.com/pdf_files/rubric.pdf). At first, all faculty participated in scoring samples of papers from all FYI sections, but in the last three semesters this task has been assigned to an ongoing committee of 10 faculty who have been specially trained in essay scoring. Faculty have also struggled with specific questions on the nature and procedures of the assignment: How can students think critically on a topic before they know anything about it? What is a good topic for this exercise? Should the first paper count as part of the student's course grade? Should students know that their papers might be read by a scoring team? Should students know the rubric against which their work will be placed? Grappling with these questions has strengthened the faculty's sense of owning and collectively managing a complex program.

The before-and-after essay exercise serves as a tool in program assessment and is not intended to assess instruction. Quantitative measures of critical thinking are available, but there is considerable debate about the applicability of these instruments and whether they can show demonstrable change within a single semester. In addition, the qualitative essay exercise provides rich information about the students' ability to think critically. The essays reveal evidence of the students' developing ability to grapple with significant global issues by analyzing and evaluating an argument and drawing judicious conclusions based on available sources.

Each semester, FYI and CHASS FYS students and faculty also respond to questionnaires about their experience. We ask students to report on the nature of their classroom experience: for example, the incidence of class discussions, breakout groups, and other opportunities for inquiry-guided learning. Students' reflections about specific aspects of their experiences in the courses serve to assess the program objectives of FYI and CHASS FYS, namely, that students will improve their ability to think critically, will develop responsibility for their own learning, will advance toward intellectual maturity, and will become skilled inquirers. On average, 70% of FYI students' reflections about a time when they were called upon to think critically during the course and to give details reveal a clear understanding of what critical thinking requires; however, 30% do not reflect a clear understanding of critical thinking.

Responses to questions about changing as learners during an FYI course indicate a trend toward taking greater responsibility for one's own learning. Students' comments include: "I am better at speaking out." "I am a better listener." "I listen more carefully and longer than I used to." "I am better at writing essays." "I am more internally motivated." "I question things more often." "I am more open to different points of view and find different points of view more quickly." "I see all sides of a question." "I am able to make connections." "Now I learn by interacting with my fellow students." "Now I know how to go deeper into a subject, and also look more broadly for what is seen from different points of view." "I know how to read." "I get beneath the surface of what is said in the lecture or in the reading." "I know how to take notes." "I learned how to use sources." "The course has changed my outlook on class and shown how I can be a better student." "When looking at data I now think, 'Is the source reliable?' 'Was it written for a certain audience?' I analyze the information through these lenses rather than just accepting everything." "*All* of the work involved critical thinking. Simply memorizing data wasn't required or used and therefore this class was more challenging." "I've learned *so* much more than facts. I've learned to *think . . .*"

In reflecting on their CHASS FYS experience, student comments included the impact the seminars had on their sense of connection to the College of Humanities and Social Sciences, to the college experience, and to larger world issues. "I found the size of the class helpful. It is easier to adjust with fewer students and understand concepts. I felt united with the CHASS program and everything I learned was extremely useful." "It was a very interesting course that got me acquainted with the library and uses a LOT of deep, critical thinking. It is very helpful in preparing me for what is to come in the next 3 years at NC State." "I have really enjoyed being part of my CFYS. The challenges that await our generation are looming not so far in the distance. I feel that it is *so* important to have discussions like today's where students are forced to evaluate their *own* positions on cross-cultural differences, globalization, Americanization, and the effects of their own culture. Perhaps the questions we have asked today will go on and mystify and confuse many others after us. But the point is not to arrive at answers as much as it is to do the thinking and struggle with the ideas and conflicts along the way. *This* is true learning, and the most valuable kind."

IGL, the Campus Community, and the Future

Innovations continue in the NCSU effort to expand inquiry-guided learning opportunities for first-year students. For three years, the FYI Program has partnered with the First Year College (FYC), an intensive advising program for first-year students, to offer first semester students a living/learning experience. Students who enter NCSU via the First Year College select one of two FYC resident halls. They are then randomly assigned to FYI sections and co-enrolled in a paired section of the First Year College orientation course. In addition to the shared living community and co-enrollment in two classes, faculty lead field trips and experiential learning opportunities relevant to the FYI class topic. FYI faculty and First Year College advisers who have taught in the learning community model report a higher level of engagement and responsibility among these students. Analysis of grade point averages indicates students in the paired classes have a significantly higher grade point average for their first semester than students in nonpaired sections taught by the same adviser. The FYI students in learning communities are more likely to report that they know more students in their class and know them better than students who are not in the learning community. Future learning community assessment plans include a comparative study of noncognitive aspects of development. A longitudinal study is planned to examine the FYI Program's impact on student engagement, retention, and graduation.

Several FYI faculty members have created partnerships with various campus units, including the Faculty Center for Teaching and Learning's Service-Learning Program, the Center for Student Leadership, Ethics and Service, and the Study Abroad Office to incorporate an off-campus engagement component into their FYI courses. Targeting spring break for an extended "field trip" component of the FYI course, faculty have led trips to destinations as diverse as the Navajo Nation in Tuba City, Arizona; Guatemala; Spain; and Cuba.

Inquiry-guided learning experiences for first-year students continue to evolve at NCSU. The major thrust, however, remains focused on developing students' ability to think critically and to inquire intelligently. As each semester passes, FYI and CHASS FYS faculty renew their commitments to nurturing first-year students as they and their students continue to deepen their understandings of inquiry-guided learning. It would be a mistake to conclude that at NCSU interest in student-focused, learning-centered pedagogy began in the mid-1990s or that the institutionalization of the FYI or CHASS FYS Programs depended exclusively on either the Hewlett Program or the Faculty Center for Teaching and Learning's support. The immediate and widespread faculty response to these programs indicates that many faculty members were already concerned and prepared to address first-year students' learning issues. These efforts helped people find one another. The new programs provided a place where people could meet, discover commonalties, air differences, negotiate agreements, and move forward together.

Conclusion

The cognitive psychologist Ausubel and his colleagues (1978) wrote about the importance of meaning and problem solving in the construction of human learning. They present an explanation and rationale for the importance of learning by discovery and through problem solving consistent with the approach to inquiry-guided learning found in the two university programs described in this chapter. True and lasting learning is developmental and proceeds by stages leading the students to self-motivated and independent learning. The First Year Inquiry Program and the CHASS First Year Seminar Program, therefore, support student learning in a profound way. They represent the kind of meaningful learning that NCSU is trying to promote in the early academic experiences of first-year students at our university.

References

Ausubel, D. P., Novak, J. D., & Hanesian, H. (1978). *Educational psychology: a cognitive view* (2nd ed.). New York: Holt, Rinehart, & Winston.

The Boyer Commission on Educating Undergraduates in the Research University. (1999). *Reinventing undergraduate education: A blueprint for America's research universities.* Stonybrook, NY: State University of New York at Stonybrook.

Wiggins, G., & McTighe, J. (1998). *Understanding by design.* Alexandria, VA: Association for Supervision and Curriculum Development.

17

THE HEART OF THE MATTER

WRITING, SPEAKING, AND INQUIRY-GUIDED LEARNING

By Chris M. Anson and Deanna P. Dannels

An Internet search for classroom strategies that support inquiry-guided learning yields dozens of useful sites with a wealth of creative ideas. In almost every case, writing and speaking play a significant role, enhancing each learning activity through moments of critical written reflection, verbal exchanges of ideas and observations, or group activities involving writing and discussion. For example, R. Russell Wilke's course component paper, "Inquiry Learning Strategies for Busy Science Practitioners" (Russell, 2002) describes several ways to support the processes of scientific inquiry that are a crucial part of his biology courses, processes such as observing, classifying, measuring, predicting, inferring, summarizing, collecting data, and interpreting evidence. The strategies, organized sequentially to realize certain goals of inquiry, include written and oral responses to instructor-generated questions, "think-pair-share" activities, and one-minute reflective papers. Although Wilke's goals are strongly focused on the teaching of science, his inquiry-based activities are almost entirely dependent on writing and speaking for their success. Put simply, writing and speaking are the heart and lifeblood of inquiry-guided learning, driving and sustaining virtually all its intellectual and social processes. Although it is possible for students to become active learners through non-language-based activities, such activities are rare, and are themselves rarely used independently of writing and speaking.

In this chapter, we first sketch an approach to communication across the curriculum (CAC) oriented toward inquiry-guided learning. This approach requires that we see writing and speaking as tools for student learning and development, not simply as ways to demonstrate (and assess) acquired knowledge and ability. We then describe how the Campus Writing and Speaking Program (CWSP) at NCSU supports inquiry-guided learning by helping faculty to infuse language activities into their courses in new and creative ways.

From Output to Input: Rethinking the Role of Writing and Speaking

A glance at any typical syllabus in a college or university course shows that writing and speaking assignments are almost always used to grade student performance. We ask students to write papers so that we can judge something—the evidence of their accumulated knowledge of a subject, their ability to support an argument or position about the course material, their ability to express themselves in writing. When students give oral presentations, their performances are likewise evaluated for the clarity of their ideas, the way they have translated information and can present it effectively to an audience of their peers, or even their demeanor, eye contact, and hand gestures. Our predominant focus on assessment is often reflected in elaborate rubrics or scoring guides that accompany the assignment: We give (or take off) points for the formal characteristics of finished products, such as organization, style, thoroughness of research, evidence for assertions, and elegance of presentation.

Although writing and speaking serve an important evaluative purpose in our classrooms—after all, there are only a few nonverbal ways for students to show us what they have learned—when we restrict ourselves to these purposes, we lose valuable opportunities to engage students more fully in the content and methods of our disciplines and subject matter. For students to become actively engaged in their own learning, they need to use language processes as input as well as output, as a means to articulate and explore what they know as well as a means—much later in the process of learning—to express their accumulated knowledge and expertise to others for consideration.

This reorientation from output to input requires us to reconsider the nature and role of writing and speaking in our classrooms, including especially their level of formality. Formally assessed products of language are admittedly final and finished—carefully rehearsed or revised, with attention to audience response, style, and accuracy. Writing-to-learn and speaking-to-learn activities, in contrast, are used spontaneously and often quickly at early stages of topic exploration, without opportunities to revise or rehearse. For this reason, they do not lend themselves to formality either in presentation or in assessment. It would be bizarre for us to ask students to write (or speak with others) for three minutes to begin exploring a complex topic, and then evaluate their performances for elegant style, careful organization, or adherence to the conventions of academic prose or elocution. Instead, we would want to look at their work as evidence of engagement—of inquiry and active exploration.

By way of illustration, consider some of the activities used by NCSU Psychology instructor Karen St. Clair. She uses informal writing and speaking constantly in her courses, as a way to engage students in their own learning and to help them to acquire certain skills of inquiry common in her field of psychology. In her Psychology 201 course, "Controversial Psychological Issues," such activities include the following:

- *Anticipatory writing and speaking about an upcoming topic.* Students informally explore a topic area to gauge the degree of their knowledge or test out their assumptions and beliefs.
- *"Evaluating the evidence."* St. Clair provides the students with published empirical research and asks them to consider and report informally on the validity of the methods and conclusions.
- *"Applying the critical thinking process."* Students informally report on analyses of controversial statements chosen from a list, such as "most women are natural mothers."
- *"The main point."* Students informally write or speak for a minute or two, focusing on the main point of a mini-lecture, reading, or class discussion.
- *Illustrations and explanations.* Students use visual media, such as paper, symbols, or props, to convey the meaning of certain principles or concepts to an audience.
- *"Voices."* Students convey different types of people's stances on controversial topics—a mother, a clergyman, a child—in order to tease out stereotyped responses or examine the relationship between position and belief. (St. Clair, 2002)

In these and other informal activities, St. Clair's goal is to support the process of inquiry, which, in a general education course in psychology, includes developing the ability to research, analyze, evaluate, and make decisions about the details of complex contemporary issues in the field. She uses writing and speaking as "input" to help her students to acquire these skills. At the same time, St. Clair's observations of the students' products—informal freewrites, brief reports and presentations, and the like—allow her to assess how effectively students are achieving these goals. In this case, evaluation is not entirely about student performance; just as importantly, St. Clair is also inquiring into the effectiveness of her own instruction. The evidence of learning, or lack thereof, guides her subsequent decisions as a teacher, both in the course itself and in her overall efforts as a teacher.

St. Clair's use of these informal writing and speaking activities supports students' learning as an end in itself; the "products" are improved learning on the part of her students, and enhanced teaching on the part of St. Clair, as illustrated in Figure 17.1.

Another inquiry-based use of informal writing and speaking, however, supports the development of formal papers and presentations. As shown in Figure 17.2, the writing and speaking activities comprise a process of inquiry that yields a formal written or orally presented product. Breaking down a large, formal project into many smaller episodes of discovery, invention, and sharing—all of which can be done quickly and informally—leads to more polished, insightful work and subverts the allure of preformulated material (including entire papers) readily available to students on the Internet.

This inquiry-based use of writing and speaking that culminates in a formal product is illustrated in NCSU Professor Helga Braunbeck's course, jointly listed in Foreign Languages and Literatures and the Department of English (Braunbeck, 2001). The course, "Literatures of the Western World II," covers a number of "masterpieces" of mostly European literature (in translation) from Enlightenment to the early 20th century. In Braunbeck's version of the course, students complete a number of short assignments that give them practice in the processes of literary inquiry. Small group work on focused questions demonstrates the processes of careful reading and analysis of a literary work. Students write informal responses and share these orally in the groups; each student also takes notes during the meeting and may be asked to give a brief report of the group's process and conclusions. A series of brief writing assignments leads up

Figure 17.1   Learning-based Writing and Speaking Model.

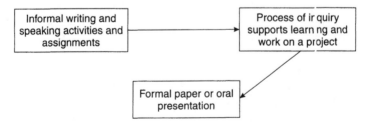

Figure 17.2   Process-based Model of Writing and Speaking in Support of Formal Projects.

to drafts of two formal papers, each of which is discussed in peer critique sessions before the students prepare revised versions to turn in. The informal assignments include practice annotating original texts to capture ideas for analysis; sample outlines of analysis that could lead to papers; freewrites about images or metaphors in passages of text; and practice describing and analyzing the physical setting of a story or novel. By the time students begin to work on a formal paper or oral presentation of their analysis, they have engaged in a number of low-risk writing and speaking activities that have honed their skills of literary inquiry. By looking at the results of this informal work, Braunbeck can also gauge the need for mini-lectures, resources, or further practice in those areas of inquiry with which the students continue to need help.

Supporting IGL in a Communication Across the Curriculum Program

Since their inception, communication across the curriculum (CAC) programs have focused mainly on improving the writing and speaking abilities of undergraduate students. The need for such work is important and still pressing, as students move from college into professional arenas that increasingly demand the ability to communicate effectively in complex, often team-based environments. In support of these skills, many CAC programs work with faculty and students to enhance writing and speaking competencies that will benefit students both in college and beyond.

Like many similar programs around the country, the Campus Writing and Speaking Program at NCSU supports the goal of improving students' abilities to write and speak effectively. Yet the program does not restrict itself to a skills orientation. In addition, it also helps faculty to engage students more actively as learners by linking classroom strategies and activities to the processes of discovery and inquiry that characterize specific disciplines. The mission of the CWSP, therefore, includes an explicit emphasis on learning in addition to the emphasis on communicative competence in the disciplines.

Recognizing the dual aspects of this mission, the CWSP uses a goal-based approach in working with faculty on incorporating writing and speaking into their courses. As faculty work to improve their courses, the program encourages them to choose writing and speaking strategies that best match their own course goals. The overarching framework, as depicted in Figure 17.3, is based on a three-stage instructional design model: (1) identifying learning goals; (2) designing assignments and teaching strategies to meet those goals; and (3) informally evaluating the extent to which students have met those goals. The model is recursive; as teachers assess the outcomes of their activities, they often modify their goals and/or create new strategies to realize those goals, ensuring that students are fully engaged as inquirers into the subject of their courses and that this inquiry is leading to gains in their knowledge and abilities.

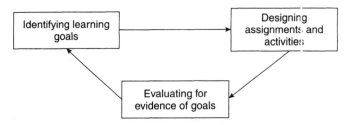

Figure 17.3   A Goal-based Model of Writing and Speaking Activities.

When working with faculty interested in inquiry-guided issues, we first encourage them to begin by creating writing and speaking goals that are inquiry guided in nature. These goals typically focus less on communication competence and more on the processes that lead to learning course content. Some sample course goals related to inquiry-guided learning include the following:

- Students will develop the ability to consider alternative views, perspectives, or positions on a subject.
- Students will develop the ability to find support for claims and use that support judiciously and ethically.
- Students will be able to develop the ability to deepen understanding or analysis through heuristic processes.
- Students will be able to develop the ability to relate new information to other areas of thought or inquiry.

Next we provide faculty with a framework within which they can create a variety of writing and speaking assignments that can potentially meet their inquiry-guided goals. This framework places activities and assignments along a continuum from the most informal (those explicitly used to achieve learning-based goals) to the most formal (those explicitly used to achieve competence-based goals), as depicted in Figure 17.4.

As faculty work with the continuum, they recognize that activities on the left side of the continuum are designed and used explicitly to encourage active, critical, and analytical learning in the classroom, processes fundamental to inquiry of all kinds. In this way, writing and speaking activities are not used to test communication competence, nor are they assessed by using formal, traditional standards of professional writing or speaking. Rather, they are assessed according to the extent to which that learning occurs.

In the middle of the continuum are strategies that are still done quickly—usually overnight, without revision or rehearsal. But unlike the freeform, spontaneous, and often associative responses on the leftmost side of the continuum, these assignments are more sharply focused, sometimes specifying certain audiences or purposes, or constrained by form (e.g., a letter, a mini-presentation

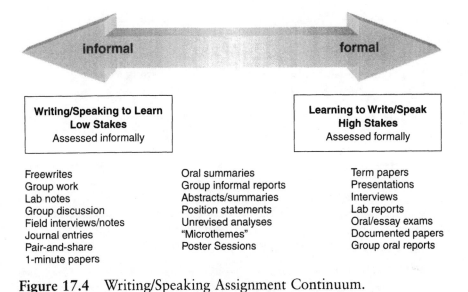

Figure 17.4   Writing/Speaking Assignment Continuum.

whose notes must fit on one 3" × 5" card, an annotation of no more than 50 words). Because there are some minimal requirements for such assignments, they are sometimes graded using an informal rubric, the results contributing in small (but cumulative) ways to the student's overall grade.

On the right end of the continuum, writing and speaking strategies support the development of communicative competence—learning the conventions, genres, and discourse that characterize a skilled writer or speaker in a discipline. Although we encourage faculty to locate their own course goals along the continuum, we hope they consider the continuum fluid—that they understand the ways in which all writing and speaking activities (regardless of where they lie on the continuum) potentially support learning-based goals of inquiry. For example, more formal strategies that focus primarily on teaching writing and speaking competence also compel students to inquire into the course content in complex, learning-rich ways. Typically, though, faculty interested in inquiry-guided instruction design assignments that are best located along the left side of the continuum. Some sample writing and speaking assignments related to inquiry-guided learning include:

- Mini-presentations to encourage thoughtful reading or analysis
- Brief, journal-like responses to integrate new subject matter into existing knowledge
- Writing or oral responses to cases that students must analyze using new tools

- Collaborative poster sessions that present the results of processes involving inquiry
- Small group sharing that anchors or extends learning
- Process journals that illustrate the learning happening as students prepare for formal writing or speaking assignments

The final step in the design framework involves creating assessment measures to evaluate students' writing and speaking activities (and hence their learning). In this step, we ask faculty to look back at their goals and decide what counts as evidence that students have achieved those goals. In this way, we challenge faculty to shift their thinking about grading writing and speaking—to pay less attention to the form or delivery and to pay more attention to the evidence of learning and the processes of inquiry that students engage in when they complete the assignment or activity. Sample assessment processes that emerge for inquiry-guided goals and assignments include

- Self-evaluations focused on personal intellectual gains
- Parallel texts that explain the students' intent and processes involved with creating a product
- Portfolios that display processes of learning that happen throughout the course
- Spontaneously given tasks designed to gauge the acquisition of critical-thinking processes and skills

Although the CWSP uses a goal-based approach in all faculty development activities, we also design specific faculty development workshops that are more explicitly devoted to inquiry-guided writing and speaking assignments. The following faculty development workshops illustrate some of the CWSP programmatic activities that have been designed to focus on learning-based goals.

- "Are Your Students Really Thinking? Using Writing and Speaking to Improve Learning"
- "Beyond a Reasonable Doubt: Using Writing and Speaking to Enhance Analysis of Arguments"
- "If Only They Were Better Readers: Writing, Speaking, and Assigned Reading"
- "Writing, Speaking, and Problem-based Learning"
- "A Case for Writing and Speaking in Context: Using Case Studies in the Classroom"

Driven by the CWSP focus on writing and speaking, these and other workshops all have at the core a focus on active learning in which students become participants in their own understanding of and inquiry into course content.

In its support of the IGL initiative on the NCSU campus, the Campus Writing and Speaking Program has been blessed with faculty and administrators in other programs who are passionate about collaboration. As we have teamed up with others to support improvements in the climate for undergraduate education, we have realized that in spite of slight differences in terminology or in focus, all of us are united in common educational goals. The Campus Writing and Speaking Program has benefited from these partnerships in innumerable ways, rethinking our approaches to instruction and the role of writing and speaking. In turn, we have been able to bring new perspectives and strategies to faculty interested in providing the best instruction they can to their students, regardless of their fields.

References

Braunbeck, H. (2001). ENG/FL 222: Masterpieces of the Western Tradition II (course materials). www2.chass.ncsu.edu/CWSP/fac_seminar/sem_archives/for_lang_lit.html.

St. Clair, K. (2002). PSY 201: Introduction to Controversial Issues (course materials). www2.chass.ncsu.edu/CWSP/fac_seminar/sem_archives/psych.html.

Wilke, R. R. (2002). Inquiry learning strategies for the busy science practitioner. TxCEPT Course Component Paper, National Science Foundation Grant No. DUE 9987332. www.sci.tamucc.edu/txcetp/cr/ InquiryLearningStrategies.pdf.

18

SERVICE-LEARNING

INTEGRATING INQUIRY AND ENGAGEMENT

By Sarah L. Ash and Patti H. Clayton

As a land grant institution, NCSU has a long history of service to society. However, a recent Kellogg Commission cited the need to redefine "outreach"—moving beyond the traditional unidirectional model of transference of research-based knowledge—to a more reciprocal relationship among faculty, students, and the community. In this new model of "engagement," faculty and students partner with members of the community to identify and address social concerns. The NCSU Service-Learning Program has grown out of our institutional commitment to become one of the nation's premier "engaged" universities, and it plays an important role in harnessing the power of students' energies and abilities to contribute to this reconceptualized engagement mission. Service-learning (SL) itself explicitly uses inquiry-guided learning to help accomplish the goals of this civic mission, because it gives students first-hand experience in applying the process of inquiry to inform action on important social issues.

As we will describe more fully in this chapter, SL exemplifies all of the basic objectives of IGL: critical thinking, independent inquiry, responsibility for one's own learning, and intellectual growth and maturity. In fact, Boyer and Hechinger foreshadowed the important relationship between SL and IGL over 20 years ago when they described institutions of higher learning as places for faculty and students "to come together to gather data, test ideas, reflect upon deeper meanings, and weigh alternative conclusions" in order "to help shape a citizenry that can weigh decisions wisely and more effectively promote the common good" (1981, p. 60). Thus our two campus-wide initiatives, inquiry and engagement, have been mutually reinforcing. Engagement offers undergraduates unparalleled opportunities to investigate important questions and to do so within a concrete context that has meaning and relevance to their lives. In addition, applying principles of IGL to community involvement makes engagement a much more powerful experience for the students and the community alike. It improves the quality of both students' learning and their service and produces more meaningful outcomes for the community by enhancing student service with careful inquiry into the complexity of the issues at hand. In other words, SL effectively integrates inquiry and engagement with the result that "SL opportunities available through engagement . . . not only strengthen [our students'] academic programs but enhance their positions as citizen-leaders" (Commission on the Future of NC State, 2000).

Service-learning as a Model for Inquiry-guided Learning

Engagement with the Community as the Context for Inquiry

Service-learning is a form of experiential education in which students render meaningful service in community settings that present complex issues related to academic material. Through guided reflection, individually and collaboratively, students critically examine their experiences from academic, as well as personal and civic, perspectives, thereby deepening their understanding of course material, their self-awareness, and their capacities as citizens and change agents.

As an example, students in "Contemporary Science, Technology, and Human Values" partnered with local assisted living facilities. The course content places scientific development and technological change in a social context, examining the impact of scientific and technological development on society and vice versa and focusing especially on the ways in which leadership is being redefined in the information age. In their SL project, students solicited donations of computer equipment, worked with the staff of the facilities to install it, and then helped the residents gain confidence in using the computers to search the web, play games, send email, or make birthday cards for family members. Through systematic reflection, the students explored such issues as intergenerational perspectives on technological change (academic), the assumptions and skills they bring to interaction with the elderly (personal), and the challenges involved in working to effect change within the constraints of their partner organizations (civic).

Because students are full partners in SL, they have an equal voice with faculty and community partners in defining project objectives and in conceptualizing the problem or issue to be addressed. Given their relative inexperience with the issues in question, however, effectiveness in this role requires meaningful inquiry into the nature of the problem or issue in question, not only before beginning the service but continuously throughout the project. Repeated interactions during the project yield new dimensions of the issue and demand additional layers of understanding. In the case of the computer project, questions such as the following helped to frame the issues: In what ways are the lives of the elderly limited and how can they (and can they not) be enhanced through access to computers? What particular challenges do they face in using computer technology? And, more fundamentally, why are so many elderly members of our society not involved in processes of technological change, and with what consequences?

Students also evaluate the range of possible approaches to serving the population in question. They consider what factors influence the choice of responses, in what ways the issues call for "quick fixes" or for long-term systemic change, and what resources are available and how they can be mobilized. In the case of the computer project, students evaluated the costs and benefits of bringing laptops to the facilities during each visit versus permanently installing donated equipment in a public space, and they struggled with the trade-offs between responding in the short term to the interests of the residents and developing the facilities' capacity to support computer access over the long term. Coming to both expect and respect the difficulties inherent in the process of problem-definition and problem-resolution, the students often find multiple and even contradictory answers to important questions. In the process they struggle with ambiguity and complexity as inherent characteristics of real-world inquiry and of change agency.

Reflection as the Central Mechanism for Inquiry

Guided, integrative reflection is key to helping students learn to deal with the complex problems that can arise when working with others in an actual community setting. Finding appropriate resolutions is often, at best, a matter of trade-offs. Students need to make sense of and sort through multiple perspectives and interpretations before they can bring a critical perspective to bear on the process of taking action that has real consequences. Reflection, which takes service activities out of the realm of strictly volunteerism, is itself a process of inquiry, defined over 70 years ago by Dewey as "active, persistent and careful consideration of any belief or supposed form of knowledge in the light of the grounds that support it, and the further conclusions to which it tends" (1910, p. 6).

Structured reflection mechanisms help students make connections and deepen their learning, but in such a way that the students themselves often identify which elements of their experience are most reflection-worthy and what aspects of course material or of their personal lives are most relevant to the analysis. With reflection occurring continuously (i.e., before the project begins, throughout the project, and after the project concludes) and in multiple forums, over the course of the semester students internalize the reflection process and learn to observe and even manage the evolution of their own thinking. By the end of the semester, we hope they will be able to reflect on all their experiences (service and otherwise) independently and evaluate the quality with which they articulate their own learning outcomes. Reflection makes explicit the importance of taking responsibility for one's own learning. By its very nature it helps students to become increasingly aware of themselves as learners and increasingly adept at critical thinking.

Faculty and students at NCSU have developed a rigorous reflection framework that maximizes the learning potential of community engagement and helps to refine reflective and critical-thinking skills. Designed at the program level, the framework is applicable to classes in any discipline and has been used on our campus in a wide range of courses, from animal science to environmental ethics to engineering. It is structured as a series of questions that focus the students' attention on particular analytical perspectives consistent with the academic, personal, and civic objectives of SL. However, the framework also gives them substantial freedom in the selection of experiences to explore and even more independence in the substance of the conclusions they reach. We have used the framework to support multiple approaches to reflection in a variety of settings: during in-class activities, facilitated by the instructor or by the students themselves using worksheets to guide small group conversation, or out of class, either in the form of guiding questions for individual journal writing or as a structure for small group reflection sessions led by a trained upperclassman. Thus both writing and speaking, at the heart of any inquiry-guided learning process, are potential vehicles for reflection (see Chapter 17).

Figure 18.1 provides a schematic overview of our model for guided integrative reflection. Students begin each reflection activity by objectively describing their service experiences, considering, for example: Where was I and why? Who else was there? What was done? What was said? This *description* phase is followed by *analysis* of their experiences, structured to include academic, personal, and civic perspectives.

- When analyzing from the academic perspective, students identify the course concepts that relate to the experience and consider the ways in which those concepts emerged, for example, through deliberate application on their part. They consider similarities and differences between what they experienced and what they expected based on their understanding of the concepts. And if there are differences, they look for reasons behind those differences [e.g., a lack of understanding on their part or an assumption or bias on the part of the author(s)].

- Analysis from the personal perspective supports the students in exploring a new awareness of a characteristic such as a strength, weakness, or assumption that emerged in interpersonal interaction during the service experience. The students also assess whether and how they might use or compensate for that characteristic in their ongoing process of personal growth and what challenges they will face in doing so.

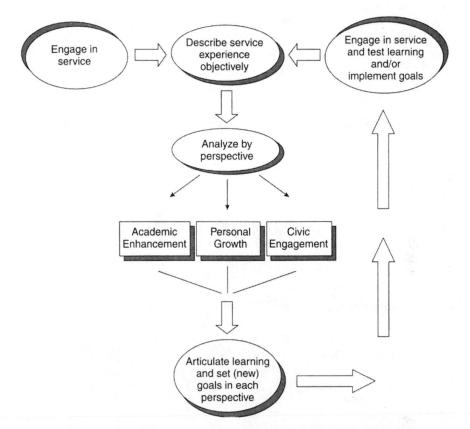

Figure 18.1   Schematic Overview of NCSU's Model for Guided Integrative Reflection.

- Civic analysis involves consideration of actions taken (or not taken) in the context of collective social change objectives. Students examine these actions in light of their consequences for the common good, consider alternative approaches, and evaluate their appropriateness in light of the possibilities for and constraints on long-term systemic change.

In our most rigorous implementation of this model, the reflection activity occurs six times over the course of the semester in two-hour, out-of-class, peer-facilitated, small group reflection sessions, with the reflection leader increasingly handing responsibility for the use of the framework over to the students themselves as the semester proceeds. Optimally this collaborative reflection occurs in conjunction with journal-based reflection exercises, often tailored to focus on course-specific objectives and allowing for more private reflection.

The ultimate goal of this combination of collaborative and individual reflection is to help students "develop a habit of critical reflection on their experiences, enabling them to learn more throughout life" (Kendall et al.,

1990, p. 38). Such ingrained reflectiveness fosters the IGL goals of developing self-motivated inquiry, responsibility for one's own learning, and habits of life-long learning. The students discover that while taking action is important, learning to become "reflective-in-action" (Schön, 1983) provides continuous opportunities for growth and thus can be equally valuable.

Articulating Learning as the Culmination of Inquiry

Whatever the forum for reflection (e.g., in-class or out-of-class discussion, journal writing), in our model each reflection activity comes to a close with the articulation of learning. Producing a written product, or *articulated learning (AL),* supports students in recognizing what they have learned through reflection on experience, placing it in context, expressing it concisely, and acting on it in the future. In other words, it supports them in thinking about their own learning.

The AL is structured in accordance with four guiding questions:

1. What did I learn?
2. How, specifically, did I learn it?
3. Why does this learning matter, or why is it significant?
4. In what ways will I use this learning, or what goals shall I set in accordance with what I have learned in order to improve myself, the quality of my learning, or the quality of my future service or other experiences?

A complete AL is a series of well-crafted paragraphs that address each of the four prompting questions. It is specific to just one of the categories of learning objectives (i.e., academic, personal, civic).

While the reflection framework supports students in surfacing the core of important learnings, writing and then refining an AL—and then subsequently reflecting on their attempts to enact its goals or test its conclusions—helps them fully develop and refine those learnings. Several characteristics of the AL process encourage students to take ownership of their learning. First, although the instructor may need to help them refine their thinking, the focus of the learning is initially left to the students' determination—a significant shift away from the more traditional model of students' responsibility for learning being limited only to what the teacher tells them they need to know. In addition, the linkages they make in exploring the sources and significance of their learning are individualized to their own experiences and understanding of the broader context for the learning. The goal setting in particular makes overt the students' responsibility to find an important consequence or outcome of the learning and then to act accordingly, holding themselves accountable for further reflection in the evaluation of their attempts to bring the learning to life in a meaningful way.

The AL process both requires and flourishes in the presence of careful feedback and opportunities for students to refine the learning. We have developed two tools that are key to maximizing the AL process. The first is a set of program-level learning objectives, written in accordance with the reflection framework (see Appendix 18.A). We present the objectives as a hierarchy with prompting questions within each perspective (i.e., academic, personal, civic), from the identification of knowledge to a judgment based on critical evaluation (cf. Bloom's taxonomy of the cognitive domain). Students do not have to follow the questions in sequential fashion. However, by presenting them in this way, we help to model the thought processes at the heart of IGL: identifying and examining the problem or issue at hand, generating possible solutions or conclusions, and selecting the best solution or conclusion with appropriate justification. Instructors and students alike use these learning objectives formatively in assessing a draft AL, as they consider how the thinking being articulated can be improved by meeting the higher levels of the objectives.

The second tool helps students apply the standards of critical thinking that are necessary to move effectively from identification to evaluation. As outlined by Paul (1993), these standards include accuracy, clarity, relevance, depth, breadth, logic, and significance. We have found that the learning objectives alone are not sufficient guidance regarding, for example, the use of evidence to support a claim, nor do they reinforce the importance of clarity in its presentation or encourage students to consider whether their conclusions represent the most significant learning. The appropriateness of any reasoned judgment likewise rests on thinking that remains relevant to the issue, addresses additional questions that arise, considers alternative points of view, and proceeds logically to the conclusion(s) being drawn. We have developed materials with definitions of these standards along with sample AL passages that exemplify each one, to support students' integration of these standards into their own thinking process as they develop their own ALs. Faculty, in turn, help to reinforce the standards by drawing upon them in their feedback.

Taken together, the learning objectives and the critical-thinking guidelines support students in articulating powerful learning outcomes from reflection on service experiences.

- A sophomore working on the computer project described previously reflected on her group's failure to anticipate problems with the donated equipment in light of a class reading about the significance of leaders having foresight. The author suggested that a leader is apt to have her hand forced by external circumstances if she doesn't practice adequate foresight. The student, on the other hand, suggested that in fact her group still had a range of options available to them despite increasingly constraining external circumstances. Further, she noted that the author's view had not considered the possibility that mistakes, if identified immediately, could be corrected in time to maintain a leadership role. She thus proposed a reason why, in this case, theory had not played out as expected in practice.

- Another student, serving at a local high school, reflected on the challenges his group faced in motivating high school students to engage fully with their own community-based projects. He articulated a civic learning regarding the tension between appealing to "baser" motives, such as the students' grade orientation, which may be effective in the short term, and nurturing "higher" motives, such as the love of learning and the desire to contribute meaningfully to the community. These higher motives may take longer to become effective but may be more apt to shape the students' long-term development as adult learners and citizens. His goal setting reflected the need to recognize and honor "baser motives" while identifying specific ways to promote "higher ones." In so doing he reflected an understanding of the complexities inherent in taking action in a real-world setting.

Challenges of Implementation

Tensions Between the Process of Inquiry and the Outcomes of Service

Sometimes there is a tension between the learning objectives of inquiry and service objectives, especially in terms of the meaning and significance of both time and success. Inquiry-guided learning focuses on process; it acknowledges that student learning rarely proceeds in an orderly fashion, and it honors failure or error as a source of substantial learning. Community partners, however, often operate on explicit time frames at odds with an inquiry-guided process that unfolds at a pace determined by the particular skills and interests of the learners. IGL nurtures abilities that will continue to develop and evolve over the student's lifetime. While community partners often have a similar investment in the long-term development of social consciousness, specific community projects may include important short-term outcomes as well.

Sometimes progress toward these outcomes does not proceed as expected, given the complexity of collaborative social change processes and the limitations of student expertise. From the perspective of the community, significant shortcomings in the students' work may mean that organizational objectives important to their constituents remain unrealized. This lack of "success," however, provides students an opportunity to reflect on the reasons for unmet objectives, alternative approaches that might be more effective in the future, and the ambiguous nature of problem definition.

Resolving these tensions requires that students, instructors, and community partners understand each others' goals and limitations and, in many cases, that they adopt a long-term perspective on both sets of objectives (i.e., inquiry and service). Sometimes trade-offs are necessary to achieve optimal learning objectives *and* optimal service objectives. We have found that open communication among closely collaborating partners is crucial in maintaining this important balance.

Institutional Culture Oriented Toward Research/Technology

Particularly in research- and technology-extensive institutions such as ours, another challenge to the implementation of SL is the emphasis on course content over learning process in highly technical, content-laden curricula. An unwillingness to trade off content in order to make room for a more explicit focus on process makes it especially critical to closely match service activities with academic material and to structure reflection carefully to promote rigorous academic outcomes. However, well-integrated design itself can be a challenge in disciplines in which service based on technical expertise easily translates to the unidirectional model of "outreach" that the "engagement" initiative is struggling to transform.

The focus on content also makes the development of reflective abilities a relatively steep learning curve for many instructors, as well as for students. Traditional teaching approaches tend to focus on information and job skill acquisition (the learning product) rather than on the acquisition of critical-thinking skills and the development of the whole person (the learning process). In response we have designed intensive faculty development workshops that include immersion in service and subsequent reflection activities. The workshops help faculty deal with the nuts and bolts of implementing service-learning in their courses, but even more importantly, help them understand and embrace the distinct nature and purpose of reflection specifically and of SL more generally.

Service-learning is not completely at odds with our institution's research focus. It offers faculty substantial opportunities to conduct research in the context of the scholarship of teaching and learning. And it can serve as a mechanism for the integration of research and teaching when, for example, a SL project involves a population with whom the instructor already has a research partnership. Further, service learning offers opportunities for students themselves to participate in research, in projects conducted on behalf of and in partnership with the community. For example, SL projects in marketing and communications courses are part of a large-scale grant designed to promote sustainable farming practices and will include student-led research to determine and appropriately respond to citizens' understanding of and commitment to alternative food products.

Adapting Core Models to Fit a Range of Student Populations and Objectives

The breadth of both disciplines and student population at NCSU, combined with our commitment to high-quality implementation of service-learning, has also posed significant challenges in the evolution of our program. At the same time it has also, however, encouraged us to experiment with adaptations and has led us to refine our understanding of best practices and expand the range of approaches used.

As described, instructors of SL-enhanced courses adapt the program's core model for reflection in a variety of in-class and out-of-class reflection mechanisms, depending on their objectives, constraints, and student population. Faculty can also work with community partners to structure the service experience to meet the needs and/or the limitations of the particular course objectives and student population. For example, in a First Year Inquiry course, the SL component involved just two discrete service activities—cleaning up a local park with senior citizens and habitat construction at an animal sanctuary—followed by instructor-guided reflection in the classroom and a short analytical essay. In a class on life cycle nutrition, students served a minimum of 25 hours over the course of a semester at sites that presented diet-related issues relative to pregnancy, childhood, and older adulthood. They also kept an extensive guided journal, participated in six out-of-class reflection sessions, and gave a final public presentation. In its most comprehensive form, the SL project can function as the primary structure of the entire course. For example, students in a senior-level Chemical Engineering course collaborated with a North Carolina community concerned about air quality, meeting with local advocacy and policy-making groups, researching methods to monitor air quality and to compare pollution levels across municipalities, participating in out-of-class reflection sessions, and presenting their findings at town meetings and to local school children.

Service-learning-enhanced courses at NCSU have run the gamut from first-semester freshman orientation classes to fourth-year graduate courses, and from elective courses taken to meet General Education requirements to required courses in the major. As with other forms of IGL, service-learning involves navigating the tensions between the flexibility required for such breadth of implementation and the adherence to core principles and guiding values required for programmatic coherence and quality implementation.

Conclusion

The challenges posed in implementing SL at an institution like NCSU have provided the impetus for experimentation with this pedagogy and subsequent improvements in our ability to help students put their knowledge to work for the betterment of the community. As with other approaches to IGL, SL also gives students the tools to participate as partners in the shared process of intellectual discovery; it provides the support necessary for them to grow and mature as thinkers and to learn to make and act on reasoned judgments in the face of uncertainty and ambiguity. The students themselves become more aware of the nature of this shift. They internalize the standards of critical thinking as they learn to give examples in support of their claims, to gauge the logic of their conclusions, to adopt perspectives other than their own, and to qualify their judgments. They demonstrate their growing ability to reflect meaningfully on their service-learning experiences as they come to realize how complex and "messy" life really is and to accept that "easy answers" are rarely the only or the best answers. By evaluating their own learning and engagement in the community, service-learning students have significant opportunities to develop those qualities that are at the heart of inquiry-guided learning (i.e., critical thinking, independent inquiry, responsibility for one's own learning, and intellectual growth and maturity) and that help "lead to the discovery of larger meanings that can be applied with integrity to life's decisions" (Boyer & Hechinger, 1981, p. 62).

References

Boyer, E. L., & Hechinger, F. M. (1981). *Higher learning in the nation's service*. Washington DC: Carnegie Foundation for the Advancement of Teaching.

Commission on the Future of NC State. (2000, June). *The new NC State: Becoming the nation's leading land-grant institution*. Raleigh; North Carolina State University.

Dewey, J. (1910). *How we think*. Boston: DC Heath and Company.

Kendall, J., et al. (1990). Principles of good practice in combining service and learning. In J. Kendall & associates (Eds.), *Combining service and learning I* (pp. 37–55). Raleigh, NC: National Society for Internships and Experiential Education.

Paul, R. (1993). *Critical thinking: What every person needs to survive in a rapidly changing world*. Santa Rosa, CA: Foundation for Critical Thinking.

Schön, D. (1983). *The reflective practitioner: How professionals think in action*. New York: Basic Books.

SERVICE-LEARNING PROGRAM-WIDE LEARNING OBJECTIVES

Academic Dimension

1. **Identify and describe course-related concepts in the context of your service-learning-related activities.**

    - Describe the course concept that relates to your service-learning experience. [Note: Be explicit and detailed in your description of the concept.] —AND—
    - Describe what happened in the service-learning experience that relates to that course concept.

2. **Apply course-related concepts in the context of your service-learning-related activities.**

    - How does the course-related concept help you to better understand, or deal with, issues related to your service-learning experience? —AND/OR—
    - How does the service-learning-related experience help you to better understand the course-related concept?

3. **Analyze course-related concepts in light of what you have experienced in the context of your service-learning-related activities.**

    - In what specific ways are a course-related concept (or your prior understanding of it) and the experience the same and/or different? —AND—
    - What complexities do you see now in the course-related concept that you had not been aware of before? —AND/OR—
    - What additional questions need to be answered or evidence gathered in order to judge the adequacy/accuracy/appropriateness of the course-related concept when applied to the experience?

4. **Synthesize and evaluate course-related concepts in light of what you have experienced in the context of your service-learning-related activities.**

- Based on the analysis above, does the course-related concept (or your prior understanding of it) need to be revised and if so, in what specific ways? Provide evidence for your conclusion. —AND—

- If revision is necessary, what factors do you think have contributed to the inadequacy in the concept as presented or in your prior understanding of it? (e.g., bias/assumptions/agendas/lack of information on the part of the author/scientist or on your part) —AND—

- Based on the analysis above, what will/might you do differently in your service-learning or other academic-related activities in the future?

Personal Dimension

1. **Identify and describe an awareness about a *personal* characteristic that has been enhanced by reflection on your service-learning-related activities.**

   - What personal strength, weakness, assumption, belief, conviction, trait, etc., have you become aware of as a result of reflection on your service-learning-related activities? [Note: Be explicit and detailed in your description of the strength, weakness, etc.]

2. **Apply this awareness to interactions with others in the context of your service-learning-related activities or other areas of your life.**

   - How does/might this characteristic affect your interaction with others? —AND/OR—
   - How is/might this characteristic be affected by others?

3. **Analyze the sources of this characteristic and the steps necessary to use or improve on it in your service-learning-related activities or other areas of your life.**

   - What are the possible sources of/reasons for this personal characteristic? —AND—
   - In what specific way(s) can you use this strength, improve upon this weakness, etc., in your service-learning-related activities or other areas of your life? —AND—
   - What are the potential personal benefits *and* risks or challenges you might face as you do so?

4. **Develop and evaluate your strategies for personal growth.**

   - Based on the analysis above, what is an appropriate and significant way to use this new awareness in your service-learning-related activities or other areas of your life? —AND—

- How will you deal with any challenges or setbacks you might face? —AND—
- How will you assess or monitor your progress or success?

Civic Dimension

1. Identify and describe the approach (e.g., decision or action) you or others took or, looking back on it, could have taken. [Note: This might be a deliberate approach or an approach that was not intentional at the time but that you now see as having an effect on collective objectives.]

   - What was/were the collective objective(s)? —AND—
   - What kind of approach was undertaken with respect to those objectives? (e.g., Did you (they) initiate action or follow others? Did you (they) accept objectives established by others, challenge them, or establish new objectives?)

2. Apply your understanding of your (others') approach in processes of collective action to the relationship between social action and social change.

   - What alternative actions/decisions were available for moving toward the meeting of the objective(s)? (e.g., directing action toward an individual versus a group; toward a symptom versus a root cause; toward a short-term versus long-term solution)

3. Analyze the appropriateness of the approach taken and the steps necessary to make any needed improvements in the approach.

   - What specific factors explain the approach to change you (they) took in this action? (e.g., attitudes, interests, agendas, assumptions, knowledge, resources) —AND—
   - Would an alternative approach have been more effective, and if so, why was it not chosen? If not, why was the approach taken the most effective? —AND—
   - In what specific ways can you (they) improve on your (their) involvement in processes of collective action? What are the challenges associated with doing so?

4. Evaluate your (others') role as an agent(s) of systemic change.

   - What would be involved in moving future action in the direction of long-term, sustainable, and systemic change? (e.g., change that addresses underlying causes and that does not cause inappropriate dependencies) What challenges would be associated with such movement?

PART IV
SUPPORTING AND ASSESSING INQUIRY-GUIDED LEARNING

Part IV documents the faculty development effort that has supported the inquiry-guided learning initiative as well as various ways of disseminating inquiry-guided learning to a broader group of faculty. It also explains the methods we've used to assess the impact of inquiry-guided learning on our students, faculty, and the institution as a whole.

19

MASTERING INQUIRY-GUIDED LEARNING ONE STEP AT A TIME

FACULTY DEVELOPMENT AND DISSEMINATION

By Virginia S. Lee

As a collection of instructional practices that support a very active learning process based on inquiry, engagement, and personalization, inquiry-guided learning represents a pedagogical Everest for many faculty. Quite secure in the lowlands of traditional instruction, many faculty scale the heights of inquiry-guided learning only gradually, one new practice at a time, pausing to rest, acclimate, and assess frequently along the way. As a result, faculty development has played an essential role in the inquiry-guided learning initiative at NCSU. This chapter describes the range of approaches we have used to develop and then continually improve the capacity of instructors to support inquiry-guided learning in the classroom. (Readers may wish to read this chapter in conjunction with Chapters 1, 17, and 20 for a more complete picture of our faculty development effort.)

The Role of Faculty Learning Communities in the Inquiry-guided Learning Initiative

Faculty learning communities (Cox, 2002, 2001) have played a vital role in each of the projects that have fed the IGL initiative at NCSU over the past several years (i.e., Hewlett Initiative, Hewlett Continuation, Hewlett Campus Challenge). They have also played an ongoing role in sustaining the campus-wide First Year Inquiry Program and increasingly the First Year Seminar Program based in our College of Humanities and Social Science (CHASS). They have provided an environment in which cross-disciplinary groups of faculty have explored issues and topics related to inquiry-guided learning, revitalized their teaching practice, and begun to engage in the scholarship of teaching and learning. Members of these communities have exerted an important influence on their departments and other university-wide programs and initiatives related to teaching and learning as well.

In addition to the participating faculty themselves, of course—anywhere between 12 and 60 faculty from a range of disciplines, the core of each faculty learning community is a program comprising one or more common elements (see Appendix 19.A for a representative project program). Each element of the program makes its own special contribution to building the learning community whether building *esprit de corps,* establishing a common language and shared understanding of learning and teaching practices, sharing ideas and successful classroom practices, problem solving, or presenting teaching innovations to a wider audience for feedback and as part of the practice of the scholarship of teaching.

Retreats

Whether facilitated by on-campus or off-campus experts, retreats provide an opportunity for project participants to gather and interact in a relaxed manner at an off-campus site away from the pressures and commitments of regular campus life. Retreats are effective at the beginning of a project to build community and establish a foundation of common understanding and experience. Depending on the duration of the project, they are also helpful at regular intervals (e.g., per semester, annually) to reinforce community and build upon an established foundation. The focus of the retreat will depend on the needs of the project and community; we have had retreats on a variety of topics including intentional course development using inquiry-guided learning, disseminating inquiry-guided learning in the department, teaching strategies consistent with inquiry-guided learning, and the scholarship of teaching and learning. While the venue is important, we have held retreats at a Holiday Inn directly off an interstate and a hotel on the beach, both to good effect. While we have had effective retreats facilitated by on-campus experts, off-campus experts have been more effective. Most bring the caché of a national reputation and, of course, novelty, a wonderful galvanizer of interest and attention. Outside facilitators have included Peter Frederick (Wabash College), Craig Nelson (Indiana University), Tim Riordan and Ann van Heerden (Alverno College), and Carnegie Scholars Stephen Jacobs (University of Notre Dame) and Larry Michaelsen (University of Oklahoma). As busy as faculty are, most project participants have been able to attend retreats if convinced of their value and given sufficient notice.

Workshops

During the regular semester, workshops provide another opportunity for participants to convene and renew community, to support one another, to consider new ideas and strategies, and to share with one another their successes and failures. Particularly with larger projects (i.e., 50 to 60 participants), finding a time during the week when all participants are available has been challenging. But we have held workshops during these times as well as on "reading days" and during exam periods or the week following exam periods. Workshops have ranged in length from one to three hours and have been facilitated both by on-campus and off-campus experts including Barbara Walvoord (University of Notre Dame), Stephen Brookfield (University of Saint Thomas), Richard Paul (Sonoma State), and Peter Facione (Loyola University).

Working Groups

In all of our projects and programs small working groups have served an important role. Faculty enjoy getting together in cross-disciplinary groups with other faculty and talking about teaching. In the process, they share and vet ideas and strategies with one another and offer support. In some programs, small groups of instructors facilitated by other instructors, who have more experience supporting inquiry-guided learning, has been the predominant faculty development strategy (see Chapter 16; Odom & Greene, 2003). For example, during monthly meetings First Year Inquiry faculty members share ideas and approaches with colleagues from different disciplines. Topics of faculty meetings include characteristics of writing assignments that encourage demonstration of critical-thinking skills, rubrics for evaluating written work, classroom strategies for encouraging student discussion, designing experiential learning components, and meeting the particular needs and challenges of first-year students. Focusing on teaching and learning has been a shared challenge that has allowed cross-curricular discussion and the refinement of teaching practice.

Presentations

Faculty share their classroom practices with one another informally all the time, but we've also found that more formal presentations are effective, too. Presentations provide a vehicle for faculty to make their teaching public and practice one aspect of the scholarship of teaching. Formats we've found effective are luncheon gatherings in which a few faculty present more formally on the innovations they've made in their classrooms. Campus-wide symposia in which faculty showcase their work to a wider audience have also worked well (see below).

Informal Gatherings and Celebratory Events

Informal gatherings and celebratory events such as receptions and end-of-project dinners provide another opportunity for faculty to mingle informally and build community with no other agenda in particular. More formal celebratory events are important, because they mark important achievements and dedication of time and effort, no mean accomplishment given the packed schedules of most faculty members.

Conference Attendance

We have had some funds to support the participation of several faculty at national conferences as both attenders and presenters. Conference attendance has been a positive experience for participating faculty: an opportunity to practice the scholarship of teaching, receive external recognition of their work, and to hear about comparable initiatives on other campuses. And, traveling together represents yet another bonding experience for those who participate.

As the work of Kember (1997) suggests, faculty development is a slow process. Because assumptions about teaching and learning are so deep seated and often unconscious, adopting teaching practices consistent with inquiry-guided learning is not like turning a light switch on—one moment using traditional teaching approaches, the next an entirely new and expanded repertoire of practices. In funded projects like those that have propelled our initiative, faculty enter with different levels of teaching expertise, commitment to changing their teaching practices, and time to devote to teaching. Even for the most dedicated faculty, change is an iterative process. It sometimes begins with a systematic reappraisal of one's teaching, but oftentimes starts with localized experiments—one assignment here, a class session there—that gradually proliferate over time resulting in a more complete transformation of one's teaching (see also Chapter 1). Even in a one- or two-year funded project with an extensive, carefully planned program like the one detailed in Appendix 19.A, many faculty only begin to make changes in their teaching during the actual project period. Hopefully with continued support they will continue to extend and refine their experiments in teaching consistent with inquiry-guided learning.

Sustaining and Disseminating the Work of the Initiative

A critical challenge we currently face is sustaining the initiative—supporting experienced faculty, extending it to more faculty, and deepening our understanding of instructional practices that promote inquiry-guided learning. A difficult budget environment and several worthy, but competing, campus initiatives heighten the challenge. We have experimented with several less resource-intensive models including an *Inquiry-guided Learning Seminar* for five two-person departmental teams. The Faculty Center for Teaching and Learning offered the two-semester seminar during the spring and fall 2002 semesters. All seminar participants attended a one-day retreat in early January before classes began, followed by three monthly supper meetings. Each participant prepared a set of exercises leading up to a full-course syllabus that incorporated inquiry-guided learning explicitly. In the fall 2002 semester, participants taught the course they had planned. Team members observed each other's classes at least two times in the semester, and participants planned and conducted at least one classroom-based assessment to explore a question concerning student learning that had arisen in their classroom.

Other less resource-intensive models included a four-session workshop series, *Introduction to Inquiry-guided Learning,* and a one-day workshop for new faculty co-facilitated by experienced IGL faculty. Faculty who have participated in the various IGL projects and programs have strongly advocated workshops for new faculty on inquiry-guided learning as setting an expectation for teaching at the university.

In addition we have held two symposia on inquiry-guided learning and are planning a third as a way of celebrating achievement, raising visibility, and educating ourselves and others on the progress and promise of inquiry-guided learning at the university.

March 2001 Campus-wide Symposium on Inquiry-guided Instruction. At the conclusion of the Hewlett Continuation Project, we organized a symposium open to the entire campus community to showcase the efforts of project participants as well as related efforts on campus. The symposium began with a keynote address by Sheila Tobias, author and science education consultant. Twelve breakout sessions organized in three consecutive blocks of four sessions each held throughout the morning and early afternoon and led by faculty, staff, graduate students, and undergraduate students followed (see Appendix 19.B). The symposium enhanced the pride of project participants in their accomplishments and extended awareness of inquiry-guided learning to a wider audience.

January 2002 Institute on Inquiry-guided Learning. Attended by approximately 60 instructors at the university as well as key administrators, the institute explored the implementation of IGL on our campus at four levels: individual course, sequence of courses in the major, program, and span of general education to the major. Presentations of best practice at each level provided a stimulus for focused, small group discussions on the challenges and opportunities in implementing comparable changes at the individual course and department curriculum level (see Appendix 19.C).

January 2004 Third Symposium on Inquiry-guided Learning: Institutionalizing Inquiry-guided Learning at NCSU. To further increase the visibility of the inquiry-guided learning initiative on our campus, to educate the campus on the dynamics of the initiative as a major undergraduate reform effort, and to garner the support of higher administration, we are organizing a one-and-a-half day campus-wide symposium. Working with Al Guskin and Mary Marcy of the Project for the Future of Higher Education (PFHE), we will both celebrate the achievements of the initiative and also explore it more critically, looking at the factors that have both helped and hindered its progress over the years at various levels. A particular focus will be how to grow and sustain the initiative in a time of scarce resources. The symposium's varied format will include keynote addresses, special planning sessions with IGL leadership and PFHE staff, and presentations by campus IGL innovators. Representatives from nearby universities (i.e., Duke University, University of North Carolina at Chapel Hill) and from an inquiry-guided learning project based in the public schools will also join us.

Dissemination within Departments

In addition to campus-wide dissemination efforts, we have also developed approaches for extending IGL work within the department through the Hewlett Campus Challenge Project. Two departments—Microbiology and Paper Science and Engineering—have implemented particularly successful approaches (see Chapters 11 and 12). For example, roughly midway through the funding period for the Hewlett Campus Challenge Project, the Department of Microbiology team planned a retreat for the rest of its undergraduate teaching faculty and any other departmental faculty who wished to attend. The purpose of the retreat was twofold: (1) to discuss the results the team was seeing in their IGL courses, and (2) to explore how the IGL work tied in with the department's undergraduate curriculum learning outcomes and program assessment. In perhaps the most useful exercise at the retreat, participating faculty first mapped individual courses to broader curricular-level outcomes. They discussed each of the undergraduate courses in the curriculum, the types of assignments given to the students, the types of exams, and the overall mixture of lecture, class discussion, and group work. The faculty agreed that the learning experiences provided by the IGL courses were what they wanted for their students, and all of the faculty teaching undergraduate courses agreed to move toward incorporating IGL into their courses. They then attempted to determine how well the courses were preparing students to achieve intended learning outcomes. This discussion highlighted the sense of ownership the whole faculty felt toward the curriculum, and the importance of seeing the courses as part of a larger learning experience rather than stand-alone faculty domains.

Summary

Faculty development has played a critical role in growing and sustaining the inquiry-guided learning initiative at NCSU. In order to support inquiry-guided learning effectively, most faculty have had to reexamine their fundamental assumptions about the teaching and learning process and slowly adopt a range of initially unfamiliar instructional practices. To support this complex change process, we have used a variety of approaches to faculty development—multisemester projects, faculty learning communities, workshops, presentations, discussion groups, conference attendance, faculty-led departmental retreats, campus-wide symposiums, advocacy, and more. In addition, course-based assessment has played an important role in sustaining faculty development and engagement with inquiry-guided learning among those faculty and departments that have embraced it with some enthusiasm. And we continue to seek new, less resource-intensive approaches to faculty development.

References

Cox, M. D. (2001). Faculty learning communities: Change agents for transforming institutions into learning organizations. In D. Lieberman & C. Wehlburg (Eds.), *To improve the academy: Vol. 19, Resources for faculty, instructional, and organizational development* (pp. 69–96). Bolton, MA: Anker.

Cox, M. D. (2002). Achieving teaching and learning excellence through faculty learning communities. *Essays in Teaching Excellence: Towards the Best in the Academy, 14,* 4. Fort Collins, CO: The POD Network.

Kember, D. (1997). A reconceptualisation of the research into university academics' conceptions of teaching. *Learning and Instruction, 7*(1), 255–275.

Odom, J., & Greene, D. (2003). The first year inquiry program: A faculty led teaching and learning initiative at NC State. *Emphasis, 12*(4). Raleigh: The Faculty Center for Teaching and Learning, NC State University. Available at www.ncsu.edu/fctl/Services/Emphasis_Teaching_And_Learning/

APPENDIX 19.A

HEWLETT CONTINUATION PROJECT PROGRAM

NORTH CAROLINA STATE UNIVERSITY

Semester/Month	Event
SPRING 2000	
January	• 21—Opening Reception with all Hewlett Fellows
February	• 4/5—Retreat at Wilmington w/ **Peter Frederick** • Hewlett Seminars 1 & 2 • Working Group meetings ongoing
March	• Hewlett Seminars 3 & 4
April	• 17—The Course as an Investigation of Learning Session • 18—Hewlett Principles and the Advising Process
May	• 5—Hewlett Working Dinner • 10—Evaluation Workshop w/ **Barbara Walvoord**
FALL 2000	
August	• 15—Pre-Fall Lunch w/ **Ephraim Schechter**
September	• 29/30—Fall Retreat w/ **Alverno College faculty** • Seminars (as needed) • Teach/assess "transformed" courses ongoing • Working group meetings ongoing
October	• Seminars (as needed)

| November | • 15—Being a Critically Reflective Teacher Workshop w/ **Stephen Brookfield**
• Seminars (as needed) |
| December | • Late November/early December Lunch with Presentations |

SPRING 2001

January	• 31—Lunch with Presentations
February	
March	• 1—Lunch with Presentations • 19—Campus-wide IGI Symposim w/ **Sheila Tobias**
April	• 19—Final Celebratory Dinner
ONGOING	• Website, videotaping

APPENDIX 19.B

INQUIRY-GUIDED INSTRUCTION AT NCSU

A Campus-wide Symposium

Breakout Session Schedule

Location	South Gallery	North Gallery	Brown Room	Blue Room
Time/Track	Classroom Teaching Practices and IGI	Technology and IGI	Assessing the Effects of IGI on Students and Faculty	Other Undergraduate Education Reform Efforts and IGI
10:15–11:00	"Scaling Up IGI from the Small to the Large Classroom"	"Use of Distance Learning Technology to Further IGI in a Service Learning Enhanced Course"	"Inquiry-Guided Instruction and the First Year Inquiry Courses: The Faculty Perspective"	"The Alcoa Project: Teaching and Learning in the Diverse Classroom"
	Oliver-Hoyo/Beichner	Clayton/Dehoney/Lyon	Odom	Leonard/Griffin/ Williams/ Patterson/ Malloy-Hanley/ Stallings/DeJoy

11:15–12:00	"Putting IGI into Practice in the Classroom"	"Cross-Cultural Reflection on Work-Based Learning: Using Online Instruction to Facilitate IGI"	"Inquiry-Guided Instruction: The Student Perspective"	"Service Learning as an Example of IGI"
	Zimmer/Cowen/ Spence	Williams/Crawford	Conley/Davis/ Early/Evans/Pless/ Powell/Welf/Pless	Clayton/Ash/ Moore/Odom
12:15–1:00	"Writing and Speaking at the Core of IGI"	"Replacing the Borg Collective with a New Learning Community: Introducing Students to IGI"	"Challenges in Assessing IGI at NCSU: A Historical Review of Methods"	"International Programs and IGI"
	Anson/Dannels	Slatta	Schechter/Lee	Greene/Gustke

INSTITUTE ON INQUIRY-GUIDED LEARNING

COLLEGE OF TEXTILES, NORTH CAROLINA STATE UNIVERSITY
FRIDAY, JANUARY 22, 2002, 8:30 A.M.–4:15 P.M.

8:30–9:00	Registration/Continental Breakfast
9:00–9:15	Welcome and Orientation *James Anderson, Vice Provost, Undergraduate Affairs* *Virginia Lee, Associate Director, FCTL*

Inquiry-Guided Learning: Transformation of Courses & Faculty Development Issues

9:15–10:15	Presentations Transformation of a Single Course *Arlene Malinowski, Foreign Languages* *Erin Malloy-Hanley, MDS* Transformation of a Sequence of Courses *Adrianna Kirkman, Wood & Paper Science*
10:30–11:15	Small Group Discussions
11:30–12:15	Large Group Report Back and Discussion
12:15–1:15	Lunch

Inquiry-Guided Learning: Transformation of Curricula & Organizational Development Issues

1:15–2:00	Transformation of Program Presentations *Michael Shearer, Mathematics* *Mike Hyman, Microbiology*
2:15–3:00	Individual Reflection and Small Group Discussion

3:15–3:45 Span of General Education to Completion of the Major
Lynn Turner, Food Science
Jonathan Kramer, Music
David Greene, Director, First Year Inquiry Program

3:45–4:10 Large Group Discussion

4:10–4:15 Closing Remarks
Doug Wellman, Director, FCTL

20

ASSESSING THE IMPACT OF INQUIRY-GUIDED LEARNING AT NCSU

By Virginia S. Lee

Introduction

The IGL initiative resides in a vibrant and relatively enlightened assessment culture at NCSU, and we have taken a variety of approaches to assessment with respect to inquiry-guided learning. In the early stages of the initiative we utilized more traditional, quantitative approaches to assessment conducted centrally. But as the initiative progressed, we shifted to smaller scale, classroom-based assessments conducted by instructors themselves. This trend is consistent with a shift in the assessment movement over the past 15 years to the increased use of such assessments conducted by faculty using existing classroom assignments and feedback from colleagues and students (Ewell, 2002; Schilling & Schilling, 1998). It is also consistent with the assessment approach of our campus' unfolding Undergraduate Academic Program Review (UAPR) process. In this process, programs identify the kinds of specific student learning they value and how they will assess that learning directly. After assessing students, analyzing patterns of student performance, and noting discrepancies between expected and actual student performance, programs "close the loop" by identifying strategies to more closely align expected and actual student performance. Ideally programs are constantly striving to improve student learning through an iterative process of defining learning outcomes, teaching, assessing, analyzing, and refining.

Three Areas of Assessment

In the IGL initiative we have experimented with assessment in three broad areas: faculty learning, student learning, and to a lesser extent, institutional learning. Enhancement of learning in each of these areas is essential in order for an educational reform initiative like the IGL initiative to succeed. Current approaches to assessment tend to emphasize student learning, and certainly the quality of student learning is a critical indicator of the quality of instruction. But faculty as the primary drivers of student learning are a critical part of the equation. Their closely held assumptions about teaching and learning directly affect their instructional practices, which in turn affect the quality of student learning. Therefore, we should try to assess the quality of faculty learning with respect to teaching and learning as well. Finally, there is institutional learning or the extent to which an institution is able to alter organizational structures and reallocate resources to support educational reform initiatives like inquiry-guided learning.

The alignment of structures and resources to serve learning is one of four key characteristics of learning institutions identified in a national project funded by the Pew Charitable Trusts based on the experience and practice of 27 institutions of higher education including NCSU (Doherty et al., 2002). However, the failure of institutions of higher education to alter their core structures in response to curricular and programmatic initiatives like the IGL initiative was cited in a recent *Chronicle of Education* column (Marcy, 2003) as a primary reason why foundations have cut back their support of higher education in recent years. Without such alignment of fundamental structures, undergraduate reform efforts like IGL are "enacted parallel to, and on a much more modest scale than, the traditional curriculum." What results are "pockets of innovations" that have "little effect on the overall fabric of higher education" (Marcy, 2003).

In the following sections we describe the approaches we have taken in each of these areas, what we found, and what we did as a result.

Faculty Learning

Hewlett I

Following the first major inquiry-guided learning project on our campus, Hewlett I (see Chapter 2), an assessment team of two faculty members and a graduate student conducted a study that used pre/post test surveys of instructors who had taken part in the project and student ratings of classroom instruction for both Hewlett Fellows and a comparison group. The comparison group included comparable courses taught by instructors who had not participated in the first Hewlett project. Because of the difficulty in finding comparable classes, only 18 of the 35 Hewlett Fellows and their classes were included in the study (Lindblad, 2001). The study did not really measure either faculty or student learning directly. Instead it tried to measure faculty learning indirectly by asking students to assess the degree to which certain kinds of instructional practices known to be consistent with inquiry-guided learning occurred in the classes they had taken. The focus on instructional practices reflects the emphasis of the first Hewlett Project on inquiry-guided *instruction* rather than inquiry-guided learning.

The survey asked students to rate their instructors' teaching style and emphasis on critical-thinking skills. (Early phases of the inquiry-guided learning initiative emphasized the acquisition of critical-thinking skills more heavily than inquiry.) Conceptually related items were summed to create five scales: traditional teaching, nontraditional teaching, emphasis on basic skills, inquiry-guided instruction, and Bloom's taxonomy (i.e., students' perception of the degree to which instructors consciously cultivated higher levels of the taxonomy). Hewlett-group scores were significantly higher than comparison scores for basic skills, inquiry-guided instruction, and Bloom's taxonomy. Further analyses indicated that participation in the Hewlett Initiative contributed to higher student ratings for inquiry-guided instruction and Bloom's taxonomy rather than other explanatory variables (i.e., the faculty member's teaching experience, course enrollment). However, as Hewlett classes got larger relative to the comparison classes, the differences in students' ratings of how strongly the course emphasized basic skills decreased.

Despite certain shortcomings of the study noted by the researchers (e.g., selection bias, small sample size), the analysis suggested that instructors participating in Hewlett I adopted teaching practices consistent with at least one outcome of inquiry-guided learning as defined on this campus: critical thinking. The researchers made several recommendations for future assessments including placing less emphasis on summative evaluation of the effectiveness of the intervention and more on faculty development, faculty-driven course-based assessment, and ongoing rather than only summative assessment at the end of the project period.

The Hewlett Continuation Project

A subsequent IGL project funded by the Office of the Provost, the Hewlett Continuation Project (see Chapter 2), used a two-pronged assessment effort: an external report conducted by two faculty members from Alverno College midway through the project and faculty self-reports of changes made in their courses due to their involvement in the project at the end of the project period. Through these assessment efforts, we wanted to describe (and ultimately increase) the extent to which faculty transformed their courses through the introduction of outcomes related to inquiry, critical thinking, and student responsibility for their own learning and the types of teaching practices that promote them (i.e., teaching methods, assignments, exams, readings).

Midway through the project we were fortunate to have two faculty members from Alverno College come and facilitate a weekend retreat with project
participants. In a series of guided discussions, exercises, critiques of course
materials brought by project participants, and a sharing of practices at
Alverno College, they helped participants explore the extent to which they had
intentionally integrated the IGL outcomes into their courses. Following the
retreat they submitted a report that summarized their observations of the
progress participants had made toward this goal.

1. Participants could identify what the Hewlett principles would look like as
   learning outcomes. They focused not only on the content they were
   expected to teach, but also on forms of pedagogy that truly engaged
   students in the practice of their disciplines. They had also begun to move
   beyond statements of learning outcomes to more specific criteria they could
   use to assess whether students were actually demonstrating these outcomes.

2. Participants had begun to identify strategies they could use to help
   students become more active learners. As a result their students were
   beginning to change their approach to their own learning. Participants
   had also become more conscious of the role grades play in the learning
   environment and were beginning to explore how to foster a spirit of
   inquiry in students in the context of a graded system.

3. Participants expressed varying degrees of satisfaction with the effectiveness
   of the instructional strategies they were using, but agreed it was important
   to approach course design with their course learning outcomes in mind.
   The examples of teaching outcomes they provided focused as much on
   what students were doing as on what they themselves as teachers were
   doing. This is an important shift because it emphasizes the role of the
   student as practicing the discipline he or she is studying, not just hearing
   and memorizing what the teacher has to say about the subject.

4. Participants had taken first steps toward designing assessments that require
   students to perform in ways that would actually demonstrate the ability to
   think critically and inquire within and across disciplines. But most agreed
   that they still had plenty of work to do in this area (Riordan, 2001).

The format of the final assessment report (see Appendix 20.A) represented
a compromise recommended by an evaluation subcommittee of project participants from an earlier assessment plan that was far more comprehensive. The
earlier plan asked instructors to reflect on key features of their courses (e.g.,
outcomes, classroom assignments, teaching strategies) and how they integrated
the Hewlett principles and to support their claims with relevant course materials (e.g., syllabi, assignments) or selected samples of their own and student performance. Given competing demands for project participants' time, the plan
was too ambitious. While some project participants did selected portions of the
assessment (e.g., peer observation of classrooms), very few completed the entire

assessment. In the end, a core group of active project participants submitted final assessment reports. This group included 10 of the 26 faculty members and 3 of the 11 graduate students.

Based on a qualitative analysis of the submitted reports, the impact of the project on participants' teaching practices varied depending on several factors including time available for teaching, rank, discipline, prior teaching experience, formal teaching preparation through participation in workshops or other projects, prior use of alternative teaching methods, and prior reflection on teaching. In all cases, however, participants did change their teaching practices in ways that would help facilitate Hewlett principles and they intended to continue and, in many cases, increase these changes in all of their courses.

Although a few project participants had employed classroom practices consistent with Hewlett principles earlier, most had used very traditional teaching practices for the most part. As a result of the Hewlett Project, participants reported changes in their teaching in five key areas.

- *More explicit use of outcomes as a planning tool.* Some participants reported being more conscious of the student learning outcomes they were attempting to achieve and using these to guide the planning and implementation of instruction. Using Bloom's taxonomy, participants began to consciously build higher level outcomes into their courses. Using Perry's stages of intellectual development, participants became more aware of students' level of intellectual development and then consciously tried to move them to higher levels of development. In addition to so-called "content" outcomes, participants began to explicitly introduce outcomes related to thinking in the disciplines, critical thinking, and other outcomes (e.g., professional development, networking). Related to the use of outcomes, some participants also tried to organize their entire course around a central question and/or lessons around an individual question or "key word." And one participant reported using classroom time more strategically to advance explicitly stated student learning outcomes.

- *Increase in the use of alternative teaching strategies and a decrease in the use of the lecture method.* The extent to which participants implemented alternative teaching strategies varied on a number of factors described previously. Some continued to rely on the lecture method primarily, but made their lectures more interactive, interspersing "mini-lectures" with thought experiments, "think-pair-share" exercises, group work, and the like. Others adopted a more inductive approach to teaching, working from specific examples to the general, rather than a more traditional deductive approach. Depending on the discipline, some participants began to make greater use of primary, as opposed to secondary, materials, forcing students to read and analyze these as, for example, a historian would.

- *Shift in focus from the teacher and content to the student and their learning.* Participants expressed this in a variety of ways: through the conscious use of outcomes, the use of teaching strategies that required more active participation and engagement on the part of students, giving students more decision-making responsibility, and the like. Participants became more aware of the sources and meaning of student resistance and welcomed it as an indication that true learning was occurring. One participant reported adopting a more holistic view of student needs that moved beyond cognitive to affective needs as well. Several participants reported more systematically soliciting student feedback about how various aspects of the course were going.

- *Making more explicit and transparent for students the reasons for the instructional decisions that had been made and expectations about how these would contribute to student learning.* For example, participants discussed with their students the nature of the outcomes, the selection of teaching strategies, the types of classroom assignments, and expectations for student performance. Several instructors underscored the importance of learning as a partnership and made more explicit the responsibilities of both students and instructors. Others began to draw more explicit linkages between course material presented at different points during the semester and even in other coursework. A few began to experiment with the use of concept maps to help students become more conscious of the relationships between key course concepts. Others consciously talked about the learning process, introduced students to the language of Bloom's taxonomy, had students describe their problem-solving process rather than merely report solutions, and the like. A number of participants began to use scoring rubrics that made explicit standards of performance for students.

- *Increase in the variety of student assignments and assessment methods used.* Moving from a heavier reliance on traditional examinations, participants began to make greater use of written assignments, oral presentations, projects, and homework assignments, for example. Participants also provided more explicit guidance to students on these types of assignments.

Of course, there is some overlap and interaction among these areas. For example, as faculty became more aware of students (e.g., their stage of intellectual development, academic preparedness, prior knowledge), the better they were able to consciously design instruction in a way that intentionally guides student learning. As instructors became more conscious of student learning, they became more conscious of manipulating instructional variables to influence student learning rather than merely covering content, however orderly that coverage may be. As instructors began to use more active learning strategies and solicit student feedback on instruction, they became more conscious of how and what their students were thinking, which in turn allowed them to become more intentional about their teaching. In the following section, we discuss participants' observations of changes in students' behavior.

The findings of the midproject external assessment and the final self-reports of project participants support Kember's (1997) findings that instructors are slow to relinquish underlying assumptions about teaching and learning and the kinds of instructional practices that emerge from them. Like any complex competency, approaches to teaching change slowly over time and at different rates for different instructors. In the context of education reform efforts like the inquiry-guided learning initiative, therefore, the use of formative, classroom-based assessment or action research at the curricular level (Kember, 2000) seems particularly appropriate not only as a means of assessment, but as a reflective mechanism to aid instructors' development as teachers.

Student Learning

First-year Programs

Over the past few years the First Year Inquiry (FYI) Program—and, more recently, the College of Humanities and Social Science (CHASS) First Year Seminar Program—has used various methods to assess their courses for first-year students. Because these methods are described fully in Chapter 16, we will only highlight them briefly here. In the very early stages, the FYI program compared pre- and post-tests of various student learning outcomes of interest (e.g., moral reasoning) in FYI and non-FYI courses. Later, due to the difficulty in identifying comparison groups, a less useful statistical analysis compared each FYI instructor with all other FYI instructors. These studies provided some insight into the effectiveness of the program, but neither provided guidance that individual instructors could use to improve their teaching practices to further critical student learning outcomes more effectively.

For the past few years, the FYI program has used the Facione and Facione (1994) holistic critical-thinking rubric to evaluate development of students' critical-thinking ability evidenced in student essays. Instructors assign essays designed to assess critical-thinking ability at both the beginning and end of the semester. They submit ungraded "beginning" and "end" essays from four randomly assigned students for assessment by an independent group of reviewers. The reviewers have been trained in the use of the Facione and Facione rubric and are blind as to when the essays were written. Ratings are compiled to assess aggregate change in students' critical-thinking ability over all FYI courses for the semester. In addition, faculty self-reports of changes made in their classes and student self-reports of learning complement the direct assessment of student learning. From semester to semester, these various assessments have yielded mixed results on growth of students' critical-thinking ability with some semesters indicating more growth than others. However, the assessment has been exceptionally useful as a faculty development effort; it has spawned extremely useful conversations about a range of issues including accommodating disciplinary differences in interpretations of critical thinking and inquiry; establishing measures of performance that reflect the complexity of learning and critical thinking expected in higher education; and the types of teaching practices that promote key learning outcomes most effectively.

Hewlett Continuation

In addition to self-reports of changes in their own teaching practices (see previous section), participating instructors also reported on perceived changes in student behavior and learning that they attribute to their changed instructional practices, although they did so with qualified confidence. Together these changes indicated greater student engagement in the learning process.

- Better attendance and greater use of office hours
- Increased student participation, interaction, and positive affect in classes
- Increasingly positive attitude as the semester continued from an initial position of resistance or indifference
- An evolving student buy-in and *esprit de corps*
- Increased student self-confidence
- Better retention of key concepts
- Better quality student work, grades, and improvement in writing assignments
- Growing professionalism

In contrast to these more positive changes, however, some instructors noted continued resistance, at least from some students. In informal feedback, some students complained that there was not enough lecturing and that in-class exercises were a "waste of time." And despite changes in classroom practices, some students still did not attend class and remained unengaged.

In reflecting on their expectations for students at the outset of the semester based on the changes they had made, some instructors reported being pleasantly surprised while others were disappointed in varying degrees. One instructor had anticipated student resistance at extra homework, but found that students did the extra work willingly. Others were surprised by higher-than-expected attendance levels, greater participation in class, greater use of office hours, and heightened enthusiasm. On the other hand, one instructor had such high expectations and was so proud of the changes that she had made that she was surprised by the level of student resistance. As a result of this resistance, however, she tried to view her instructional practices from the students' perspective in a way that she hadn't previously. Other instructors had anticipated greater improvement in student performance on written assignments and exams, for example, and were disappointed to find that this was not the case.

Despite instructors' reluctance to make strong claims about changes in student performance and behavior, without exception those project participants who prepared final assessment reports were excited about the changes they made and convinced of their efficacy. They reported intending to make additional changes in their classroom practices consistent with principles of inquiry-guided learning and to extend similar classroom practices to other courses they teach. Instructors planned on extending and deepening the use of active learning strategies. They planned on introducing more sophisticated assignments and projects that force students to think critically within the framework of their disciplines: for example, designing experiments and surveys, larger research projects, student presentations. Some instructors wanted to become even more explicit in defining learning outcomes, while others hoped to achieve a better balance between structure and flexibility and to do a better job determining what students already knew and designing the course accordingly. One participant expected that her department would soon adopt more broadly the types of changes she had initiated.

Hewlett Campus Challenge Project

Unlike the earlier two initiatives whose primary focus was general education and the individual course, the focus of the Hewlett Campus Challenge Project was a sequence of courses in the departmental major. Departmental teams identified a sequence of three to four courses in the major to transform through the introduction of inquiry-guided learning. In transforming these courses each team had to consider how these courses were related to one another including how to develop the key IGL outcomes developmentally. In addition the project had other important projected outcomes as well: coordinating the efforts of four units on campus and disseminating the work of the departmental teams within their own departments.

At the outset of the project we were not prepared for the additional complexity of working with a team of instructors at the curriculum level as opposed to individual instructors at the individual course level. The work of the teams was subject to all the vagaries of events within the departments including unpredicted curriculum revisions, elimination of targeted courses, difficulties in finding regular times for the teams to meet, and the like. As a result, their progress varied substantially. Also, the scope of the project was very ambitious, and all project participants were on a steep learning curve. Not only were we grappling with assumptions and methods that challenged many participants' assumptions about teaching and learning, we were also grappling with the equally daunting challenges of assessment and coordinating still poorly understood campus efforts like the UAPR process. It all presented a very tall order. While all save one departmental team that dropped out in the middle of the project made good progress, some teams made greater progress than others. As a result, toward the end of the project, we gave teams quite a bit of latitude in how they assessed their project work. In keeping with the requirements of the UAPR process, however, we asked teams to try to assess student learning directly through the use of instructor-designed classroom assignments.

Following is a selection of assessments, results, and follow-through conducted by the teams.

Accounting. Dovetailing its project assessment with the UAPR requirements, the team used a combination of direct assessment of student learning and student and employer surveys. It had targeted three courses in the curriculum—ACC 310 "Intermediate Accounting," ACC 320 "Cost Accounting," and ACC 490 "Senior Seminar on Accounting"—and worked actively on the first and third course. The team focused on two curricular-level outcomes that also corresponded to the general IGL outcomes: (1) promoting familiarity with the structure of the professional literature, problem-solving ability, and research ability; and (2) promoting effective written accounting and business communications. From both student comments and examples of assignments, they learned that students initially did not respond well to less-structured assignments (i.e., not multiple choice or short answer) but did a better job on these assignments as they progressed through the semester. Also as a result of introducing more open-ended assignments in earlier courses, students performed better on similar kinds of assignments in later courses. As a result the department has begun to incorporate IGL principles in introductory courses through less structured assignments completed in a group environment. They have also changed writing assignments in earlier courses to require more student responsibility for task completion.

Biological and Agricultural Engineering. The team targeted three courses in the undergraduate curriculum—BAE 200 "Introduction to Biological Engineering and Computing," BAE 401 "Bioinstrumentation," and BAE 451/2 "Engineering Senior Design I"—and dovetailed project assessment work with UAPR as well as the Accrediting Board for Engineering and Technology (ABET) requirements. They used various types of assessments including student self-evaluations, direct assessment of student learning using classroom assignments and problem solving in a lab environment, and senior and course survey results. The team posed different questions concerning learning depending on the individual course: how students used the textbook to figure out details when implementing programs (BAE 200), the perceived value of laboratory experiences (BAE 401), and the perceived value of a team approach to project work (BAE 451/2). As a result of these assessments the department recognized that students needed more step-by-step guidance in the introductory course and instituted a just-in-time learning concept, added additional inquiry-guided problems, supplemented formal exams with a practical lab-based problem-solving component, and affirmed the use of teamwork in the senior design course.

Mathematics. The team used a variety of approaches to assessment including graded homework, in-class group assignments, in-class tests, and a midterm questionnaire designed to assess the effectiveness of new teaching strategies in the three targeted courses: MA 225 "Foundations of Advanced Mathematics," MA 407 "Modern Algebra," and MA 425 "Math Analysis I." Initially spurred by the Hewlett Project, in the spring 2003, the department undertook new assessment strategies for the UAPR process. Results from the questionnaire indicate that students were much more engaged in the class than previously. They also reported enjoying the format more than conventional classes. It appears that test scores were affected only marginally by the different style, but it seems that average students are encouraged to work harder under the newer format with some achieving a better grade as a result. The department will investigate this finding further in future assessment work.

Microbiology. The team used various forms of course-based assessment (e.g., homework, lab reports, posters, group discussion reports) to evaluate the impact of changes made in three courses: MB 103 "First Year Seminar," MB 351/2 "General Microbiology and Lab," and MB 411 "Medical Microbiology." Through these assessments the department has learned that beginning students value having multiple types of reading assignments. As a result instructors continue to assign a variety of readings and discuss topics related directly to microbiology as well as to the entire university learning experience. In addition students need opportunities to practice new concepts outside the examples given in textbooks, so instructors have made homework assignments in MB 351 required rather than voluntary. Finally students enjoyed spending time in their groups discussing case studies and research reports, and their performance on exam questions was as good as prior years. As a result the instructor of MB 411 intends to decrease lecture time next year and introduce more discussion sections.

The various threads of this complex project came together toward the end of the extended project period in exciting ways. In addition to becoming convinced of the benefits of inquiry-guided learning and its positive effects on student performance and attitudes toward learning, many project teams have come to appreciate the value of course-based assessment and the benefits of coordinating courses and communicating more fully with one another in the interests of student learning. Several teams have disseminated their work more broadly in their departments and have become models for other departments within their colleges and for the university as a whole in curriculum and assessment work.

Institutional Learning

As noted, ultimately the success of the inquiry-guided learning initiative here will depend on the extent to which we are able to alter key organizational structures and reallocate resources to support inquiry-guided learning. The need to align structures and resources has not escaped participants in the various IGL projects here. To paraphrase one faculty member: "I know I'm doing the right thing, but inquiry-guided learning takes more time. Often students are resistant initially, and course evaluations are lower. And I haven't really told my department head I'm involved in this project, because I know he won't support my participation. I'm beginning to think I'm pretty stupid for doing this." Clearly for many faculty members to persist with an initiative like this and for others to engage at the outset, we need to change structures as fundamental as the incentives for faculty. Without alignment of fundamental structures, undergraduate reform efforts like IGL will be "enacted parallel to, and on a much more modest scale than, the traditional curriculum." The result will be "pockets of innovations [with] little effect on the overall fabric of [the institution]" (Marcy, 2003).

To date we have not conducted a formal assessment of NCSU's capacity to support inquiry-guided learning, but we have taken some steps in that direction. On January 22, 2002, we convened an *Institute on Inquiry-guided Learning* that brought together approximately 60 faculty and staff who had participated in one or more IGL projects or programs. The level of analysis and discourse at the institute was at a substantially higher level than the *Campus-wide Symposium on Inquiry-guided Instruction* (see Chapter 19) held just a semester earlier, itself an indicator of our learning as an institution. At the institute we examined examples of best practice in inquiry-guided learning at four levels: the individual course, sequences of courses in the major, the program, and the undergraduate curriculum as a whole. Small group discussions and follow-up discussion by the whole group analyzed the challenges and opportunities in implementing inquiry-guided learning at each level. Opportunities and challenges existed at both the individual course level for the isolated faculty member and at the program or curricular level with the faculty member in the context of a larger departmental effort. Further, participants perceived many and pervasive (i.e., occurring in multiple departments) conditions in departments that support or hinder instructional innovation through inquiry-guided learning. These conditions are as follows:

Supporting Conditions

- Tradition of commitment to teaching within the department and/or a core of faculty dedicated to innovation in teaching
- Involvement in other parallel initiatives on campus
- Requirements of accrediting bodies
- Nature of discipline conducive to IGL approaches
- Small class size
- Support of department head and/or college dean
- Assessment efforts
- Development of capstone courses that inherently incorporate IGL
- Focus on technology
- Shift in department structures for faculty roles and rewards

Hindering Conditions

- Commitment to traditional, teacher-centered teaching approaches emphasizing lecturing and content coverage exclusively
- Resistance from senior faculty burnt out on teaching
- Perception that IGL is time consuming and anxiety about using it from faculty already stretched too thin
- Lack of shared understanding of IGL and/or perception that the department faculty are already doing it
- Faculty autonomy
- Lack of support from department head and/or dean
- Relatively high numbers of nontenured and adjunct faculty
- Size of classes, the department, and the number of faculty
- Lack of teaching assistants
- Limitations in physical facilities
- Rigidity of curriculum
- Decentralized curricula dispersed over many departments
- Transfer students
- Resistance from students
- Competition from other initiatives
- Lack of convincing assessment evidence
- Difficulty of implementing alternative, student-centered methods of evaluating teaching
- Reappointment, promotion, and tenure criteria that recognize research over teaching
- Requirements of accrediting bodies

Essentially the institute provided examples of good practice in inquiry-guided learning at different units of analysis within the institution and then explored the broader capacity of the institution to support comparable levels of practice more pervasively.

Further the Student Learning Initiative in which NCSU is a participant (see above) has developed a framework that identified four characteristics of learning institutions (i.e., institutions that place student learning at the core of their mission and actually practice it). These characteristics include achieving clarity about student learning outcomes, pairing teaching and assessment, aligning structures, and continuous improvement. Within the IGL initiative we have helped participants put into practice the first, second, and fourth characteristics. As we have noted throughout this volume, a shared understanding of four broad student learning outcomes—critical thinking, independent inquiry, responsibility for one's own learning, and intellectual growth and maturity—is the mortar of the inquiry-guided learning initiative at NCSU. And in all of the IGL projects and programs we have tried to help participants use these outcomes to select appropriate assignments and teaching strategies to support student learning. Further we have encouraged participants to use a variety of course-based assessments to evaluate and improve their ability to promote inquiry-guided learning. However, participants have spontaneously brought up the third characteristic—alignment of structures and resources—as an impediment to inquiry-guided learning, because it is not really practiced at the university. That is, key structures such as the incentive structure for faculty and mechanisms for resource allocation do not widely support inquiry-guided learning.

A number of us at the university believe the unfolding undergraduate academic program review process provides a mechanism for promoting institutional learning by supporting these characteristics across the institution as a whole and fortifying the inquiry-guided learning initiative in the process (Lee, 2001). As we noted at the start of this chapter, through the review process departments are defining curricular-level outcomes, developing a variety of ways to assess these outcomes (e.g., classroom assignments, student focus groups, surveys), and then "closing the loop" (i.e., noting discrepancies between desired and actual student performance and developing strategies to narrow these discrepancies). Essentially these steps mirror the first, second, and fourth characteristics of the Student Learning Initiative framework. And to the extent that the university has supported this process, it is also furthering the alignment of resources and structures in support learning. Further, as we describe more fully in Chapter 15, because many curricular-level outcomes being developed by departments actually describe modes of inquiry in the disciplines, the potential exists for the implementation of inquiry-guided learning very broadly throughout the university. To realize this potential, faculty within departments must coordinate their efforts more extensively and use curricular-level outcomes as a tool to guide the selection of teaching strategies and assignments to further these inquiry-guided learning outcomes.

Summary

Since its inception more than seven years ago, we have used a variety of methods to assess the impact of inquiry-guided learning on our faculty, students, and the institution as a whole. Together these methods have demonstrated the effects of inquiry-guided learning. At the same time, they've underscored the sizable challenges of managing an effort like this across an institution of this size and complexity. The challenges exist on many fronts: the assumptions faculty carry about teaching and learning, comparable student attitudes toward learning, the complex mission of the university, and inflexible organizational structures. At the same time, using inquiry-guided learning has galvanized many instructors' teaching and their excitement about it, promoted enhanced conversations about teaching and learning, engaged students more deeply in the learning process, and deepened our understanding of students' capacity for learning and how to bring it about. We have also become increasingly aware of the need for more broad-based institutional support as we try to extend inquiry-guided learning more widely throughout the university.

References

Doherty, A., Riordan, T., & Roth, J. (Eds.). (2002). *Student learning: A central focus for institutions of higher education: A report and collection of institutional practices of the student learning initiative.* Milwaukee, WI: Alverno College Institute.

Ewell, P. T. (2002). An emerging scholarship: A brief history of assessment. In T. W. Banta & Associates, *Building a scholarship of assessment* (pp. 3–25). San Francisco: Jossey-Bass.

Facione, P. A., & Facione, N. C. (1994). Holistic critical thinking scoring rubric. Available at www.insightassessment.com/pdf_files/rubric.pdf.

Kember, D. (1997). A reconceptualisation of the research into university academics' conceptions of teaching. *Learning and Instruction, 7*(1), 255–275.

Kember, D. (2000). *Action learning and action research: Improving the quality of teaching and learning.* London: Kogan Page.

Lee, V. S. (2001). NC State's undergraduate program review process: Promoting sustained inquiry about student learning. *Emphasis, 11*(2). Raleigh: Faculty Center for Teaching and Learning, North Carolina State University. Available at www.ncsu.edu/fctl/Services/Emphasis_Teaching_And_ Learning/

Lindblad, M. (2001). Internal analysis of the Hewlett I project. Raleigh, NC.

Marcy, M. B. (2003, July 25). Why foundations have cut back in higher education. *The Chronicle of Higher Education,* B16.

Riordan, T. (2000). External assessment of Hewlett Continuation project. Milwaukee, WI.

Schilling, K., & Schilling, K. (1998). *Proclaiming and sustaining excellence: Assessment as a faculty role.* ASHE-ERIC Higher Education Report, 26(3). Washington, DC: The George Washington University, Graduate School of Education and Development.

Acknowledgments

I would like to acknowledge the important contribution of Ephraim Schechter, Associate Director, University Planning and Analysis, and University Director of Assessment to the inquiry-guided learning assessment effort at NCSU as well as his careful review of this chapter. I am also grateful to Marilee Bresciani, Director of Assessment, Division of Undergraduate Affairs, and Joni Spurlin, Director of Assessment, College of Engineering for their comments as well.

HEWLETT CONTINUATION PROJECT

FINAL ASSESSMENT REPORT

Purpose

The Project assessment plan has a dual focus:

1. to describe the various changes faculty have made in their courses to enhance students' ability to inquire, think critically, and take responsibility for their own learning
2. to describe the impact of these changes on students and student learning

The assessment effort should also help us

1. develop a growing, common understanding of the kinds of teaching practices that promote students' ability to inquire, think critically, and take responsibility for their own learning
2. provide information and evidence that individual instructors can use to continue to change their courses in ways that continue to improve students' ability to inquire, think critically, and take responsibility for their own learning
3. provide an account of the project to the Provost that he can use to justify his continued support of inquiry-guided instruction

Individual Instructor Classroom Assessment

By **December 1,** please complete a 2–4 page written assessment of your course using the guidelines below. This will complement the individual and working group assessments completed in preparation for the retreat, the preliminary project assessment at the retreat (see **Retreat Summary**), and Alverno College's external assessment review (sent via campus mail).

1. **Briefly describe your course** (i.e., number, title, level, target student population, format—online, in class, curricular purpose, content/process description)

2. Briefly describe how you taught the course pre-Hewlett (i.e., outcomes, classroom assignments, teaching strategies, texts and/or other instructional materials including technology)

3. Describe how you have changed the course as a result of your participation in the Hewlett Program. Please focus on the following areas: a) outcomes; b) classroom assignments; c) teaching strategies; d) texts and/or other instructional materials (e.g., technology). In some areas you may have made significant changes, in others few if any.

4. Describe and provide some evidence of at least 2–3 changes you have noticed in your students' behavior/learning over the course of the semester. This could include changes in use of office hours, attendance, attitude, classroom participation, views of learning, or quality of student work, for example.

5. Briefly compare these changes in students' behavior/learning with your expectations at the outset of the semester. Describe possible factors that you believe either enhanced or impeded the effects of the changes you made in your course on students' behavior/learning.

6. Describe your future plans for this course and what effect you hope these additional changes will have on students' behavior/learning. Once again, please focus on each of the four areas above (i.e., outcomes, assignments, teaching strategies, texts and/or other instructional materials).

CONTRIBUTORS

VIRGINIA S. LEE was the Associate Director of the Faculty Center for Teaching and Learning, North Carolina State University, from January 2000 through February 2004. She played a significant leadership role in the Inquiry-guided Learning Initiative as well as other campus-wide initiatives related to teaching and learning. She has presented and published on a range of topics related to teaching and learning in higher education.

CHRIS M. ANSON is Professor of English and Director of the Campus Writing and Speaking Program at North Carolina State University. A scholar of writing, language, and literacy, he has published 12 books and over 75 articles and book chapters, and has led faculty workshops at colleges and universities across the United States and abroad.

ALISON ARNOLD joined the NCSU Music Department as an adjunct Assistant Professor in the fall 2000. She earned her doctorate in musicology and ethnomusicology at the University of Illinois, Urbana-Champaign, in 1991. She has also worked as an editor, most recently editing *The Garland Encyclopedia of World Music*, South Asia volume (2000).

SARAH ASH is an Assistant Professor in the Departments of Animal Science and Family and Consumer Sciences at NCSU. She has taught courses in food history and in human nutrition from the introductory to the advanced levels. She has been active in both the inquiry-guided learning and service-learning initiatives at NCSU.

ROBERT BEICHNER, Associate Professor, Department of Physics, has a research focus on physics learning. His biggest current project is SCALE-UP, but he also developed the popular "video-based lab" approach, and his diagnostic tests of understanding are used internationally. He endeavors to reform physics instruction at a national level. His most visible work has been coauthoring the top-selling introductory calculus-based physics book in the nation.

SUSAN BLANCHARD, Professor, Department of Biomedical Engineering, teaches human physiology for engineers and introduction to biomedical engineering at North Carolina State University. She is the ABET accreditation coordinator for biomedical engineering, was a member of CUAPDRPI, chaired CUPR in 2002–2003, and is an ABET evaluator. She has published in a variety of scholarly journals and is an author of *Introduction to Biomedical Engineering*.

MARILEE BRESCIANI is the Director of Assessment, Division of Undergraduate Affairs, at NCSU and has been in higher education administration and faculty positions for over 15 years. She also teaches assessment courses in the Department of Adult and Community College Education.

MEDWICK V. BYRD, Ph.D., North Carolina State University, is Director of Applied Research and Undergraduate Coordinator. Department of Wood and Paper Science. His research interests are mechanical pulping, chemical pulping and bleaching, and nonwood pulping. He is a member of the Technical Association of the Pulp and Paper Industry.

MICHAEL CARTER, Associate Professor, Department of English, teaches writing and rhetoric at North Carolina State University. He has played an active role on his campus in academic program assessment and in assessing general education. He has published in a variety of scholarly journals and is the author of *Where Writing Begins: A Postmodern Reconstruction*.

PATTI CLAYTON is Coordinator of the NCSU Service-Learning Program and a visiting lecturer in College of Humanities and Social Sciences. Codeveloper of the program's reflection framework, assessment strategy, student leadership roles, and faculty and student guidebooks, she also consults with middle and high schools and with other universities on service-learning capacity building.

DEANNA P. DANNELS is an Assistant Professor of Communication and the Assistant Director of the Campus Writing and Speaking Program at North Carolina State University. Her research explores theoretical frameworks for communication across the curriculum and protocols for implementing and assessing communication within the disciplines.

CHRISTOPHER R. DAUBERT is an Associate Professor in the Department of Food Science at North Carolina State University. He received his B.S. from the Pennsylvania State University in 1991 and a Ph.D. (Food Science and Agricultural Engineering) from Michigan State University in 1996.

MEREDITH DAVIS is Professor of Graphic Design and teaches design studios and courses on design theory and cognition. She is author of *Design as a Catalyst for Learning* and has written numerous articles on the application of design pedagogy to teaching and learning in K–12 schools.

C. ASHTON DREW is a doctoral student in the Department of Marine, Earth, and Atmospheric Science at North Carolina State University. Ashton was a team member in "Surrogate Species Planning" and provided a student's perspective for the chapter she co-authored.

DAVID B. GREENE is the Director of the First-Year Inquiry Program, Head of the Department of Multidisciplinary Studies, Professor of Arts Studies at NCSU, and a member of the university's Academy of Outstanding Teachers. As Chair of the Council of Undergraduate Education in the 1990s, he was instrumental in the faculty development movement toward transforming undergraduate education at NCSU.

JOHN A. HEITMANN, JR., Professsor, Ph.D., Institute of Paper Chemistry, is a specialist in papermaking technology. His research interests are recycled fibers, biotechnological applications to papermaking processes, wet end chemistry, coating, and other aspects of papermaking technology. He has been selected as an Outstanding Teacher and Alumni Distinguished Undergraduate Professor.

GEORGE HESS is an Associate Professor in the Department of Forestry at North Carolina State University. George has been leading inquiry-guided, collaborative research courses since 1996. His first attempt was an abject failure. His latest offering, "Surrogate Species Planning," resulted in two manuscripts that are now in peer review for journal publication.

MICHAEL HYMAN is an Assistant Professor and joined the Department of Microbiology in 1998. His main teaching responsibility over the last five years has been MB 351 "General Microbiology." He also served as the team leader for the department's Hewlett Campus Challenge team.

HASAN JAMEEL, Ph.D., Princeton University, is Elis and Signe Olsson Professor, Department of Wood and Paper Science. He has received the NCSU Outstanding Teacher Award and the Alumni Distinguished Undergraduate Professor Award. His research interests are pulping and bleaching process analysis, process modeling and control, and chemistry of pulping, and bleaching. He is a member of TAPPI and AIChE.

ANA KENNEDY completed the Ph.D. at Duke University in Spanish Golden Age Literature. She served as Assistant Director of the Pre-Major Center at Duke before coming to teach at NCSU. In addition to teaching Spanish language and literature courses at NCSU, she serves as Coordinator of Advising for the Department of Foreign Languages and Literatures.

ADRIANNA G. KIRKMAN, Professor, Department of Wood and Paper Science and Associate Dean, College of Natural Resources, Ph.D., North Carolina State University, was awarded the 1994–1995 Teaching Excellence Award for the Department of Wood and Paper Science. Dr. Kirkman is a member of TAPPI. Her research interests are process analysis, mathematical modeling, and simulation.

JONATHAN KRAMER is Associate Director of the Music Department at North Carolina State University and Adjunct Professor of Ethnomusicology at Duke University. He holds advanced degrees from Duke and the Graduate School of the Union Institute where he completed a Ph.D. in Ethnomusicology and Performance Studies in 1994. As a cellist, he has performed widely both nationally and internationally.

GERRY LUGINBUHL, Professor, Department of Microbiology, served as the Chair of the Council on Undergraduate Education from 2002–2003. She was recognized as the department's Alumni Distinguished Professor of Undergraduate Teaching in 1990 and received the College of Agriculture and Life Sciences' Outstanding Faculty Award in 2003.

ARLENE MALINOWSKI, Associate Professor, has taught in the Department of Foreign Languages and Literatures at North Carolina State University for over 20 years, since completing a Ph.D. in Romance Linguistics at the University of Michigan, Ann Arbor. Most recently, she directed the First Year Seminar Program in the College of Humanities and Social Sciences.

KATHY MAYBERRY received her M.Ed. in Mathematics Education from North Carolina State University in 1985. She has 15 years of secondary teaching experience and 8 years experience in network and computing services. She is currently the Coordinator of Student Owned Computing in the Department of Information Technology and Engineering Computer Services in the College of Engineering at North Carolina State University.

SUSAN NAVEY-DAVIS holds a Masters of Arts in Teaching from the University of North Carolina at Chapel Hill. She now serves as coordinator of the Spanish Teacher Education program at NCSU and in that capacity teaches, advises, and supervises student teachers in Spanish. She also coordinates lower-division Spanish courses on campus. She is coauthor of the textbook, *Plazas: Lugar de Encuentro Para la Hispanidad.*

JANICE E. ODOM is currently the Director of the Caldwell Fellows Program. She has been involved with initiatives related to first-year students at NCSU since 1991. She was the Associate Director of the First Year College and the First Year Inquiry Program.

MARIA OLIVER-HOYO, Assistant Professor, Department of Chemistry, joined the faculty of the NCSU in 1999 after completing her Ph.D. in Chemistry at Drexel University in Philadelphia. Her research program in chemical education emphasizes courseware development primarily in the areas of laboratory innovations and multimedia applications.

SAMUEL B. POND, III, Ph.D., Industrial and Organizational Psychology, Auburn University, is Associate Professor of Psychology at North Carolina State University where he researches attitudes, motivation, and performance.

He has actively participated in matters of planning, teaching, and evaluation in the First Year Inquiry Program at NCSU from its inception.

SARAH A. RAJALA received her Ph.D. in Electrical Engineering from Rice University in 1979. In July 1979, she joined the faculty at North Carolina State University, where she is currently Professor of Electrical and Computer Engineering and since 2002 has served as Associate Dean for Research and Graduate Programs. Her research interests include engineering education and the analysis and processing of images and image sequences.

ROGER P. ROHRBACH, Ph.D., PE, Professor of Biological and Agricultural Engineering, has taught the capstone "Senior Engineering Design" in Agricultural Engineering for 27 years. He has been a member of the College of Engineering Computing Committee since its inception, and has chaired the committee for the past 6 years.

EPHRAIM SCHECHTER is University Director of Assessment at NCSU, and Associate Director of University Planning & Analysis. He has been a faculty member, psychology department head, and institutional researcher, and has been involved in higher education outcomes assessment for 15 years. He maintains a nationally known meta-list of Internet assessment resources at www2.acs.ncsu. edu/UPA/assmt/ resource.htm.

RICHARD W. SLATTA directs the First Year Seminar Program in the College of Humanities and Social Science. He has taught history at NCSU since completing his doctorate at the University of Texas at Austin in 1980. He is the author of seven books, and since 1984 has published dozens of articles and reviews promoting educational applications of computer technology.

JONI E. SPURLIN, Ph.D., Director of Assessment, College of Engineering, North Carolina State University, has had 22 years experience in higher education, and for the past 12 years she has provided leadership and expertise to faculty, administration, and staff in the development of tools for assessment, institutional effectiveness, and planning processes. She has worked with faculty on improving outcomes assessment for engineering, computer science, liberal arts, education, business, and nursing and allied health programs.

PAUL TESAR is Professor of Architecture and teaches design studios as well as courses in aesthetics, typology, and vernacular architecture. While his main research focuses on issues of architecture, he has maintained an active interest in design pedagogy throughout his academic career.

LYNN G. TURNER is Professor of Food Science and Undergraduate Teaching Coordinator, Department of Food Science, North Carolina State University. He received his B.S. and M.S. degrees in Dairy Science at the University of Georgia and his Ph.D. in Food Science from NCSU.

J. DOUGLAS WELLMAN is Professor and Head of the Department of Parks, Recreation and Tourism Management at North Carolina State University and a member of the university's Academy of Outstanding Teachers. From 1998–2003 he served as founding Director of the Faculty Center for Teaching and Learning. He is author or coauthor of 18 works on teaching and learning.

INDEX